Lingo

American Voices

AMERICAN VOICES

How Dialects Differ from Coast to Coast

Edited by Walt Wolfram
and Ben Ward

BLACKWELL PUBLISHING
350 Main Street, Malden, MA 02148-5020, USA
9600 Garsington Road, Oxford OX4 2DQ, UK
550 Swanston Street, Carlton, Victoria 3053, Australia

The right of Walt Wolfram and Ben Ward to be identified as the Authors of the Editorial Material in this Work has been asserted in accordance with the UK Copyright, Designs, and Patents Act 1988.

First published 2006 by Blackwell Publishing Ltd

2   2007

Library of Congress Cataloging-in-Publication Data

American voices : how dialects differ from coast to coast / edited by Walt Wolfram and Ben Ward.
    p. cm.
  Includes bibliographical references.
  ISBN-13: 978-1-4051-2108-8 (alk. paper)
  ISBN-10: 1-4051-2108-4 (alk. paper)
  ISBN-13: 978-1-4051-2109-5 (pbk. : alk. paper)
  ISBN-10: 1-4051-2109-2 (pbk. : alk. paper)   1. English language—Dialects—United States   2. English language—Variation—United States.   3. English language—Dialects—Canada.   4. English language—Dialects—Caribbean Area.   I. Wolfram, Walt, 1941–   II. Ward, Ben, 1962–

  PE2841.A77 2006
  427′.973—dc22

                   2005017255

A catalogue record for this title is available from the British Library.

The publisher's policy is to use permanent paper from mills that operate a sustainable forestry policy, and which has been manufactured from pulp processed using acid-free and elementary chlorine-free practices. Furthermore, the publisher ensures that the text paper and cover board used have met acceptable environmental accreditation standards.

For further information on
Blackwell Publishing, visit our website:
www.blackwellpublishing.com

Contents

Part IV The West

Part V Islands

Part VI Sociocultural Dialects

List of Illustrations

Preface

The collection of dialect profiles that led to *American Voices* began innocently. But it was hardly by accident. In fact, it developed from a shared vision by the co-editors of this volume. In 1997, publisher Ben Ward launched a magazine dedicated to bringing language issues to the attention of allied service professionals and to the American public in an attractive, readable format. Linguists sometimes talk about the need to make language issues more accessible to the general public; the editors of *Language Magazine* made it happen. It was a bold venture, premised on the assumption that many people were curious about language apart from the highly specialized field of linguistics. If the development and distribution of *Language Magazine* over the last several years is any indication, the assumption of interest was more than justified.

Meanwhile, Walt Wolfram's sociolinguistic research over several decades taught him that just about everyone is curious about dialects. After all, one can hardly avoid noticing and wondering about language differences in daily interactions with people from all walks of life. The problem, however, is bridging the chasm between highly technical, microscopically detailed studies of language variation and popular, broad-based levels of interest. With all due respect to linguists, they often have a way of transforming inherently interesting subject matter into jargon-laced presentations that are comprehensible only to the few thousand professional linguists in the world. This collection of articles is intended to do better. It attempts to translate the detailed research of professional dialectologists into readable descriptions for those who are curious about language differences but have neither the background nor the desire to be professional linguists. We systematically attempt to cover (for the most part) a range of North American English dialect communities, including both well-known and rarely recognized cases in which speakers may not even be thought to speak a dialect. By selecting our dialect profiles in this way, we hope to convince readers that everyone really does speak a dialect – and that they are all of interest. We also attempt to cover a few major sociocultural varieties, though our focus is on regional space rather than social place. Chapters in the book, all of which appeared originally in *Language Magazine*, are not intended to be read in sequence since they are independent articles that do not build on each other; in fact, we would suggest that the reader choose articles on the basis of interest and curiosity.

The idea for this collection was born in 2000 when Ben Ward contacted Walt Wolfram about writing an article for *Language Magazine* on the unique Ocracoke dialect spoken on the Outer Banks of North Carolina. Though Wolfram was quite happy to do so, he wondered if it might be more appropriate to write a more general article on the state of American dialects, and suggested that this might be followed up by an ongoing series of articles highlighting some of the notable dialects of North American English – and slightly beyond. The seed was planted. Germination and cultivation of the idea was another matter. Who would write these articles? Could linguists actually write trade articles without resorting to the jargon that so frequently typified their technical descriptions? Would they consider this a worthy venture given their active research lives? We hope that the articles that appear in this collection answer these questions satisfactorily.

Prominent dialect researchers on particular American English dialects were contacted to see if they would accept the challenge of writing up their sophisticated research for a broad-based audience. Amazingly, practically everyone accepted, despite the fact that the presentation was a journalistic challenge. The incentive was simply the offer to tell their story in a way that might be comprehensible to their friends, family, and non-linguist colleagues and students. The reward was seeing their story attractively presented in a glossy magazine format with cool images and rapid turn-around time in publication. The response has been one of the highlights of our publishing careers. The most eminent scholars in the field wrote their dialect stories and, in the process, also subjected themselves to editing decisions on behalf of the audience. Happily, the authors greatly exceeded our expectations. A great debt of thanks goes to each of the authors, not only for their splendid contributions in terms of content and presentation but also for being such good sports in accommodating the editorial process sometimes necessary to ensure readability and comparability. Thanks also to Sarah Coleman and Tami Kaplan at Blackwell for encouraging us in this project, even though it was slightly different from the usual book project. We hope that the collection will be of interest both to the leisure reader interested in language differences and to undergrad students in courses on the English language, American dialects, and sociolinguistics.

For convenience, the articles are arranged in broad-based sections that may stretch traditional notions of region. A section is also devoted to island dialects, a favorite breeding ground for distinct language maintenance and development, and another section is devoted to some prominent sociocultural varieties. Admittedly, the collection does not include all of the dialects that might have been covered, and we can image the reader asking, "But what about the X dialect?" In most cases, this is probably a valid concern, and we can only apologize for our sins of omission. We fully recognize that there are many other regional and social dialects of North America beyond those described here. To a large extent, coverage was dictated by the availability of active researchers to write about the dialects they were researching, with an eye toward regional and ethnic representation. Since we follow a case study format, it is bound to exclude many situations worthy of inclusion. Perhaps our oversights will inspire the description of other worthy dialect cases so that we can produce a second volume in the future.

If nothing else, we hope that readers will understand that American dialects are alive and well – and that they remain every bit as interesting today as they were during their presumed heyday, whenever that was supposed to have been. In fact, our point is that dialects are not artifacts of the past, but ongoing, contemporary social statements about people and place. We also hope that some of the excitement that inspires dialectologists and sociolinguists to devote their entire lives to the description of a speech community will rub off on the reader. If these descriptions do that, then we will have succeeded beyond our imagination. Dialects are such fun – and such an essential part of who we are and what America is. Don't believe the myth that dialects in American society are dying!

Walt Wolfram
William C. Friday Distinguished Professor
North Carolina State University

Ben Ward, Editor
Language Magazine

Language Evolution or Dying Traditions? The State of American Dialects

Walt Wolfram and Natalie Schilling-Estes

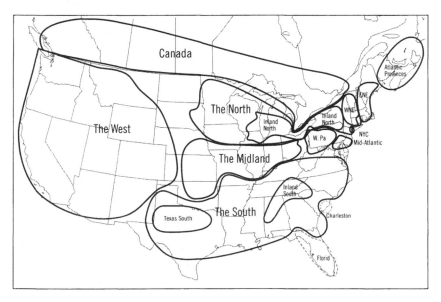

1 Dialect areas of the United States, based on telephone survey data (from Labov, Ash, and Boberg 2005). © 2005 by William Labov, Sharon Ash, and Charles Boberg from *Atlas of North American English* (New York/Berlin: Mouton de Gruyter).

Most people find dialects intriguing. At the same time, they have lots of questions about them and often have strong opinions as well. Probably the most common question we encounter about the condition of American dialects is, "Are American dialects dying, due to television and the mobility of the American population?" Certainly, media, transportation, and technology have radically compressed the geography of the United States and altered American lifestyles over the last century. So what effects do these significant changes have on America English dialects? What about the future of American dialects as English assumes a global role?

Basic Dialects of American English

The methodical collection of data on regional dialect variation in America began in earnest in the 1930s when the Linguistic Atlas of the United States and Canada was launched and dialectologists began conducting large-scale surveys of regional dialect differences. This effort was buoyed in the 1960s through an extensive national survey that has now led to the publication of the first four volumes of the six-volume *Dictionary of American Regional English* (Cassidy and Hall 1985, 1991, 1996, 2002), the premier reference work on regional American English dialectology. These surveys focused on the regional vocabulary of older lifetime residents of rural areas and so captured a picture of dialect differences as they existed in the late nineteenth and early twentieth centuries. The result was a number of useful dialect maps of the primary and secondary dialect areas of the mainland US, including the one featured at the beginning of the chapter.

To a large extent, traditional dialect divisions in the US reflect differences first established in Colonial America by people from different parts of the British Isles. These differences were cemented in early cultural hubs such as Richmond, Philadelphia, Boston, and Charleston and later diffused outward as English speakers moved inland. But do these differences still hold at the beginning of the twenty-first century, after a century of demographic shifts, economic growth, and sociocultural change? Linguist William Labov and his colleagues at the University of Pennsylvania are currently conducting an extensive telephone survey of dialect pronunciations throughout the US. Though still ongoing, his survey reaffirms the persistence of the same major dialect boundaries that were established in earlier studies. However, Labov's research reveals more than the mere maintenance of fundamental dialect boundaries; it shows that in some ways the major dialects of the US are actually becoming more different from one another rather than more alike.

In large Northern cities such as Chicago, Detroit, Cleveland, and Buffalo, certain vowel pronunciations are changing in ways that distance them from Southern vowels. For example, the *augh* sound of a word like *caught* is now pronounced more like the vowel of *cot*. Meanwhile, a word like *lock* sounds something like *lack*, while *tack* sounds a little like *tech*. At the same time, Southern vowels are changing in different ways. For example, *red* sounds something like *raid*, and *fish* sounds almost like *feesh*. So much for the presumed homogenization of Northern and Southern speech.

Changing Trends in Dialects

The continuity and enhancement of basic dialect boundaries during a century of demographic and social change is certainly a feature story, but there are some sidebars that point to change in the dialects of American English as well. Several factors have had a significant impact on the repositioning of American English dialects at the turn of the millennium. These include changing patterns of immigration and language contact within the US, shifting patterns of interregional movement within the US, and expanded transportation and communication networks. To go along with these demographic and technological developments, changes in social structure and cultural values have affected the development of dialects.

Language Contact

One factor that has always contributed to the distinctive flavor of American English is the influence of other languages, from the earliest Native American influences on the vocabulary of general American English (*raccoon, moccasin, pecan*, etc.), to the later influence of Scandinavian languages on the pronunciations of the Upper Midwest, to the influence of African languages on Ebonics. But the languages influencing American English change as the cultural mix changes.

The languages of more recent immigrant populations from Asia and different areas of the Hispanic world are now affecting English just as various European languages have done throughout the history of the US. Furthermore, new ethnic varieties of English are arising from more recent language contact situations. For example, there are various types of

Hispanic English in regions of the Southwest and Southeast with heavy concentrations of Hispanics. And these dialects are spoken not only by those who learn English as a second language but by those whose first and primary language is English as well.

Long-established ethnic varieties also change, as patterns of contact among ethnic groups shift. The desegregation of ethnic communities is an ongoing process in American society that continually brings speakers of different groups into closer contact. However, the result of contact is not always the erosion of ethnic dialect boundaries. Ethnolinguistic distinctiveness can be remarkably persistent, even in face of sustained, daily inter-ethnic contact. Ethnic dialect varieties are a product of cultural and individual identity as well as a matter of simple contact. One of the dialect lessons of the twentieth century is that speakers of ethnic varieties like Ebonics not only have maintained but have even enhanced their linguistic distinctiveness over the past half century. In addition, Ebonics has become a supra-regional dialect that unites African Americans across urban and rural areas that range from Boston to Los Angeles.

Population Movement

Dialect boundaries often follow the migratory routes of the major population movements. Historically, the significant migrations of English-speaking people in the US have run along east–west lines. However, the last half of the twentieth century was characterized by some different patterns of population movement. For example, some areas of the South have been inundated by speakers from Midland and Northern dialect areas. At first glance, the effect of this trend seems enormous, especially in areas such as Miami, Houston, and the Raleigh–Durham area of North Carolina, where Southerners are overwhelmed by non-Southerners to such a degree that it is becoming increasingly rare in these areas to locate young people with genuine "Southern accents." But there are also factors that work to counter the "dialect swamping" that may result from such situations.

Many Southerners view their dialect as a strong marker of regional identity and a source of cultural pride. Such feelings may help preserve certain dialect features even in the face of massive linguistic pressure from outside groups. Dialectologist Guy Bailey and his team of researchers have found that some Southern dialect features in Oklahoma and Texas, including the use of *fixin'* to in *They're fixin' to go the mall*, have persisted and even spread in the face of increasing settlement by non-Southerners. The nature of regionalized American English is certainly changing, but we can hardly say that regional dialect forms are subsiding.

Expanding Transportation and Communication Networks

The broadening of transportation and communication networks throughout the twentieth century now provides access to even the most remote dialect areas. These locations were once the sites of some of America's most distinctive dialect traditions. A potential linguistic consequence of this increased accessibility is dialect endangerment, in which a distinctive variety spoken by relatively small numbers of people in a once isolated community is overwhelmed by encroaching mainstream dialects. For example, a number of island communities on the eastern seaboard of the US are currently in grave danger of extinction. These communities have been transformed from small, self-contained marine-based communities into service-based tourist meccas in a matter of decades. The traditional dialect features of some of these communities are receding rapidly, often within a couple of generations. At the same time, though, some communities, or sub-groups within a community, may maintain and even enhance certain noticeable dialect features in order to distinguish themselves from outsiders.

Shifting Cultural Centers

Throughout its history, the US has undergone a number of major population shifts as its economic and social structures have changed. In the process, its centers of cultural influence have shifted as well. In the latter part of the twentieth century and the early twenty-first, the major stream of population movement is no longer toward the heart of the city but into the suburbs. As cultural centers shift, so too does the locus of linguistic change. Important dialect changes often are now initiated in the suburbs, not the city proper. For example, sociolinguist Penelope Eckert of Stanford University has shown that some of the most innovative speakers in the North are suburban teens – not people from the middle of the city. In addition we find that dialect features may spread across geographic space in different ways. Whereas some dialect features may spread out from a central area in a fairly straightforward way, like ripples in a pond, others may "jump" from region to region. For example, the pronunciation changes affecting some Northern cities have been shown to spread from one major metropolitan area to another, skipping intervening areas of low population.

Populations in particular locales may also carve out new dialects as they develop a sense of regional identity. Many of the earliest maps of the United States show less dialect distinctiveness as we move from east to west, reflecting the relatively late arrival of English-speaking groups on the West Coast as well as increased dialect mixing during westward expansion. But this is changing. Linguists and non-linguists alike are recognizing quite distinctive dialects on the West Coast, including California English, whose influence has spread among young speakers throughout the US. One of the most distinctive features of this dialect (characterized in pop culture as "Valley Girl Talk" or "Valley Speak") is the pronunciation of statements with rising rather than falling intonation, so that a statement like "We went to the movies yesterday" sounds like a question: *We went to the movies yesterday?*

American Dialects in the New Millennium

Even as some traditional American dialects recede, new ones appear, reflecting the changing dynamics of American demography and social structure. But the present contours are deeply embedded in the historical origins of American English, and future developments no doubt will take their cues from the present dialect profile. Dialects mark the regional and cultural cartography of America as much as any cultural artifact, and there is no reason to expect that they will surrender their emblematic role in American life in the future.

References

Bailey, G., T. Wikle, J. Tillery, and L. Sand (1993) Some patterns of linguistic diffusion. *Language Variation and Change* 5: 359–90.
Carver, C. M. (1987) *American Regional Dialects: A Word Geography*. Ann Arbor: University of Michigan Press.

6 Language Evolution or Dying Traditions?

Cassidy, F. G., and J. Hall (1985, 1991, 1996, 2002) *Dictionary of American Regional English, Vols. I–IV.* Cambridge: Belknap Press at Harvard University Press.

Labov, W., S. Ash, and C. Boberg (2000) *A Phonological Atlas of North America.* The Hague: Walter de Gruyter.

Wolfram, W., and N. Schilling-Estes (2005) *American English: Dialects and Variation*, 2nd edn. Malden, MA: Blackwell.

PART I
THE SOUTH

Sounds of the South

Guy Bailey and Jan Tillery

2 A group of Confederate soldiers awaits orders during the re-enactment of a Civil War battle. © by Dan Brandenburg.

Southern American English (SAE) is the most widely recognized regional dialect of American English, but as most of its speakers know, widespread recognition is a mixed blessing. SAE is also the regional dialect that is most negatively evaluated. In a recent study of folk beliefs about American dialects, Dennis Preston (1996) found that 90 percent of his respondents from Michigan and Indiana and 96 percent of those from South Carolina recognized SAE as a distinct variety of American English. The Michigan and Indiana respondents, however, also evaluated SAE as the most "incorrect" variety of American English (New York City speech was the only serious competitor), and the South Carolina respondents were ambivalent about its correctness as well.

The widespread recognition and negative evaluation of SAE can have practical consequences for its users that in some cases include negative stereotyping and linguistic discrimination, just as with African American Vernacular English (AAVE), or Ebonics. While SAE almost never generates the extreme reactions and extensive prejudice that AAVE often does, its users can anticipate at least polite (and often not so polite) condescension to their speech by non-Southerners. In spite of its low status outside of the South and of standardizing forces such as interregional migration and universal education that threaten many minority languages and dialects, SAE persists.

Some Features of Southern American English

Misunderstandings about what comprises SAE are almost as widespread as the recognition of its distinctiveness. These misunderstandings in large part have been fueled by media portrayals in movies such as *Gone with the Wind* and television shows such as *The Dukes of Hazzard* that presented grossly exaggerated and inaccurate stereotypes of SAE. More recent portrayals in television shows such as *Designing Women, Evening Shade* and *Grace Under Fire* are more accurate, but their effect on the public knowledge of SAE is unclear.

Traditionally, SAE differed from other varieties of American English in some of its lexical, grammatical, and phonological features, but many of the lexical differences, which were rooted in an agrarian economy and a traditional society, have begun to disappear. For instance, most young Southerners are as likely to use *green beans* as *snap beans* and are more likely to use *dragon fly* than either *snake doctor* or *mosquito hawk*. Just as these book terms have replaced the older folk terms with the advent of universal education, a significant part of the regional vocabulary associated with farm life has become obsolete as the artifacts to which they refer have disappeared. Few Southerners under 50 know what a *singletree* is (it is the bar of wood on a wagon to which the traces are attached) or have heard the term *dogtrot* used for a type of house (usually a two-room house with an open hall down the middle). Many of the distinctive grammatical and phonological features of SAE persist however.

Some of the grammatical differences between SAE and other varieties are well known. For example, most Americans immediately recognize *you-all* or *y'all* as distinctively Southern second person pronouns, and many would know that *fixin'* to, as in *I'm fixin' to eat breakfast*, is Southern as well. The latter represents a modification of the English auxiliary system that enables Southerners to encode an aspectual distinction grammatically that must be encoded lexically elsewhere: *I'm fixin' to eat breakfast* means that I intend to eat breakfast in the next little while.

Other grammatical features are less widely known but are no less important. SAE also modifies the English auxiliary system by allowing for the use of more than one modal in a verb phrase. For instance, for most Southerners *I might could leave work early today* is a grammatically acceptable sentence. It translates roughly as *I might be able to leave work early*, but *might could* conveys a greater sense of tentativeness than *might be able* does. The use of multiple modals provides Southerners with a politeness strategy not available in other regional dialects. Although no generally agreed-upon list of acceptable multiple modals exists, the first modal in the sequence must be *might* or *may*, while the second is usually *could, can, would, will, should,* or *oughta*. In addition, SAE allows at least one triple modal option (*might should oughta*) and permits *useta* to precede a modal as well (e.g., *I useta could do that*).

All three of these grammatical features remain robust in SAE, and migrants to the South from other parts of the country often appropriate both *y'all* and *fixin' to*. Multiple modals, on the other hand, are typically used only by native Southerners. Most of the phonological features of SAE are also typically used only by natives.

The most widely recognized phonological features of SAE are the merger of the vowels like *pen* and *pin* or *ten* and *tin* (the vowel in both words has the sound of the second member of the pair) and the loss of the offglide of the *i* diphthong in words like *hide* (so that it sounds like *hahd*). SAE is also characterized by a series of vowel rotations that William Labov (1994) called the "Southern Shift." Describing the shift would require an extensive technical phonetic description of SAE vowels, but most people can hear its most important feature simply by listening to Bill Clinton's pronunciation of the vowel in *way* or *stayed*. The beginning of the vowel (which is a diphthong in SAE) will sound something like the vowel in *father*. Vowel differences such as these are hard to describe in non-technical terms, but they are what make people immediately recognizable as speakers of SAE – long before a *might could, fixin' to,* or *y'all* crops up in their speech.

Change and Persistence in SAE

Much of the research on SAE has focused on its relationship to British regional dialects – on what many linguists see as its roots. The focus is primarily a result of the assumptions that American regional dialects are a reflex of settlement history and that they were formed during the colonial period. Recent research on SAE, though, suggests that both assumptions are inadequate. A case in point is the *pen/pin* merger. This merger occurred in the American South at least as early as the second quarter of the nineteenth century (Brown 1991), but it occurred in only a relatively small segment of the population. During the last quarter of the nineteenth century, however, the *pen/pin* merger began to spread rapidly throughout the South until by World War II virtually all Southerners had the merger. This same 50-year period also saw the emergence and spread of the loss of offglide in *i* and of the distinctive vowel pronunciation in words like *way*. Moreover, during this time grammatical features such as *fixin' to* and *y'all* expanded rapidly.

The diffusion of these features after 1875, after the initial settlement of the South, may seem odd, but demographic and socioeconomic developments of this era suggest why these features may have begun to spread when they did. In *The Promise of the New South* (1992), Edward L. Ayers points out that during the last quarter of the nineteenth century the emergence of stores, villages, and towns and a dramatic expansion of the rail system set in motion a process of urbanization that would ultimately reshape the region. In 1860 less than one in ten Southerners lived in urban areas (communities with populations of 2500 or more), and only 21 towns from Virginia westward through Texas had populations of 5000 or more. By 1900 the urban population of the South had doubled, and it doubled again by the onset of World War II. What seems to have happened linguistically is that migration to towns and cities created contact among dialects that were formerly local and insular, and as a result, features that were relatively restricted in occurrence began either to spread out or to disappear. The parallel process of diffusion and extinction eliminated many local vernaculars but at the same time gave rise to the larger regional dialect known today as SAE. Vestiges of some local vernaculars persist among older residents of insular communities, as the work of Wolfram and his associates shows, but among younger Southerners they have all but disappeared.

Demographic developments since World War II raise some interesting questions about future prospects for SAE. The urbanization that began before World War II expanded dramatically during and after the war, but with some significant differences. Before World War II people in Southern towns and cities came from the surrounding countryside, and most industry involved low-wage, manual-labor operations, such as cotton mills and petroleum-processing plants. After the war, and especially after 1970, the migration to the Southern cities was as likely to come from the North as the South, and new industries often included such things as the corporate headquarters of J. C. Penney and the Dell computer production facilities. In addition, in Texas, Florida, Virginia, and large cities throughout the South, migration from outside the United States is now occurring at an astonishing rate.

The linguistic impact that the new arrivals from outside the South will have is not yet clear, but some trends are already becoming apparent. In Texas and Oklahoma, and in many metropolitan areas around the South, some national linguistic trends such as the merger of the vowels in *caught* and *cot* (both sound like the latter) are emerging. In several of the larger metropolitan areas (e.g., Dallas–Fort Worth and Memphis) some traditional Southern vowel features such as the distinctive pronunciation of the vowel in words like *way* are beginning to wane. Even as these developments take hold in metropolitan areas, however, traditional grammatical features such as *y'all* and *fixin' to* are spreading to non-Southerners migrating to the region.

While the long-term consequences of the new developments are impossible to predict, it is apparent that SAE is continuing to evolve – just as it has over the last century and a half. The extent to which the results of that evolution will yield something that is recognizably "Southern" remains to be seen.

References

Ayers, Edward L. (1992) *The Promise of the New South: Life after Reconstruction.* Oxford: Oxford University Press.
Bailey, Guy, and Jan Tillery (1996) The persistence of Southern American English. *Journal of English Linguistics* 24: 308–21.

Brown, Vivian (1991) The merger of /i/ and /e/ before nasals in Tennessee. *American Speech* 66: 303–15.

Labov, William (1994) *Principles of Linguistic Change: Internal Factors.* Oxford: Basil Blackwell.

Preston, Dennis (1996) Where the worst English is spoken. In Edgar Schneider (ed.), *Focus on the USA*, 297–360. Amsterdam: John Benjamins.

Wolfram, Walt, Kirk Hazen, and Natalie Schilling-Estes (1999) *Dialect Maintenance and Change in Outer Banks English.* Publication of the American Dialect Society 81. Tuscaloosa: University of Alabama Press.

Defining Appalachian English

Kirk Hazen and Ellen Fluharty

3 A farmer hoes beans in the mountains. © by Dan Brandenburg.

When people speak of Appalachian English, they often treat it as if it has mad cow disease and needs quarantining. As linguists, we are always saddened by the negative attention the Appalachian dialect receives. To us, all dialects are legitimate variations of English; no dialect is more "correct" or "legitimate" than another. Appalachian English, like many other American dialects, has existed for almost two hundred years and has developed its own unique vocabulary and grammar.

To regard the Appalachian dialect as deficient is therefore scientifically incorrect, and it unfairly maligns the entire social group that speaks it.[1]

Why do so many people feel Appalachian English is at best "quaint" (read "useless and outdated") and at worst stricken and deformed? Since the earliest days of settlement in America, Appalachia has been perceived as backwards and exclusively poor. Although this is by no means true, these misperceptions continue to this day. Social judgments of the Appalachian dialect, then, are often nothing more than cover for a very ugly kind of prejudice. At its root, prejudice against Appalachian English is more a social judgment of Appalachian people than of the language they speak.[2]

Who Speaks Appalachian English?

According to the Appalachian Regional Commission, Appalachia stretches from mid-state New York to the northeast corner of Mississippi, and includes 406 counties in 13 states. It has a tremendous geographic area (roughly 200,000 square miles), and a population of about 22 million. Of course, not all of Appalachia's 22 million people speak a dialect traditionally regarded as Appalachian. Traditional Appalachian English has been defined by a laundry list of features: people expect to hear *bar* for *bear* and *sodipop* for *soda pop*; they expect to hear phrases like *I was a-working when the lats [lights] went out* and *I ain't seen but one deer when we was out huntin'*. If we look for these language features among the population of Appalachia, our best estimate is that only about 30 percent of residents would have them. The reason for this is that Appalachia encompasses a great number of disparate urban, suburban, and rural communities. With such geographic diversity, there are great differences in the way Appalachian people speak. For example, growing up in southern West Virginia may or may not mean that you have a Southern accent, depending on whether you grew up in suburban Charleston or in rural Logan County.

There are also great differences between younger and older generations of speakers. The version of Appalachian English used by many teenagers, while it may share many traditional features with the speech of their grandparents, is far from identical to it. For example, a teenager who is hyperconscious of sounding Appalachian may not use *y'all* for the second person plural pronoun whereas the grandparents may have only ever used this form. Because of this problem of defining a single Appalachian English, we have begun to view it not as one dialect with a particular set of features, but as a number of dialects.

The Roots of the Dialect

One popular myth is that Elizabethan English is still spoken in the region. The varieties of Appalachian English are diverse, but Elizabethan English, which was spoken during the reign of Queen Elizabeth I (1558–1603), was never spoken in Appalachia. In 1603, the colony of Jamestown was only an idea, and major settlement in the region did not begin until the eighteenth century. Even if there had been a settlement of Elizabethan English speakers in Appalachia, and they had remained isolated until today, their great-great- . . . -great-grandchildren would not speak the same dialect as their forebears, as all living languages undergo change. We suspect that people who promote this idea within Appalachia are trying to correct the myth that there is something wrong with Appalachian English by promoting an alternative myth.

Appalachian English has roots that extend far into the past. The dialect features we hear the most about demonstrate a link to Scots-Irish heritage: *The car needs washed* (vs. the non-Appalachian *The car needs to be washed* or *The car needs washing*). Although upsetting to some, the different uses of a verb like *need* are perfectly normal. A verb is the boss in a sentence and requires certain things to come after it. For example, the verb *to kiss* generally requires a following noun, as in *The girl kissed the boy*. The verb *to need* in areas outside upper West Virginia, eastern Ohio, and western Pennsylvania requires another verb, like *to be*; inside this area, the verb *to need* only requires an adjective like *washed* or *painted*. This same bit of variation is found in parts of the British Isles, especially Scotland.

Another Scottish link is found in the Appalachian pattern of adding an -*s* in sentences like *The dogs walks* and *The people goes*. The Scots-Irish heritage of Appalachian English is further evident in the use of *a*-prefixing, as in *He went a-hunting*. *A*-prefixing is generally used to mean that the action is going on at that moment.

One often overlooked aspect of Appalachian English heritage is the dialects' relationship to Southern English and African American Vernacular English (AAVE). One of the marked speech features of both Appalachian and Southern English speakers of either African or European ancestry is a two-part vowel (diphthong) becoming a single vowel in words like *mine* (*mahn*), *mile* (*mahl*), and *bide* (*bahd*). European-American Appalachian English has been distinctive in the past for having this feature in words such as *like*, *light*, and *wipe*. AAVE, originally a Southern variety, did not have this feature before sounds like *p*, *t*, or *k*. We have found that some African American Appalachians actually have this traditional feature of Appalachian English. As with the rest of Appalachia, there is certainly change between generations of African American Appalachians. We do not find continuity between the older and younger African American Appalachian speakers in terms of the sociolinguistic features that mark their speech as African American. But there does appear to be an Appalachian variety of AAVE, blending traditionally European-American Appalachian features with traditional AAVE features: for example, habitual *be* which marks an event as happening on a repeated or regular basis, as in the sentence *Sometimes, my ears be itching*. Understanding how ethnic diversity influences language diversity helps provide for a more complete definition of Appalachian English.

Is There a Future for Appalachian English?

The question we are most frequently asked about Appalachian English concerns its future: will Appalachian English become part of the homogeneous dialect landscape of the US? The answer is "No." First, there is no threat of the United States having a homogeneous dialect. Currently, the US is experiencing grammatical and sound system alterations; these language changes ensure a wide diversity of language patterns across the US. Second, the Appalachian region's culture and identity continues to be dissimilar to that of its neighbors. As long as Appalachia remains a culturally distinct area, the English spoken here will continue to be different from other regional Englishes.

Notes

1 The prejudice against Appalachian English may be even more sinister than this would suggest. After all, the ability to acquire languages as a child is part of our genetic code; to claim that one variety of a language is deficient is like claiming that an entire social group has a genetic defect.

2 The stereotype of Appalachian English may certainly contribute to the notion that it is somehow "bad" to sound Appalachian. As anyone who has seen the spellings in a Hillbilly Dictionary knows, the public's ideas about Appalachian English have more to do with the speaker's perceived illiteracy than with sound or grammar differences. For example, spelling the word *was* as *wuz* does not indicate a sound change since it is only "eye dialect," but instead, it is supposed to indicate the "speaker's" level of intelligence and formal education.

Acknowledgment

The West Virginia Dialect Project would like to thank the National Science Foundation (BCS-9986247) and West Virginia University for supporting our research.

If These Hills Could Talk (Smoky Mountains)

Christine Mallinson, Becky Childs,
Bridget Anderson, and Neal Hutcheson

4 A creek running through the Great Smoky Mountain National Park. © by John von Rosenberg.

Driving the steep and winding roads along the border of western North Carolina and eastern Tennessee, it is easy to see why the Cherokee Indians who first settled in this mountainous region named it the "place of blue smoke." The trademark of these hills is the ever-present blue-gray mist that casts a hazy glow over the dense fir and spruce pine covered landscape. The Smoky Mountains, or the Smokies, as they are known locally, are a well-known destination for tourists from across the United States. At the same time, the lush forest, underground caves, and natural water sources provide a veil of cover under which one could easily fade into the backdrop of the mountains – as notorious fugitive Eric Rudolph did for nearly five years. The terrain has played a major role in the development of mountain life and culture, and continues to be a source of past and present local tradition.

Stereotypes abound about the people who call Appalachia their home. The common assumption is that it is a region lacking in racial and ethnic diversity, populated mostly by whites of European ancestry. But the Smoky Mountains and Appalachia in general were actually settled by diverse groups of people. Coming to the area around 1000 AD, the Cherokee Indians left a strong legacy: Oconoluftee, Nantahala, Hiwassee, Cheoah, Junaluska, Cataloochee, and Cullowhee are just a few of the places whose names pay homage to the Smoky Mountains' Cherokee settlers. Today, many flourishing communities of Cherokee Indians and other Native Americans still reside in the Smokies. For example, the Snowbird Cherokee in Graham County, North Carolina, continue to preserve their distinct ethnic and cultural identities as Native Americans and actively maintain their ancestral language. The tiny community of Snowbird contains nearly one-third of the total Cherokee-speaking population in the eastern United States, making it a significant community in the preservation and transmission of the Cherokee language and culture.

In addition to Native American groups, European Americans of varying ancestry – Scots-Irish, English, German, Polish, Swiss, Portuguese, Spanish, French and more – have populated the Smoky Mountain region since the late 1700s and early 1800s. Likewise, some African Americans were brought to the area as slaves of these white settlers, but independent, non-slave African American settlements have also existed in Appalachia since these earlier times. One small community, called Texana, was established in the Smoky Mountains as early as 1850. Located high on a mountain about a mile from Murphy, North Carolina, Texana was named for an African American woman named Texana McClelland, who founded the first black settlement in the area. Today the community has about 150 residents who still live along the same mountain hillside where the original inhabitants first settled.

As these diverse groups of white, black, and Native American founders settled in the Smoky Mountain area, they all brought with them many different ways of speaking. Because of the extreme ruggedness of the high country's terrain, the relative inaccessibility of the Smoky Mountains allowed these different dialects to blend together in isolation over the past several centuries and develop into a distinct regional variety of speech that is often called "mountain talk." Typically, outsiders who visit the area comment on the "twang" that they hear in locals' speech. Indeed, many Smoky Mountain English pronunciations are quite different from the speech that travelers might hear in the North, the Midwest, or other regions of the American South.

Pronunciation

Many of the vowels of the Smoky Mountain dialect are quite distinct from other English varieties, even those in Southern English. While these differences may sound strange to some people, they give mountain talk a distinct character or, as one early dialectologist put it, "a certain pleasing, musical quality . . . the colorful, distinctive quality of Great Smokies speech." One feature noticed by newcomers to the area is that Smoky Mountain speakers often lengthen certain vowels and break them into what sounds like two syllables. For example, the *eh* sound in the word *bear* may sound more like *bayer*, and the short *i* sound in a world like *hill* may come to sound more like *heal*. In another example, which tends to be found in the speech of older mountain folk, the short *a* vowel can split and turn into a diphthong, usually before *f*, *s*, *sh*, and *th* sounds, so that *pass* would sound like *pace* and *grass* like *grace*.

Another vowel characteristic of Smoky Mountain English speakers is their pronunciation of long *i*. The typical Smoky Mountain *i* is a broad, unglided version of *i*, so that the word *bright* would approximate the sound of the word *brat* and *right* would almost sound like *rat*. When *i* is followed by *r*, for example, the *ire* sound may sound more like *ar*, so that *fire* and *tire* will be pronounced as *far* and *tar* by Smoky Mountain speakers.

The r sound is also an important feature of Smoky Mountain English. In contrast to some Southern English varieties that drop their *r*'s, as in *deah* for *deer*, Smoky Mountain English is primarily an *r*-pronouncing dialect. Moreover, in certain cases, mountain speakers may sound like they are even "adding" *r*'s to words where standard varieties do not use them. For example, visitors to the Smokies may hear *winder* for *window*, *feller* for *fellow*, and *yeller* for *yellow*. Another pronunciation trait affects other vowels at the ends of words, so that *extra* and *soda* are pronounced as *extry* and *sody*. In fact, it was not uncommon for us to hear older mountain speakers refer to a soft drink or soda pop as *sody water*.

Grammar

Differences in pronunciation are not the only distinguishing traits of Smoky Mountain English. Distinct grammatical features characterize it as well. Perhaps one of the most well-known features is the tendency for Smoky Mountain speakers to attach the *a* prefix (pronounced as *uh*) to verbs that end in *-ing*, particularly when they are telling stories or recounting events. For example, one might hear a Smoky Mountain English speaker say *One night that dog was a-beggin' and a-cryin' to go out.* Although this sentence may occur in many varieties of American English, it is most common in Appalachian and Smoky Mountain English.

Another common feature of Smoky Mountain English is the tendency to regularize or use different verb forms in the past tense. This may take the form of using *was* where standard English would prescribe *were*, as in the sentence *We saw a bear when we was a-huntin' yesterday.* Or, speakers may use irregular past forms such as *growed* instead of *grew* or *clumb* instead of *climbed.* Although many of these sentence structures may be considered by some people to be "bad grammar" or "bad English," these non-standard dialect variations are no better or worse than any other language differences. Often, in fact, these features reflect older language patterns that were considered proper and standard at one time during the development of English.

Many of the differences in the Smoky Mountain dialect can be attributed to the linguistic legacy that was brought by the original founders to the area. Numerous early white settlers who came to the Smokies in the late 1700s were of Scots-Irish descent. In the language these settlers carried over from Ireland and Scotland, adding *-s* to third person plural verbs was an acceptable grammatical feature. As a result, we find many mountain speakers using constructions such as *The people that goes there* – not because they are speaking incorrect grammar, but because this form is similar to the way of marking agreement with certain types of verbs and plural nouns in Scots-Irish English.

Smoky Mountain English also uses special combinations of helping verbs – *can, could, may, might, must, ought to, shall, should, will,* and *would.* Speakers of many rural dialects may use one modal verb together with another, usually to mark a particular speaker frame of mind. The most frequent double modal combination is formed with *might* and *could,* as in *If it quits raining, you might could go.* In this sentence, the speaker is indicating that if conditions are right, then the action in the future may be able to take place. Although this use may create some confusion for those who are not native users of this construction and who are unfamiliar with it, these verb combinations express possibility or probability in English in a way that is not otherwise available through a simple construction. Double modals such as *might would, would might, may could*, and even such interesting combinations as *might should ought to* are used to nuance meanings in subtle ways.

The verb particle *done* is also used in significant ways. In the sentence *She done gone there already*, the verb form *done* is combined with a past verb form to emphasize the fact that an action has already been completed. Completive *done* is used quite frequently in Smoky Mountain English, but it is found in other rural varieties of American English and in African American English as well. The form *liketa* also has a special meaning in Smoky Mountain English. In the sentence *It was so cold on our camping trip last night, we liketa froze to death*, the speaker uses this construction to indicate a narrowly averted action – real or imagined; the campers knew they weren't literally going to freeze to death, but they were still worried that they would. Dialects often use unique words and phrases to represent aspects of verb tense that standard English cannot express as succinctly.

Vocabulary

One of the most obvious ways in which the Smoky Mountain dialect distinguishes itself is in its vocabulary. Like any dialect, Smoky Mountain English has terms that refer to the local way of life and are woven into its culture. Many Smoky Mountain dialect words refer to unique places in the mountains. For example, *bald* means a mountaintop with no trees, *branch* is an area or settlement defined by a creek, *bottom* is a low-lying area or valley, and *holler* is a valley surrounded by mountains. Other vocabulary items refer to inhabitants or features of the mountain landscape. *Jasper* refers to an outsider, someone who is not from the mountains. *Boomer* is the name of the red squirrel that is indigenous to the Smokies. *Poke salad* is a salad made of wild greens that grow in the mountains – poisonous unless boiled properly before being eaten. And a *ramp* is a small wild onion with a distinctive, long-lasting smell.

Still other words are variants that may or may not have counterparts in Standard English; for example, *cut a shine* for *dance, tote* for *carry, fetch* for *go get, sigogglin* for *crooked or leaning, tee-totally* for completely, and *yander* or *yonder* to mean *over there*. Other old-fashioned words, such as *dope* for *soft drink* or *soda pop*, are still used in the mountains, although elsewhere these terms have fallen out of use. Even though some of the unique words are carryovers from earlier history, especially Scots-Irish English, we also see new words being invented and the meanings of old words being changed and adapted to fit current communicative needs.

One of the most characteristic items of the Smokies is the use of *you'ns* where other Southerners might use the more familiar variant, *y'all*, pronounced more like *yuns* or *yunz* than a simple combination of *you-ones*. *You'ns* is most typically used for plural but may be used when speaking to one person in special circumstances. In fact, next time you visit the Smokies, ask for directions and you're likely to hear *Where you'ns from?*

Although outsiders may think that "mountain talk" is unsophisticated or uneducated, the complex features briefly surveyed here indicate that this dialect is anything but simple. The people of the Smoky Mountains have created and maintained a dialect that reflects both their history and their identity. This dialect is quite distinct both linguistically and socially. As you will hear when you visit the area, mountain talk displays and preserves local tradition, culture, and experience. To hear the language of the Smoky Mountains is to hear the mountains talk.

A Short Dictionary of Smoky Mountain English

afeared afraid
airish breezy, chilly
bald treeless mountaintop
bluff cliff, usually facing a river
boomer red squirrel indigenous to the Smokies
bottom flat land along a stream or riverbed
branch area or settlement defined by a creek
britches pants
cut a shine to dance
dope soft drink, soda pop
eh law! Oh well!
fair up when rainy weather clears up
fetch to get
fritter fried patty made out of cornmeal

Christine Mallinson, Becky Childs, et al.   27

haint ghost

holler valley surrounded by mountains

jasper outsider, stranger

liketa almost, nearly

mountain laurel rhododendron

painter local pronunciation of *panther*

pick to play a stringed bluegrass instrument, like a banjo or a guitar

plait to braid

poke bag or sack

poke salad wild greens boiled to leach out poisons; often mixed with egg

razorback wild hog

ramp small wild onion

right smart great in quality, quantity, or number

sigogglin tilted or leaning at an angle, crooked

tee-totally completely

tote to carry

(over) yander/yonder over there (in the distance)

young'un child

you'ns (pronounced "yunz") you (plural)

References and Further Reading

Montgomery, Michael B. and Joseph S. Hall (2003) *Dictionary of Smoky Mountain English*. University of Tennessee Press.

Neal Hutcheson (director) (2003) *Mountain Talk*. A video documentary. North Carolina Language and Life Project, North Carolina State University.

Kephart, Horace, J. Karl Nicholas, and Harold F. Farwell (eds.) (1993) *Smoky Mountain Voices: A Lexicon of Southern Appalachian Speech Based on the Research of Horace Kephart*. University Press of Kentucky.

Doing the Charleston (South Carolina)

Maciej Baranowski

5 Historic building in Charleston, South Carolina. © by Joshua Sowin.

Charleston has always been a little different, and Charlestonians have for the most part cherished their distinctiveness. Being perhaps the most Southern city of all – socially and culturally – it was of course different from any city in the North. In fact, the Civil War began with the firing on Fort Sumter in Charleston Harbor on April 12, 1861. But Charleston was also different within the South, dominating the region culturally and economically for almost two centuries. Its vast influence and the inwardness it developed after the Civil War have sometimes led to resentment in the rest of the region. In turn, that may have strengthened Charlestonians' sense of cultural identity.

It is not surprising that the city's social and cultural prominence should be paralleled by the remarkably distinct character of its dialect. That distinctiveness was first noted in 1888 by Sylvester Primer in an article entitled "Charleston Provincialisms." The features of the dialect listed by Primer were largely confirmed by the systematic study carried out by dialectologists in the first half of the twentieth century, summarized in Raven McDavid's 1955 article "The Position of the Charleston Dialect." The accent that emerges from this study, as well as from tape-recordings of Charlestonians born around the beginning of the twentieth century, is distinct not only from most other dialects of American English but also from the rest of the South. The special position that it occupies among the dialects of North America is not necessarily due to the uniqueness of any single feature, as most of its traits can be found in other dialects of English, but rather to its unique combination of features and to the sources of these traits.

The Historical Setting

When Spanish and French explorers arrived in the South Carolina area in the sixteenth century, they found a land inhabited by many small tribes of Native Americans, mostly Catawbas and Cherokees. The first permanent English community was established near present-day Charleston in 1670. Settlers from the British Isles and other parts of Europe built plantations throughout the coastal low country, growing profitable crops of rice and indigo. African slaves were brought in large numbers to provide labor for the plantations, and by 1720 they formed the majority of the population. The port city of Charleston became an important hub of commerce and culture – and a highly stratified society. By the time of the Revolutionary

War, South Carolina was one of the richest colonies, with a strong governing class of merchants and planters leading the fight for independence from Great Britain. At the same time, the region had an extensive underclass of slaves who constituted the workforce for its economic base.

Unhappy with restrictions over free trade and the call for the abolition of slavery that led to the Civil War, South Carolina became the first Southern state to secede from the Union. The City was devastated during the Civil War and its economy suffered for many years afterward. In more recent decades, it has developed into one of America's great tourist sites, connected to its past while celebrating its present. The lavish, traditional architecture of the homes inhabited by mostly upper-class whites stand side by side with former slave quarters and city markets now celebrating the Gullah culture of African Americans, with language differences still reflecting the similarities and differences of its history. In this description, the focus is on the traditional Charleston speech used by the longstanding white population; Gullah is described in chapter 28, "Gullah Islands".

Traditional Sounds of Charleston

One of the most striking features of the traditional Charleston accent is the quality of the vowels in words such as *day* and *made* on the one hand, and *go* and *boat* on the other. In most dialects of English today, these vowels are actually pronounced as a combination of two vowel sounds one after another, or diphthongs. In the case of words such as *day* and *made*, the vowel begins close to the vowel of *dead* and ends like the one in *see*. The gliding nature of these vowels is sometimes reflected in the spelling, as in *day* or *maid*. Similarly, the vowel in words such as *go* and *boat* is a combination of two vowel elements: it begins as the vowel in *bought* and ends as the vowel in *boot*. Again, the spelling sometimes reflects the two different sound qualities comprising this vowel, as in *sow* and *row*, where the *w* represents the vowel in *boo*.

In the traditional Charleston accent these vowels are produced by maintaining the quality of the first vowel element throughout the syllable (the vowel of *dead* in *day* and that of *bought* in *go*); they are monophthongs. Or, they are produced by what linguists call ingliding vowels. In such vowels the second element is pronounced with the tongue in neutral, central position, the one in which it rests when we are breathing. In the Charleston version of these two vowels, the tongue is closer to the roof of the mouth, not unlike in the vowels in *bee* and *boo*. The ingliding version of the vowel in *day*, for example, sounds like *dee-uh*, and *gate* sounds like *gee-yuht*.

Unglided versions of the vowels of *made* and *boat* are also found in Wisconsin, Minnesota, and the Pennsylvania German area, but the ingliding pronunciations of the vowel are not found in any other dialect of American English. They are, however, found in Gullah, the English-based creole spoken on the coast and Sea Islands of South Carolina and Georgia which developed as a contact language among African slaves. Gullah has also contributed some common vocabulary to the speech of white and African Americans in Charleston, such as *cooter* (turtle), *pinder* (peanut), *yard-ax* (unskilled preacher), and *hu-hu* (hoot owl).

Some of the distinctiveness of the Charleston accent may stem from the extensive contact between the two ethnic groups, which constituted two different speech communities: Charleston's English-speaking whites and Gullah-speaking African Americans. It may seem paradoxical that an upper-class white dialect like that of Charleston could be linked to the stigmatized speech patterns of ex-slaves in the plantations of the Sea Islands, but the latter were often employed in the households of Charleston's upper class, and the white children would pick up elements of Gullah from the speech of their maids and nannies.

Another element of the traditional dialect of Charleston is the softened sound of *k* and *g* in words such as *car* and *garden*, pronounced with a *y* sound after the *k* or *g*, as *kyah* and *gyahden*. This feature was present in some dialects of English in England at the time of the settlement of Charleston and may have been inherited directly from them. Another possibility is that it emerged in Charleston as a result of contact with Gullah, where it also was present.

A prominent feature of the traditional dialect in its traditional form is the quality of the vowels in words such as *rice* and *like*, and *house* and *about*, that is, before voiceless consonants (produced without vibration of the vocal folds). In Charleston, the vowel begins with the tongue in a higher position, the same as in the initial sound of *about* or *abroad*. This pronunciation has been stereotyped in spellings such as *a boot* for *about*, pronounced something like *uh-buh-oot*. This pronunciation is found not only in Charleston; Canada is known for this pronunciation, as well as parts of the US such as the Tidewater region of Virginia. The initial part of the vowel sound is also raised in the pronunciation of *like*, *rice*, and *tight*. In its most extreme form, the vowel of *like* may sound more like *lake* and *rice* more like *race*.

Another feature of Charleston is a lack of distinction between certain vowels before *r*, leading to identical pronunciation of words such as *ear* and *air*, *hear* and *hair*, and *beer* and *bear*. Both members of their word pairs sound like the latter member, so that *ear* and *air* are pronounced as *air*. Charleston is one of the few dialects of English characterized by a merger of these two vowels, though this is a prominent feature of New Zealand English and can occur in extreme forms of the New York City dialect. Yet another peculiarity of Charleston's traditional dialect is the use of the vowel of *buck* in words such as *book*, *put*, and *look*. To go along with its distinctive vowels, Charleston was until recently an *r*-less dialect, so that *pork* and *born* sounded like *poke* and *bone*.

A Changing Dialect

The combination of features made Charleston sound very distinctive indeed. However, in the last few decades most of the distinctive features have been dying out rapidly. The two most prominent features of the traditional dialect, the unglided and ingliding vowels in *day*, *came*, *go*, and *boat*, and the raised initial part of the vowels in *rice*, *like*, *house*, and *about* are now largely gone. Many Charlestonians are still aware of them and list them as the defining features of the traditional dialect, but they can only be heard in the speech of some older members of the city's upper class. This is not surprising, as the upper class has always been the locus of the most prominent features of the dialect, possibly due in part to their contact with Gullah-speaking maids and servants, which has now diminished. Charleston has witnessed great migration movements into the city in the last few decades, both from other parts of the South and from the North. This no doubt has contributed significantly to the disappearance of some of its traditional features. Although the dialect is changing, one of the features seems to be more resilient than others – the lack of distinction between the vowels in *beer* and *bear* or *fear* and *fair*.

In addition to the disappearance of the old distinctive features, dialect development in Charleston has followed the lead of other regions. The vowel in words such as *two*, *do*, and *boot* is now also pronounced with the tongue moving to the front of the mouth, so that *two* can sound like *tee-oo*. This particular feature is now found in a large number of American dialects in the South, California, and other places. Another recent feature in Charleston – one also found in the South in general and in Philadelphia

– is the pronunciation of words such as *so*, *go*, and *bone*, where the first element of the vowel is pronounced with the tongue in central, rather than the usual back, position, so that *bone* can sound like *bay-own*.

Some vowel distinctions are disappearing in Charleston today. Charleston is on its way to a merger of the vowels in words such as *cot* and *caught* and *Don* and *dawn*. The youngest speakers do not distinguish between the vowels in these words: they hear them as the same and pronounce them identically. The oldest speakers, however, clearly distinguish between them, while middle-aged speakers vary: in some words the two vowels may be identical, for example in *Don* and *dawn*, whereas in others they may make a distinction, as in *cot* vs. *caught*. The merger of these two vowels is one of the most vigorous sound changes occurring in North American English today, expanding rapidly across many dialect regions, and Charleston is participating in this change.

Another recent development in Charleston is the so-called *pin/pen* merger: a lack of distinction between the vowel of *pin* and the vowel of *pen* because of the nasal sound that follows the vowel. As a result, word pairs like *pin/pen*, *him/hem*, and *sinned/send* are produced the same. This feature is generally recognized as a Southern dialect trait.

Finally, Charleston today, as opposed to only a few decades ago, is largely *r*-ful in words like *pork* and *born*, and shares this recent development with the rest of the South.

How Southern is Charleston?

The dialect status of traditional Charleston speech is a paradox. Though it is perhaps the most Southern city in terms of its history and culture, its traditional sound system is not very Southern at all. It does not sound very Southern to most ears – in fact, Charlestonians are sometimes identified as Northerners or even Californians when they travel across the US. The sound system does not have most of the prominent characteristics of the South. The most salient element of the Southern speech is the ungliding of the vowel in words such as *my*, *pie*, and *five*, pronounced with only the first element of the diphthong, as in *mah* for *my* or *pah* for *pie*. Such pronunciations can sometimes be heard in Charleston now, but the level of usage is much lower than in, for example, Columbia, South Carolina. Charleston does not have other elements of Southern speech either, such as the lengthening and gliding of certain vowels that are associated with "the Southern drawl." For example, words such as *bid* or *bed* are pronounced as *bih-eed* and *beh-eed* in many parts of the South, but not in Charleston. Though Charleston speech may be slowly acquiring these Southern features and one day may sound like the speech of the rest of the South, for now it remains a marginal Southern dialect. It is still different from everyone else's, as it always has been.

Acknowledgment

Thanks to Bill Labov, Sherry Ash, Corky Feagin, Uri Horesh, Gillian Sankoff, Erik Thomas, and Walt Wolfram for their helpful comments and suggestions for this chapter.

References and Further Reading

McDavid, Raven I., Jr. (1955) The position of the Charleston dialect. *Publications of the American Dialect Society* 23: 35–49.
O'Cain, Raymond K. (1972) A social dialect survey of Charleston, South Carolina. Dissertation, University of Chicago.
Primer, Sylvester (1888) Charleston Provincialisms. *American Journal of Philology* IX: 198–213.

The Lone Star State of Speech (Texas)

Guy Bailey and Jan Tillery

6 A traditional Texas welcome. © by Lisa Young.

Few states have as great a presence in the popular imagination as Texas. For many Americans the mere mention of the state brings to mind oil and cowboys, glitzy modern cities and huge isolated ranches, braggadocio and excess. The popular image has been fueled to a large extent by the size of the state, its portrayal in television shows such as *Dallas* and in movies such as *Giant* and *The Alamo*, its larger-than-life political figures such as Lyndon

Johnson, and its unique history. Unlike other states, Texas was an independent nation before it became a state, had its own Revolutionary War and creation story (who hasn't heard of the Alamo?), and negotiated special considerations when it joined the Union (the Texas flag, for instance, can fly at the same level as the United States flag). Moreover, the pride of Texans in their state and its culture reinforces the idea that Texas is somehow unique. Visitors to the state are often struck by the extent to which the Texas flag is displayed, not only at government offices, but also at private residences, on the sides of barns, at car dealerships, and on T-shirts, cups, and other items. The Texas flag flies virtually everywhere, even in areas like the Rio Grande Valley, where the flag of Texas often stands alongside the flag of Mexico.

Perhaps because of the sense of the state's uniqueness in the popular imagination, Texas English (TXE) is often assumed to be somehow unique too. The inauguration of George W. Bush as President, for instance, led to a rash of stories in the popular media about the new kind of English in the White House (Armed Forces Radio ran an interview with us on the new President's English once an hour for 24 hours). The irony of the media frenzy, of course, is that the man George Bush was replacing in the White House spoke a variety of English that was quite similar to Bush's in many ways and perhaps even more marked by regional features. Actually, the uniqueness of TXE is probably more an artifact of the presence of Texas in the popular imagination than a reflection of linguistic circumstances. Only a few features of Texas speech do not occur somewhere else. Nevertheless, in its mix of elements both from various dialects of English and from other languages, TXE is in fact somewhat different from other closely related varieties.

A Short Linguistic History of Texas

Any linguistic overview of Texas must begin with the realization that English is, historically, the second language of the state. Even setting aside the languages of Native Americans in the area, Spanish was spoken in Texas for nearly a century before English was. With the opening up of Texas to Anglo settlement in the 1820s, however, English quickly became as widely used as Spanish, although bilingualism was not uncommon in early Texas. While the outcome of the Texas Revolution meant that Anglos would outnumber Hispanics for many years to come and that English would be the dominant language in the new nation and state, the early Hispanic settlement of the state insured that much of that culture (the ranching system, for example) and many Spanish words (e.g., *mesa*, *remuda*, and *pilón*) would blend with the culture and language that Anglos brought from the east to form a unique Texas mix. The continuing influx of settlers from 1840 to the beginning of the twentieth century enhanced and transformed the mix.

Anglos from both the Lower South (Louisiana, Mississippi, Alabama, Georgia, and South Carolina) and the Upper South (Tennessee, Kentucky, and North Carolina) moved rapidly into the new state after 1840, frequently bringing their slaves with them. Lower Southerners generally dominated in east and southeast Texas and Upper Southerners in the north and central parts of the state, though there was considerable dialect mixing. This complex dialect situation was further complicated, especially in southeast and south central Texas, by significant direct migration from Europe. Large numbers of Germans, Austrians, Czechs, Italians, and Poles (the first permanent Polish settlement in the US was at Panna Maria in 1854) came to Texas during the nineteenth century. In some cases their descendants preserved their languages well into the twentieth century, and they influenced English in certain parts of Texas even as they gradually gave up their native tongues.

Although the border between Texas and Mexico has always been a permeable one, migration from Mexico accelerated rapidly after the Mexican Revolution of 1910–20, slowed somewhat during the mid-twentieth century, and since 1990 has been massive. As late as 1990, only 20 percent of the 4 million Mexican Americans in Texas were born in Mexico. After 1990, however, the number of immigrants grew rapidly. During the two-year span between 2000 and 2002, for instance, foreign migration into Texas, most of it from Mexico, totaled more than 360,000. The new immigration is steadily changing the demographic profile of the state and insures that Spanish will remain a vital language in Texas for some time to come. In fact, it has led to a resurgence of Spanish in some areas. The linguistic consequences of the new migration will be worth following.

Some Characteristics of Texas English

As the settlement history suggests, TXE is a form of Southern American English and thus includes many of the lexical, grammatical, and phonological features of Southern American English. As a result of the complex settlement pattern, however, the South Midland/Southern dialect division that divided areas to the east was blurred in Texas. Throughout the history of the state, South Midland lexical items (e.g., *green bean* and *chigger*) and phonological features (e.g., constricted postvocalic *r* in words like *forty* and intrusive *r* in words like *warsh*) have coexisted and competed with Southern words (e.g., *snap bean* and *redbug*) and pronunciations ("*r*-lessness" in words like *forty* and *four*), although Southern features were and still are strongest in east Texas. In south, south central, and west Texas, a substantial number of Spanish words gained general currency. Lexical items like *frijoles, olla, arroyo*, and *remuda* reflect not only the relatively large number of Hispanics in the areas, but also the importance of Mexican American culture in the development of a distinct Texas culture. These areas of the state are different linguistically in one other way. Many features of Southern American English never became as widespread there so that hallmarks of Southern English like the quasi-modal *fixin' to* (as in *I can't talk to you now; I'm fixin' to leave*), multiple modals like *might could* (as in *I can't go today, but I might could go tomorrow*), and traditional pronunciations like the upgliding diphthong in *dog* (often rendered in dialect literature as *dawg*) have always been restricted in their occurrence in south and south central Texas, although they occurred extensively elsewhere.

Other trademarks of Southern English also occur extensively throughout most of the state, with south and south central Texas sometimes being exceptions. These include both stereotypical phonological features such as the *pen/pin* merger (both words sound like the latter) and the loss of the offglide of *i* in words like *ride* and *right* (so that they sound like *rahd* and *raht*), and also grammatical features like *y'all, fixin to*, and perfective *done* (as in *I've done finished that*). In addition, a number of lexical items seem to have originated or have their greatest currency in Texas (e.g., *tank* 'stock pond', *maverick* 'stray or unbranded calf', *doggie* 'calf', and *roughneck* 'oil field worker'), while at least one traditional pronunciation, the use of *ar* in words like *horse* and *for* (this makes *lord* sound like *lard*), occurs only in Texas, Utah and a few other places.

Change and Persistence in Texas Speech

Few states have been transformed as radically as Texas during the last thirty years. Rapid metropolitanization, the increasing dominance of high tech-industries in the state's economy, and massive migration have reshaped the demography of the state. Roughly a third of the population now lives in the Dallas–Fort Worth, Houston, and San Antonio metropolitan areas, and non-native Texans make up an increasingly large share of that population. Between 1950 and 1970, 85% of the population growth in Texas came from natural increase. With people moving rapidly into the state from other areas during the 1970s, migration accounted for 60% of the population growth. While migration slowed during the 1980s, accounting for only 35% of the growth, during the 1990s it accelerated again and accounted for more than half. Much of the migration into Texas before 1990 was from other states, but since 1990 it has been from other countries. Texas, then, has become a metropolitan, diverse, high-tech state – with significant linguistic consequences.

Perhaps the most obvious consequence is an emerging rural–urban linguistic split. Although most Southern features remain strong in rural areas and small cities, in large metropolises many stereotypical features are disappearing. The *pen/pin* merger, the loss of the offglide in *i*, and upgliding diphthongs in words like *dog* are now recessive in metropolitan areas, although the first two in particular persist elsewhere. The rural–urban split is so far largely a phonological one, though. Both *y'all* and *fixin' to* are expanding to non-natives in metropolises (and to the Hispanic population too). Those grammatical features that are disappearing in metropolises (e.g., perfective *done* in *They done left*) seem to be disappearing elsewhere as well.

Even as some traditional pronunciation features are disappearing, some interesting new developments are taking place. Especially in urban areas, but also in rural west Texas, the vowels in words like *caught* and *cot* are becoming merged (both sound like *cot*), as are tense/lax vowel pairs before *l*: *pool* and *pull* are now homophones or near homophones throughout much of the state, and *feel/fill* and *sale/sell* are increasingly becoming so. The *caught/cot* merger is particularly interesting in Texas since it should signal the movement of the phonological system away from the "Southern Shift" pattern. In the Texas Panhandle, though, things are not quite so simple. Even as the *caught/cot* merger has become the norm among those born after World War II, the loss of the offglide in *right* and *ride* and Southern Shift features remain quite strong. What seems to be emerging on the west Texas plains, then, is a dialect that combines features of Southern speech and another major dialect. The development of such a mixed pattern is not what a linguist might expect, but this is Texas, and things are just different here.

Further Reading

Atwood, E. Bagby (1962) *The Regional Vocabulary of Texas.* Austin: University of Texas Press.

Bailey, Guy, Tom Wikle, Jan Tillery, and Lori Sand (1996) The linguistic consequences of catastrophic events: An example from the southwest. In Jennifer Arnold et al. (eds.), *Sociolinguistic Variation: Data, Theory, and Analysis*, Stanford, CA: CSLI Publications, 435–51.

Labov, William (1994) *Principles of Linguistic Change: Internal Factors.* Oxford: Basil Blackwell.

Thomas, Erik R. (2001) *An Acoustic Analysis of Vowel Variation in New World English.* Publication of the American Dialect Society 85. Durham, NC: Duke University Press.

Tillery, Jan, Guy Bailey, and Tom Wikle (2004) Demographic Change and American Dialectology in the 21st Century. *American Speech* 79: 227–49.

7

Speaking the Big Easy (New Orleans, LA)

Connie Eble

7 Bourbon Street, New Orleans during Mardi Gras. © by EauClaire Media.

A new Roman Catholic bishop was recently installed in New Orleans. The ceremony culminated in a recessional from the cathedral with the bishop clad in all the finery of his office and accompanied by richly vested altar servers and clergy as well as governmental and civic leaders. A local resident thought that the event would be a memorable occasion for his two-year-old daughter and took her to Jackson Square. As the procession made its way through the onlookers, he lifted her onto his shoulders so that she could see. When the bishop came into view, she knew just what to do. She started waving energetically and called out, "Throw me something, mistah." Because of Mardi Gras, the child had already learned the proper linguistic response at a parade – to call out to the people in costume asking to be thrown beads or other trinkets. Knowing local lore and practicing local customs and language – whether from the cradle or as a convert – are essential for an authentic New Orleanian.

New Orleans has always considered itself *sui generis*. Its very survival on a strip of alluvial land below sea-level between a shallow lake and the mighty Mississippi River is a source of pride. Founded in 1718 about 100 miles from the mouth of the Mississippi River to anchor the French colony of Louisiana, the port stood sentinel between the Gulf of Mexico to the south and almost half a continent to the north. Although its location made the city prone to diseases like yellow fever, to springtime flooding from the rising river, and to tropical storms, it also made the port strategically important to European colonial powers and later to the United States of America, which, in order to acquire the port of New Orleans, purchased the vast Louisiana territory from Napoleon.

Even though Louisiana was officially a colony of Spain for over thirty years (1769–1803), and even though slaves from Africa and immigrants from German-speaking Europe and from British America made up a sizable portion of the population, New Orleans was mainly French-speaking at the time of the Louisiana Purchase in 1803. Americanization and the English language soon permeated, creating a social division that remained important up to the twentieth century. After the Louisiana Purchase, the term *creole* was used to mean "native," distinguishing locals whose families had lived in colonial Louisiana from those whose families arrived after the port became a part of the US. Most of the people to whom the term applied were speakers of French or Spanish, and many were of African or mixed African and European ancestry, including many free people of color. Currently, Creole is the term that many descendants of mixed African and French or Spanish ancestry prefer for themselves. As a linguistic term, a creole is a type of language that developed from a pidgin, and a tiny number of African Americans in Louisiana still speak a creole of French. Another type of French still in limited use in Louisiana is a development of the dialect spoken by the Acadians, or Cajuns, who came to Louisiana from formerly French Canada in the 1760s. For the most part, the Acadians did not remain in the port city of New Orleans but spread into the swamps and plains of southern Louisiana and remained largely a rural people.

In the course of the nineteenth century, New Orleans absorbed in great numbers the same groups that helped build the urban centers of the North – the Germans, Irish, and Italians. In the four decades before the Civil War, New Orleans ranked second after New York as a port of entry for immigrants. By 1900 New Orleans was an English-speaking city, though many people used another language at home. Without adopting the French language, many of the immigrant groups adopted customs and cultural perspectives that had been established when the city was French, e.g., cleaning and whitewashing graves on All Saints' Day; baking king cakes in observance of Twelfth Night; setting aside a period of revelry between January 6 and Mardi Gras and a period of sobriety and somberness between Ash Wednesday and Easter Sunday; educating females and people of color separately, if at all; developing a fine cuisine using the abundant game, seafood, and vegetables of southern Louisiana. The groups in turn contributed to the unique cultural amalgam that is today greater New Orleans and that sustains varieties of the English language that sound different from those of northern Louisiana and from Cajun English.

Next to nothing based on scholarly research has been published on the speech of New Orleans. Two brief encyclopedia entries by Mackie Blanton (1989) and by Richard W. Bailey (1992) summarize the well-known characteristics of New Orleans speech and the complex cultural heritage and intricate social stratification that still influence it.

To be sure, New Orleans shares many linguistic features with its neighbors in other parts of southern Louisiana, particularly vocabulary. Most New Orleanians would recognize, if not use, many words claimed to be Cajun English, such as *boudin* 'sausage of pork, rice, and seasoning', *cush-cush* 'browned cornmeal eaten as a cereal', and *make do do* 'go to sleep'. Other words like *armoire* 'large upright wardrobe for clothing', *lagniappe* 'something extra', *lost bread* 'French toast', and *mirliton* 'vegetable pear' are used throughout southern Louisiana, both in Cajun country and around New Orleans. But even though both developed against the backdrop of French and have many French-derived vocabulary items in common, New Orleans and Cajun dialects of English sound quite different.

A New Orleans Glossary

alligator pear avocado

batture land between the levee and river

bobo minor sore, cut, or lump on the skin

brake tag automobile safety inspection sticker

cayoodle a dog of low pedigree

chickory root that is ground and roasted and added to coffee

cook down the seasoning slowly sauté small pieces of onions, celery, and bell peppers together as a step in the preparation of many dishes

crab boll/crayfish boll social gathering, usually out of doors, at which crabs or crayfish are boiled and eaten; the spices used to flavor boiling shellfish

deadmen's fingers inedible lungs of crabs

den warehouse where Mardi Gras floats are decorated and stored

devil beating his wife raining while the sun is shining

doodlebug little bug with lots of legs that rolls into a ball

dressed served with lettuce, tomatoes, and mayonnaise

flying horses carousel, merry-go-round

go-cup paper or plastic cup for drinking alcoholic beverages on the street

gris gris magic formula to bring bad luck, e.g., put the gris gris on someone

hickey knot or bump on the head or forehead

homestead financial institution that deals in home mortgages

locker closet

lost bread french toast, translation of *pain perdu*

muffaletta large Italian sandwich of ham, Genoa salami, Provolone, and olive salad on a round, seeded bun

nectar pink, almond-flavored syrup in a soda or on a snowball

pané meat breaded and fried veal or beef

pass by visit briefly, e.g., "I'll pass by your house after work."

second line mass of people who follow behind a funeral procession dancing in the streets. Now applied to a particular dance and music which has become a favorite part of wedding receptions as the bride and groom lead the assembled guests in a snake-like procession throughout the hall

stand in a wedding serve as a bridesmaid, groomsman, or usher in a wedding

shoe sole flat, glazed pastry shaped roughly like the sole of a shoe

Zatarain's popular brand of New Orleans foods, sometimes used generically for creole mustard or for the spices used to boil crabs and crawfish

The best record of the dialects of New Orleans is the 29-minute documentary film *Yeah You Rite!* (Alvarez and Kolker 1984). The voices of the film ring true to natives of the city, who love to analyze and explain the uniqueness of their city and often complain that the movies never get the New Orleans accent right. The natives interviewed in the film are quick to give their opinions about linguistic distinctions based on class, color, and neighborhood, voicing the popular perception that New Orleans has three dialects: uptown white, downtown white (also known as *Yat*), and black. In fact, language variation is much more complex than that three-part division implies, linked in part to a middle-class population that traverses neighborhood boundaries to attend old, established, parochial high schools. The linguistic situation among African Americans in New Orleans is particularly complex. Although many speak a variety of African American Vernacular English (AAVE) similar to that of urban areas throughout the United States, members of the longstanding middle-class community often speak a kind of English indistinguishable from that of middle-class whites. Regardless of pronunciation and grammatical differences, all varieties of New Orleans English include a common core of local vocabulary (see p. 45).

Local identity is a performance art in New Orleans, and people work at it. An email circulating among displaced New Orleanians lists hundreds of ways that "You know you're from New Orleans." Many are linguistic: People say you sound like you're from Brooklyn. You know it's *ask*, but you purposely say *ax*. You call tomato sauce *red gravy*. You *wrench* your hands in the *zink* with an onion to get the crawfish smell off. You can't stand people who say *the* Mardi Gras or *the* Jazzfeast. You write *eaux* for the sound *o*, as in *Geaux* Zephyrs or *Alfredeaux* sauce. New Orleanians are also sentimental about street names (Chase 1949). Part of local identity is knowing that, for example, Milan Street is pronounced *MY-lan*, Burgundy is *bur-GUN-dee*, and Calliope is *KAL-ee-ope*.

Over the past twenty years, a name has taken hold for the distinctive lower- and middle-class vernacular of whites in New Orleans. It is called *Yat*, and for the first time merits an entry in the American Heritage Dictionary (2000). Popular lore has it that Yat is a shortening of the familiar New Orleans greeting "Where you at?" It is of fairly recent usage, possibly originating as part of Ninth Ward public high school slang in the 1950s as the name of one subgroup of the student body. By the early 1980s Yat clearly referred to a local way of speaking and is now firmly entrenched as the name of a dialect. It has the derived adjective yatty, as in

You surely sound yatty on your answer machine. Yat can also designate a person who speaks that way or, more generally, a native of New Orleans. At Christmas season in 2000 and 2001, one of the most frequently heard holiday songs was "The 12 Yats of Christmas": "On the foist day a Chrismas my Mawmaw gave ta me a crawfish dey caught in Arabi." A light-hearted website for locals is maintained by the Southern Yat Hysterical Society, the name an allusion to the city's traditional Southern Yacht Club.

Most websites dedicated to the cultivation of a New Orleans identity are allied to tourism and seek to present New Orleans as unique, carnal, and exotic – a place in the United States that even has a high-caloric way of talking the English language. A website devoted to Mardi Gras (Mardi-speak 2000: www.mardigrasunmasked.com/mardigras/mardispeak.htm), for example, has a section explaining *king cake* 'wreath-shaped coffee cake eaten during the Mardi Gras season', *krewe* 'members of a carnival organization', *Mardi Gras* 'Tuesday before Ash Wednesday, season from Twelfth Night through Fat Tuesday', and many other words pertaining to the season.

The most accessible description of the language of New Orleans is part of "The Gumbo Pages," maintained by Chuck Taggert, a New Orleans native who now lives in California. From Taggert's (2000) *Yat-speak: A Lexicon of New Orleans Terminology and Speech*, much can be extracted about New Orleans pronunciation and vocabulary.

The dialects of New Orleans often lack *r* after vowels. For example, *charmer* is pronounced *CHAW-muh*. Thus, for many New Orleanians, *water*, *quarter*, and *oughtta* rhyme, and *autistic* and *artistic* are homophones. The vowel sound *ah* merges with the sound *aw* (as in *awful*) so that *John* and *lawn* rhyme. The *th* spelling is pronounced *d*, as shown by *da QUAW-tah* for *the Quarter*. The most parodied and stigmatized pronunciation is *er* for vowels spelled *oi* and *oy* in words like *boil*, *oil*, *oysters*, and *toilet*, which are pronounced as if spelled *berl*, *earl*, *ersters*, and *turlet*. New Orleanians also place the word stress on the first syllable in *adult*, *cement*, *insurance*, and *umbrella*. Other local pronunciations are *mayonnaise* as *MY-nez*, *mirliton* as *MEL-luh-tawn*, *pecan* as *puh-KAWN*, and *praline* as *PRAW-leen*, and the infamous *ask* as *ax*. There are at least four major standard local pronunciations of New Orleans – with either three or four syllables, and either *r*-full or *r*-less.

Indeed, language variety is deliberate and thriving and perhaps even economically necessary in New Orleans now that tourism has become the leading industry.

References

Alvarez, Louis, and Andrew Kolker (1984) *Yeah You Rite!* Film. Narrated by Billy Dell. New York: Center for New American Media.

The American Heritage Dictionary of the English Language, 4th edn. (2000). Ed. Joseph P. Pickett. Boston: Houghton Mifflin.

Bailey, Richard W. (1992) New Orleans. In Tom McArthur (ed.), *The Oxford Companion to the English Language*, 690. Oxford: Oxford University Press.

Blanton, Mackie (1989) New Orleans English. In Charles Reagan Wilson and William Ferris, (eds.), *Encyclopedia of Southern Culture*, 780–1. Chapel Hill: University of North Carolina Press.

Chase, John (1949) *Frenchmen, Desire, Good Children, and Other Streets of New Orleans.* New Orleans: Robert L. Crager.

New Orleans Web (2001) *Say what?!: The Language of New Orleans.* www.experienceneworleans.com/glossary.html.

Southern Yat Hysterical Society (1998, 2000) www.southernyatclub.com.

Taggert, Chuck (2000) *Yat-speak: A Lexicon of New Orleans Terminology and Speech.* www.gumbopages.com/yatspeak.html.

Sounds of Ole Man River (Memphis, TN)

Valerie Fridland

8 Paddle steamer docked on the Mississippi river. © by Dan Brandenburg.

When people from outside the South learn I grew up in Memphis, Tennessee, I inevitably get the comment, "You don't sound like you're from Memphis – what happened to your accent?" As I consider myself a true native, my response is always to ask for a description of what a Memphian sounds like. "You know, you don't have that . . . that twang" is what usually emerges as people realize they don't really know what a Memphian, or a Southerner for that matter, specifically talks like, except that they know one when they hear one. Non-Southerners, in fact, are generally not very good at separating out the different dialects spoken within the South, viewing us as one mass lump on the American dialect landscape. While Southern dialects share much linguistically and historically, intra-regional varieties are also quite salient, differing along ethnic, social and geographic lines.

Memphis is geographically poised at the border of west Tennessee, Mississippi and Arkansas, overlooking the banks of the Mississippi River. Its name, taken from another river city, the Egyptian city of Memphis on the Nile (whose residents were also "Memphians"), reflected its location on the majestic Mississippi, an early sign that Memphis was destined to become an important trading center in the region. The city was settled in the early 1800s, by, among others, the future US President Andrew Jackson, and owes much of its linguistic history to the spread of the earlier settlement from eastern Tennessee. The city continued to grow rapidly with settlers from the Southern Coastal regions in Virginia and North Carolina who migrated first into eastern Tennessee. Originally of English and Scots-Irish descent, these settlers joined others from eastern and middle Tennessee as they moved farther west. As travel became easier through new developments such as steamboats, these early immigrants were soon joined by settlers from other Southern states such as Kentucky, Alabama, Mississippi and Georgia. The combination of intra-Southern migration, a large African American community, and the city's role as a major river port and center for national goods distribution led to the formation of a recognizable local variety of speech, one that is distinctly urban in light of the contemporary trend of rural in-migration to urban areas of the South. In fact, Memphis' position as headquarters for several major companies like Federal Express and the Coca-Cola Bottling Company has contributed to local speech, with terms such as to *FedEx* used synonymously with "to ship overnight" and *coke* used for any carbonated drink. And, when a Memphian goes shopping, we are more than likely heading to Piggly Wiggly, affectionately known locally as simply "The Pig," a locally founded grocery chain that originated the supermarket concept.

Within a region so often negatively defined by its speech, there is an inherent pride in our speech and distinctions are made among intra-regional dialects. For those of us raised in Memphis, worse than the stigma of speaking with a Southern accent was the stigma of being perceived as speaking with a rural Mississippi or Arkansas accent. Native Memphians can easily tell where non-natives from other parts of the South are from, especially those that we have high degrees of contact with. Ask a Memphian what they sound like compared to other Southerners and they will probably use these groups as references for what they do not sound like. The rural dialects, those associated with the areas of Arkansas and Mississippi near Memphis, tend to be described as more "country" sounding and have more intense use of marked features like the pronunciation of the long *i* of *bye* and *time* without the glide, as in *baa* for *bye*, *tar* for *tire*, or *ah* for *I*), flapping (*idn't, wadn't* for *isn't, wasn't*), multiple negation (*I don't see nothing*), and vocabulary items like *ain't*. Eastern Tennessee, separated from Memphis by mountainous geography and the mid-state terminus of the early railroad system, is associated with Appalachian dialects and features such as intrusive *r* as in *warsh your clothes*, voiceless *w* sounds as in *hwich* for *which* and *a*-prefixing as in *I was a-hunting*. In addition, the Scarlett O'Hara breathy-voiced Southerner who drops *r*'s as in *Well, ah nevah* for *Well, I never* would be quickly tagged as a resident of the Deep South by most mid-Southern Memphians whose *r*'s remain steadfastly intact. However, while Memphians can recognize the natives from the non-natives, it is usually also a "I know it when I hear it" kind of differentiation rather than any clear-cut criteria they can list.

Part of the difficulty in discerning the differences between Southern dialects is that it is generally a matter of degree rather than kind that separates one from another. While some features like intrusive *r* and *a*-prefixing are clearly present only in certain areas of the South and not in others, most Southern features are at least marginally present in all local dialects, with the differences between local varieties hinging on the extent to which people in different areas use them in their speech. Memphians may say *y'all* and *fixin' to* as much as the next Southerner, but they don't tend to use *ain't* and lose *l* sounds as in *caw me* for *call me* or *hep* for *help* as often as their more rural neighbors. When a native Memphian hears another Southerner speak, it is not simply one trigger word or form that cues the Memphian into that speaker's background, but a composite of a number of different dialect features used at a different frequency than a Memphian would use them in similar conversation. Since very few of the distinctive language forms are by themselves diagnostic but instead are shared by these dialects, people are not readily able to articulate what it is *per se* that makes them know where another speaker is from. It is no wonder that non-Southerners who are much less exposed to the variations that occur in the South find it hard to hear differences among Southern dialects.

In addition, the enduring myth that Southern American English is a substandard variety of Standard English tends to lead to the grouping of these dialects under the same rubric of improper speech, without much investigation into the historical patterns that laid the foundations for the dialects now spoken throughout the South and the distinctions that are maintained. All of the dialect features noted above are as linguistically principled and patterned as any of the characteristic features of Northern or Western speech and many, such as *r*-lessness and vocalic mergers, are widely evidenced in other "prestige" dialects (e.g., the *r*-less speech of the highly regarded Received Pronunciation in Britain or the Western *cot/ caught* vowel merger), yet Southern dialects remain socially disfavored. As linguist Dennis Preston showed with his research into folk linguistic beliefs about the dialects spoken within the United States and as most caricatures about the South reveal, most Americans, including Southerners themselves, have negative evaluations of the varieties of English spoken in the Southern US. In general, people have only a vague idea of the types of features that make Southern dialects distinct. Instead, only a small subset of features are widely recognized, those that are highly stereotypical such as double modals (*I might could do that*) or the Southern drawl (itself a vague cover term for a variety of distinctions in the way vowel sounds are produced) and, of course, the ubiquitous *y'all*. Since most dialects within the South share these highly salient features, outsiders are unlikely to notice the differences that set the dialects apart. The fact that most media renditions of Southern accents are spoken by actors adopting what they believe replicates a generic "Southern twang" does little to help clarify the image of a united Southern tongue.

What makes the picture of intra-regional variation even more confusing is that within each area of the South, social factors such as ethnicity, age and gender also mitigate the use of different features. For example, all Southern English speakers use *tahm* for *time* and *baa* for *bye* to some degree, but white speakers from the Deep South tend to use it more extensively than, say, a white speaker in Memphis and, in general, white Southern speakers use it more extensively than black Southern speakers. Curiously, this situation is reversed in Memphis, as black Memphians show a greater frequency of use of this feature than white Memphians, showing that generalizations about the South as a whole abstract away from intra-regional variations. Similarly, while the pronunciation of the vowels in *pin* and *pen* as the same (called a "vowel merger") is still widespread, there is evidence from recent research that speakers under 25 years of age in Memphis are less likely to merge these two sounds than their older counterparts. On the other hand, the low back vowel merger which makes indistinct the difference in pronunciation of words like *cot* and *caught* or *Don* and *dawn* is more common among young white Memphians than among their older counterparts, but is not generally considered a feature of other Southern American dialects. Black Memphians, like older whites, maintain the traditional vowel distinction in words using these two vowels. In contrast, r-dropping, a feature that characterizes older speakers in the Deep South, is found among African American, but not European American, speakers in Memphis. While often local black and white speech may differ in terms of what speech features are used, the large African American population in Memphis also contributes much to the local flavor of speech in Memphis, with terms which originated in African American speech having spread out to many in the younger European American community, contributing terms such as *Dog!* (pronounced *dawg*), as in *Dog! I'm hungry* to the local variety.

Within the South, in places such as Memphis, locals tend to have very strong feelings about the variety of their speech community and its role in identifying them as an authentic member of that community, even if it is not so easy from the outside to tell different Southerners apart. When a Memphian talks about getting some '*cue* and going to visit *the King*, you can bet we are talking about a big plate of pulled pork barbecue and a visit to Graceland, not a trip to a pool hall or a European monarchy. In fact, mentioning to a local that you have ever eaten beef barbecue, much less enjoyed it, may be considered fightin' words. Speech is as much about our culture as are our hospitality, our music and our barbecue. And, as any Memphian will tell you, don't be messing with our Barbecue! The same goes for our speech.

PART II
THE NORTH

9

Yakking with the Yankees (New England)

Julie Roberts, Naomi Nagy, and
Charles Boberg

9 A row of houses on Martha's Vineyard. © by David Owens.

Introduction

Two major New England shibboleths are the "dropping" of postvocalic *r* (as in *cah* for *car* and *bahn* for *barn* and the low central vowel in words like *aunt* and *glass* (Carver 1987). Neither pattern is found across all of New England, nor are they all there is to the well-known dialect, faithfully reproduced in the movie *Good Will Hunting*. We present a brief description of the settlement of the region and give examples of current vocabulary and pronunciation patterns to illustrate both how New England differs from the rest of the country and what region-internal differences exist.

Settlement of New England

The Massachusetts Bay coastal area, one of the country's original cultural hearths (Carver 1987), was settled by English immigrants in the early 1600s. In search of better farm land, some original settlers moved west from the coast and settled the Lower Connecticut River Valley in central Connecticut. They were joined soon after by new immigrants from eastern and southern England, and later from Italy, Scotland, Ireland, and elsewhere. Settlement spread, generally along river valleys, into New Hampshire, Vermont, Maine, and Rhode Island. New England is now comprised of Maine, New Hampshire, Vermont, Massachusetts, Connecticut, and Rhode Island. Boston is still known as the hub, referring to its position as the center from which settlements radiated in New England.

The Handbook of the Linguistic Geography of New England (Kurath 1939–43) divides the area into eastern and western New England (divided by the Green Mountains of Vermont in the north, the Berkshires in the middle, and the Connecticut River farther south), with seven sub-regions dictated by settlement patterns (Carver 1987). However, today there is little in the way of linguistic markers of these regions, aside from some distinctive characteristics of eastern New England. *A Word Geography of the Eastern United States* (Kurath 1949) divides New England into only three regions (Northeastern, Southeastern, and Southwestern), better representing linguistic differences.

Ethnic groups have had differing influences across the region. These include Native American groups, such as the Abenaki in Northern

Vermont and the Mahican in southwestern Vermont, both of whom spoke languages in the Algonquian language family. Native American languages have died out in Vermont, but the Abenaki descendants remain, particularly in northwestern Vermont, and have begun a process of revival of customs and language. Also present in New England are Franco-Americans who moved south from French-speaking parts of Canada, and large Irish and Italian groups. Upper Maine (north of Penobscot Bay) is quite distinct from the rest of the region, due to ties with New Brunswick, Canada.

Vocabulary

New England has always been nautically oriented, so ship building, fishing, and seafood vocabulary are traditionally associated with the region. For example, *nor'easters* are a type of storm typical of the region. Similarly, there is a lot of farming vocabulary particular to the region, including *carting* or *teaming a load* 'hauling a load' and *open and shut day* 'a day with variable weather'. Some gastronomic terms particular to the region are *Boston brown bread*, a dessert, *grinder* 'long deli sandwich', *hamburg* 'ground beef', *tonic* 'carbonated drink', *dropped egg* 'poached egg', as well as food introduced by Native Americans such as *hasty pudding* and *quahog* (Rhode Island) or *cohog* (Boston) for a type of edible clam. A porch may be a *piazza*, a hair bun is a *pug*, a traffic circle is a *rotary* (Carver 1987:28–36). Two common ways of agreeing with someone are to say *a-yuh* or *so don't I* (meaning 'so do I').

According to a survey completed by a small group of University of New Hampshire students, words still widely used and recognized by residents of New Hampshire today include *grinder, hamburg, rotary*, and *notch* 'mountain pass'. On the other hand, *belly-bunt* 'ride a sled face-down', *pung* 'sleigh for hauling wood', and *pug* 'hair bun' are recognized by few people. Words which were not included in the older dialectological research but which are heard today include *bubbler* 'drinking fountain', *bulkie* 'round sandwich roll', and *spa* 'convenience store' in Boston; *directional* 'turn signal' and *frappe* 'milk shake' in eastern Massachusetts and New Hampshire; *dooryard* 'where you park your car' and *numb as a hake* 'not very bright' in downeast Maine; and *soggie* 'greasy hotdog', *cabinet* 'milkshake', *take a heart* 'have a heart attack' in Rhode Island.

Pronunciation

A feature of eastern New England, also exhibited by speakers in the Virginia and North Carolina hearth areas, is the vocalization (locally referred to as "dropping") of r in post-vocalic position. People talk about "New Hampsha" and "Woosta" instead of New Hampshire and Worcester. The distinction between word-initial *wh* and *w* sounds, as in *which/witch*, is retained to some extent in parts of New Hampshire, Vermont, and Massachusetts. Eastern New Englanders also traditionally make a distinction between pairs such as *for* and *four*, or *horse* and *hoarse*, which is not heard in most of the rest of the US. As a result of this distinction, combined with r-dropping, a Boston pronunciation of *short* sounds the same as *shot*; *north* rhymes with *moth*. This distinction may be disappearing among young people.

Words such as *cot* and *caught*, *stock* and *stalk* sound the same in most of eastern New England, both having a more or less rounded vowel pronounced in the low-back corner of the mouth. (An exception to this pattern is Providence, Rhode Island, where the two vowels are distinct.) Many speakers in eastern Massachusetts and northern New Hampshire have three distinct vowels in the words *Mary* (the vowel of *ban*), *merry* (the vowel of *bet*), and *marry* (the vowel of *bat*), while those in Vermont and southern New Hampshire pronounce the three words alike (Nagy 2001). Bostonians and northern New Hampshirites generally maintain a distinction between the vowels in the first syllables of *bother* and *father* (the *a* of *father* is produced further back in the mouth), while many residents of Vermont and southern New Hampshire, especially younger people, have merged those vowels (Nagy 2001).

In western New England, quite a different phonological system holds sway. As in New York City and upstate New York, speakers in Hartford and Springfield retain the distinction between *cot* and *caught*, *stock* and *stalk*. But western New England is less uniform in its speech than eastern New England. People in Vermont are likely to make no difference between *cot* and *caught*, like speakers east of them, while people in western Massachusetts are likely to disagree on this point: older people retain the difference while younger people have lost it. As for the eastern New England shibboleths mentioned above, r is regularly pronounced throughout western New England, and the broad *a* is much less common – *laugh* and *dance* have the same vowel as *lap* and *Dan*.

In Vermont, articles have been appearing regularly in the local press questioning and worrying about the possibility that the Vermont dialect may be dying. This is thought to be caused by the modern influx of people from elsewhere in the US, known as *flatlanders*, either temporarily, for skiing (such people are sometimes called *coneheads* in Vermont) or for *leaf-peeping* (admiring the fall foliage), or as permanent settlers seeking a more rural way of life. Early evidence shows that the dialect may, in fact, be changing toward a more standard-sounding one. Two of the most talked-about Vermont vowels are *ou*, as in *cow*, which is pronounced *kyou*, and long *i* as in *kite*, which is pronounced more like *koit*. Women and younger speakers are pronouncing these vowels more like they are said elsewhere in the country whereas older rural men tend to retain the more traditional Vermont pronunciations. However, not all of the news is bad for those bemoaning the fate of the heritage of Vermont, including its dialect. Another prominent feature is known locally as "*t*-dropping" or, more technically, as glottal stop (ʔ) replacement of *t*. This feature has been widely studied in Great Britain, where it is found in many dialects including the Cockney dialect demonstrated most famously by Eliza Doolittle (or Dooliʔl). Even children, including those relatively new to Vermont, are learning and using glottal stop. This is a feature of Vermont speech that doesn't appear to be going away!

Summary

Like many older parts of the US, New England, and eastern New England in particular, is characterized by a distinct local dialect that is gradually receding due to the influence of "general American" speech used in the mass media and by newcomers to the region. Much of the distinct New England vocabulary was connected with traditional occupations that are less important in today's economy. As people move from all over the country to take advantage of higher education and high-tech jobs in the Boston area, young New Englanders sound increasingly like young people in other parts of the country. However, some local features remain, especially in rural areas and in city neighborhoods with large proportions of local people. Many people in these areas still drop their *r*'s, though no longer as consistently or in as many words as they used to. As for the lack of a distinction between the vowels in *cot* and *caught*, it is actually the rest of the country that is becoming more like eastern New England.

How to Talk Like a New Englander: A Brief Dictionary

belly-bunt	ride a sled face-down	You'd be crazy to belly-bunt on a pung. (NH)
bubbler	drinking fountain	I'm thirsty. Where's a bubbler? (MA/NH)
creemee	soft ice cream	The creemee machine is broken. (VT)
dooryard	where you park your car	Park in the dooryard. (ME)
flatlander	outsider	He's a flatlander from New Jersey. (VT)
frappe	milkshake	I want a chocolate frappe. (Boston, NH)
leaf peepers	autumn tourists	You can't go out. The roads are full of leaf peepers. (VT)
nor'easter	storm typical of the region	There's a nor'easter coming. (all)
pung	sled for hauling wood	We teamed a load of wood on the pung. (NH)
quahog	type of edible clam	Let's go out for quahogs. (RI)
sliding	sledding	Grab your sled, and let's go sliding. (VT)
tonic	carbonated drink	Cola is my favorite kind of tonic. (MA)
woodchuck/ chuck	Vermonter, local	The chucks and flatlanders mix most at town meeting. (VT)

Sources: Carver 1987 and students from the Univercity of New Hampshire and the University of Vermont.

References

Carver, Craig M. (1987) *American Regional Dialects: A Word Geography*. Ann Arbor: University of Michigan Press.

Kurath, Hans (1939) *Handbook of the Linguistic Geography of New England*. Providence: Brown University.

Kurath, Hans (1949) *Word Geography of the Eastern United States*. Ann Arbor: University of Michigan Press.

Nagy, Naomi (2001) Live free or die as a linguistic principle. *American Speech* 76: 30–41.

Telsur Website 2000: www.ling.upenn.edu/phono_atlas.

Beantown Babble (Boston, MA)

Jim Fitzpatrick

10 Boston street scene. © by Andrei Tchernov.

Ever'body says words different . . . Arkansas folks says 'em different, and Oklahomy folks says 'em different. And we seen a lady from Massachusetts, an' she said 'em differentest of all. Couldn' hardly make out what she was sayin'.

John Steinbeck's appraisal of Massachusetts speech in *The Grapes of Wrath* is one of the most often cited quotes in dialectology. It addresses the reality of differences in American English. From the North End to South Station, from West Roxbury to East Milton Square, the Boston dialect is one of the most widely recognized throughout the United States. While the city itself has changed significantly since the arrival of Europeans in the Hub in the early seventeenth century, the Boston dialect has remained a hallmark of the area, with its dropped *r*'s (*Pahk the cah*), lowered and broadened vowels (*I'm going to the bahthroom*), and distinctive vocabulary (*That's wicked pissa!*, i.e., very good). Visitors to the city can hardly escape its distinctive character, and lifetime residents have come to acknowledge it as part of what makes Boston unique. So grab a tonic, come on into the pahlar, and pull up a chay-ah. Next stop, Pahk Street!

Boston, Past and Present

The dialect history of Boston begins with a rock – more specifically, Plymouth Rock, the landing site of the ship *Mayflower*, which came ashore in Plymouth, Massachusetts, in 1620. The 102 English Separatists who arrived on the ship helped establish the Massachusetts Bay Colony under Governor John Winthrop in the early 1630s. The first group of settlers in Boston proper were about 150 English Puritans who had fled from their native Lincolnshire to escape religious persecution. Boston quickly established itself as one of the major cultural, educational, and commercial centers of the original thirteen colonies; its fine harbor allowed for the development of shipping and maritime industry, and also set the stage for such historical events as the Boston Tea Party. Additionally, the Hub was home to such integral patriotic figures as Benjamin Franklin, Paul Revere, and John Hancock. The founding of Harvard College in 1636, sixteen years after the original landing of the *Mayflower* at Plymouth, established a rich educational tradition that is to this day one of the landmarks of the Boston area. With over 70 colleges and universities in the vicinity, it is the most densely populated region of higher learning in the United States, attracting many residents from other regions. But few mistake the voice of a native Beantowner.

While the Massachusetts Bay Colony's original population was almost exclusively Puritan, this did not last. By the second half of the nineteenth century, Boston was in the midst of an immigration explosion. Many of the Irish immigrants uprooted by the potato famine landed in Boston, and by 1920 the Irish were joined by large groups from Italy, Russia, and Poland, as well as several thousand Lithuanians, Greeks, Armenians, and Syrians. In total, foreign-born immigrants constituted one-third of Boston's population in 1920. Within a generation, immigrants and their children made up three-quarters of the city's population. Restrictions on immigration policy after World War I caused the immigrant population of Boston to remain somewhat static over the next half-century or so, and by 1970 only one out of eight Bostonians was a foreign-born immigrant.

Contemporary Boston is an ethnically diverse city, from its Chinatown area to the distinctly Italian North End. Boston's ethnic history gives the city its working-class flavor, but also sustains the divide between the immigrant-descended working class and the descendants of the original Puritan settlers, a divide that is manifested linguistically even in the present day. There is also dialect variation among different ethnic groups, so that, strictly speaking, there is not a single "Boston accent." While some dialect traits are shared by many Bostonians, there are other features that occur more frequently in different parts of the city or among different ethnic groups. The perceptive listener can, in fact, learn a lot about a speaker of Boston English by paying attention to some of the finer details of speech.

In one study of subdialectal variations in Boston, Laferriere (1979) draws some interesting conclusions about the connections between ethnicity and linguistic behavior. The segment -or- in the word *short*, for example, may be produced a variety of ways. Some speakers pronounce the *r* fully though many do not; speakers may also glide the vowel to pronounce it closer to the *o* found in *boat*, resulting in something like *show-uh*. Still others pronounce the vowel lower and unglided so it sounds like *shot*. Furthermore, there are differences based on ethnic group membership. Jewish groups tend to shy away from complete *r*-dropping, identifying it as socially stigmatized. Italians, however, predominantly drop the *r*, while the Irish fall somewhere along the middle of the continuum, dropping more *r*'s than the Jewish groups but fewer than the Italians. The fact that groups who retain their *r*'s still identify *r*-dropping as a feature of Boston Irish speech shows how speakers are inclined to attribute marked linguistic features to the dominant sociopolitical group of the area. This feature is also associated with the accent of East Boston, which is an area dominated by Italians, showing a strong connection between ethnicity and regional location in the city.

Boston continues to be a popular destination for transplants from around the country and around the world. Year after year, students flock to the Hub to attend the many colleges and universities in and around the city, and this phenomenon has given rise to a new group of young and middle-aged professionals who have settled in Boston but maintained their own linguistic backgrounds. From 1998 to 1999, over 75,000 people converted to Massachusetts driver's licenses from out of state, almost double that of a few years earlier. Because of these new arrivals, some observers have speculated that the Boston dialect is dwindling in scope and intensity; however, a walk down the streets of Southie (South Boston) will reveal that this is hardly the case – the Boston accent is alive and well.

Major Features of the Dialect

The icon of the Boston accent is its *r*-dropping after a vowel sound, so that Spider Man's alter ego is "Petah Pahkah." However, some of these *r*'s are not lost forever; they reappear across word boundaries when the following word begins with a vowel. The stereotypical Bostonian phrase, "Pahk the cah in Hahvahd Yahd," is thus not quite right; though the *r* would be dropped if *cah* were said in isolation, when following a vowel it is inserted. In fact, it is sometimes inserted where it wouldn't occur in other dialects, so that, "I know, the idear of it!" is an appropriate response to "The Red Sox ah lookin' good, they'ah goin' all the way this yeah!"

In addition to *r*-lessness, another particularly salient feature of the Boston dialect is the vowel shift that occurs in the speech of the Brahmins, a slowly disappearing group of upper-class Bostonians, and even among some non-Brahmins. The broad *a* sound, as in *can't* and *bath*, is produced somewhat lower and further back in this dialect than in Standard American English, so that they approach the *a* sound in *father*.

The Boston dialect also follows some of the features associated with eastern New England speech on a broader scale, including the merger of the vowels in words like *cot* and *caught*. Throughout eastern New England, these words are pronounced identically, and some New Englanders even have trouble fathoming how these vowels could ever be pronounced differently. In this respect, Bostonians align with the majority of Western dialects in the United States that merge these vowel sounds, but for the Eastern coast, this feature is quite distinct.

Vocabulary

Perhaps the best resource currently available on the Boston lexicon is Adam Gaffin's *Wicked Good Guide to Boston English*, available online at www.boston-online.com. Boston mainstays include *frappe* 'milkshake', *spuckie* 'submarine sandwich', *tonic* 'pop' or 'soda', and *bubbler* 'water fountain'. A day in the life of a Bostonian might center around a shopping trip to the *Bahgie*, or the Bargain Center in Quincy, which is now sadly defunct; in the past, an insult commonly hurled among Boston children was "Ya motha shops at the Bahgie!" On the way there, a driver in Boston might remark that the traffic is *wicked* (a general intensifier, stronger than *very*) by *The Common* (the green in the center of town), backed up near the *rotary* (a traffic circle), and that he should have taken the *parkway* (a divided highway). After a hard day of shopping, it would be time to go home for *suppa* (the third meal of the day), which, in most large Irish Catholic Boston families, would involve some kind of *p'daydas* (a staple of the Irish diet, served mashed or baked). Or, it might be *American chop suey*, a dish consisting of macaroni, hamburg (ground beef), tomato, onion, and green peppers. Other distinct Boston word uses include the "negative positive" *So don't I*, which is used by Bostonians in place of *So do I*. The Boston lexicon is, of course, also constantly evolving; words such as *nizza* (roughly "great"), which was a favorite of my mother's in West Roxbury in the 1970s, have faded somewhat from view but still pop up occasionally, while new terms are being coined and adapted for different uses all the time.

Some lexical items in Boston are crucial for getting around in the city. Visitors are often confused by the *Big Dig* (a notoriously slow construction project meant to improve traffic and beautify the city), and it's impossible to find *Dot* (Dorchester) or *Rozzie* (Roslindale) on a map; sometimes it is better to avoid negotiating the Big Dig traffic and just take the *T* (Boston's subway train) – remembah, *inbound* trains head towahd the city cenna, *outbounds* head away from it, wheah you'll find moah people who pronounce theiah ah's. Some days, you may get to ride on a bluebird, an old style Red Line train.

Boston-to-English Phrasebook

The Bs The local NHL team. Also known as Da Broons.

Brahmin A member of the WASP overclass that once ruled the state. Typically found on Beacon Hill. Cleveland Amory's *The Proper Bostonians* remains the definitive study of this group.

The Cape Massachusetts has two capes – Ann and Cod – but only the latter is *The Cape*.

Curse of the Bambino A Red Sox fan's nightmare. During the eight years Babe Ruth played for the Red Sox, the team won four World Series. The last of these wins came in 1918, when the then owner Henry Frazee sold the Sultan of Swat to the New York Yankees to finance a production of *No No Nanette*. Until their luck changed in 2004, the Red Sox had not won a Series since that time, and many fans blamed this sale for the long drought. The phrase regained the national spotlight during the team's 2003 playoff run, which culminated in the Red Sox blowing a 5–2 lead against the hated Yankees when a win would have sent them back to the Series.

Dunkie's Dunkin' Donuts, so prevalent in Massachusetts that the author of this article grew up in a town with more Dunkin' Donuts stores than traffic lights.

Frappe A milkshake or malted elsewhere, it's basically ice cream, milk and chocolate syrup blended together. The "e" is silent. Despite the chocolate syrup, it actually comes in many flavors.

Green Monster This monster would never fit under the bed or in the closet. Standing 310 feet down the left-field line at Fenway Park, it towers 37 feet above the ground, and is a favorite target for hitters. The 2004 baseball season marked the first year of the *Monster Seats*, the hottest buy in Boston sports tickets, with their bird's-eye view from on top of the wall.

Hoodsie A small cup of ice cream, the kind that comes with a flat wooden spoon (from H. P. Hood, the dairy that sells them). On finishing them you'd suck and then fold the wooden spoon, risking splinnahs from the folded wood.

Jimmies Those little chocolate thingees you ask the guy at the ice-cream store to put on top of your cone.

Na-ah No way!

No SUH! ("No sir!") "Really?!?" or "What did you say?!?" Often answered with "Ya huh!"

Packie Wheah you buy beah.

The Pike The Massachusetts Turnpike. Also, the world's longest parking lot, at least out by Sturbridge on the day before Thanksgiving.

Pissa Cool. Often paired with *wicked.* "Jimmy's got a pissa new cah, an '83 Monee Cahlo with a 350, headiz, anna new leathinteriah."
Rawrout Meteorological condition characterized by low temperatures and a biting wind: "Boy, it's wicked rawrout theah!"
U-ey A U-turn – the Official Turn of Boston drivers. The proper expression for "make a U-turn" is "bang a u-ey."
Wicked A general intensifier: "He's wicked nuts!"

For the citizens of Boston, their language is a marker – a symbol of solidarity recognized throughout the country. Popular Boston disc jockey Eddie Andelman says of the dialect, "It signifies where you're from. It means you're an individualist, you're street smart, you save money, you read literature, and you're a passionate sports fan" (quoted in Bombardieri 1999). And while not all Bostonians are well versed in Shakespeare or live and die over the Red Sox, Andelman's statement captures the cultural essence of the Boston dialect. Many Bostonians are proud of the way they speak, and this linguistic pride has allowed the Boston dialect to remain strong despite the challenge of a changing city. The Boston dialect remains a badge of "honah" for many who speak it.

Further reading

Amory, Cleveland (1947) *The Proper Bostonians.* New York: E. P. Dutton.
Bombardieri, Marcella (1999) It's still a mahk of distinction: The accent sets Bostonians apart. *Boston Globe,* 23 September: B1.
Gaffin, Adam. *The Wicked Good Guide to Boston English.* www.boston-online.com/glossary.html.
International Institute of Boston. *Immigration to Boston: A Short History.* www.iiboston.org/immigrant_history.htm.
Laferriere, Martha (1979) Ethnicity in phonological variation and change. *Language* 55: 603–17.
Metcalf, Allan (2000) *How We Talk: American Regional English Today.* New York: Houghton Mifflin.

11

Mainely English

Jane S. Smith

11 The joys of eating Maine lobster. © by Angela Sorrentino.

Mainely Audio, Maineland Motel, Project Mainestay, Meals for ME (postal abbreviation for Maine). . . . The creative incorporation of the state moniker into business trade names is just one of the ways in which Maine differs from other states. No other state's name is so readily available for word play. At the same time, these naming practices reflect the pride that Mainers, who sometimes call themselves *Maine-iacs*, feel about their home state.

And while all other mainland states share a border with at least two other states, Maine juts up into Canada, with French-speaking Quebec to the north and west, bilingual (English-French) New Brunswick to the east, and the Atlantic Ocean forming an extensive diagonal northeast–southwest coastline. To the west lies Maine's single neighboring state, New Hampshire. This unique geographical position, together with its earlier and recent history, played an important role in the development of English in Maine.

A Brief History

English colonists began to establish settlements along the coast of New England during the early seventeenth century, beginning in the 1620s, and, until Maine achieved statehood in 1820, it was part of Massachusetts. Given their common history and geographical proximity, many English speakers in Maine share some of the dialectal features found in Boston and the rest of New England. Its northern boundary was undetermined until the only bloodless war in American history, the Aroostook War, was settled by the Webster–Ashburton Treaty between the United States and the United Kingdom in 1842.

Before the arrival of the English colonists, however, the French were exploring the coast of present-day Maine and an area known as *Acadie*, or Acadia, currently New Brunswick and Nova Scotia in Canada. In 1604, the first French settlement was established on St. Croix Island (now on the border between Maine and New Brunswick), but in 1605 it was moved to present-day Nova Scotia following the extremely harsh winter and loss of life that first year. Acadia passed from French control to British and back again several times over the next century until the territory was finally ceded to the British in 1713. In 1755, the French Acadians were exiled by the British, some being shipped off to other American colonies, others to England, and some of them eventually made their way to Louisiana. However, a small group of Acadians managed to escape deportation, eventually settling in the upper St. John River Valley, the disputed territory that was later divided between the United States (Maine) and the United Kingdom (New Brunswick, Canada) in 1842. That area of Maine has been and continues to be largely French-speaking, though the shift to English began when the use of French as a language of instruction in public schools was outlawed in the 1920s. The law was repealed decades later.

In addition to the Acadians, a large number of French speakers immigrated to Maine during the period from 1840 to 1930, when hundreds of thousands of French Canadians from Quebec Province came to the northeastern US in search of work in the factories or mills. Thanks in large part to the establishment of bilingual parochial schools, French continues to be spoken by a number of people in central, southern, and western Maine, as well as in the St. John Valley in the north.

Although both of these groups of *Francos*, short for "Franco-Americans," continue to speak French, those whose families immigrated from Quebec tended to settle in areas already populated by English speakers, and in the shift to English they have adopted the language as it is spoken within their local communities. In the case of the Francos in northern Maine, however, their geographic isolation from the rest of New England and their proximity to French-speaking New Brunswick and Quebec led to the creation of a regional English accent that is still influenced by French.

The Classic Maine Accent

Having moved to Maine "from away," I was always the person identified as "the one who has the accent," so I had to listen carefully for the dialect differences that set me apart. I've been told that I sound like I'm from the West, and from a Maine perspective, it's not that far off the mark. I do, after all, come from western New York. In the process of acclimating to the physical conditions and social environment of Maine, I have been exposed to a fascinating – and often complex – range of English and French.

As in Boston, New York City, and parts of the South, many Mainers do not pronounce an *r* that occurs following a vowel. Words like *fork* and *fear* need not have an *r* but the vowel itself seems to be slightly lengthened as a result, and words such as *lobster* and *door* end in a vowel. Instead of simply dropping out, the *r* is replaced by a vowel sound and words like *door*, *more*, *somewhere* and *frontier* seem to get an extra syllable. This pronunciation is sometimes spelled as *ah* in advertisements featuring local foods and products, as in *lobstah* and *bumpah stickahs*. Some one-syllable words ending in *l*, for example *real* and *hole*, also may be pronounced with an extra syllable, so that *real* becomes *re-ahl* and *deal* becomes *de-ahl*.

Like lots of other vernacular dialects in English, this dialect may also "drop" the *g* from verb forms and nouns that end in *-ing*, like *hunting* and *logging*. Instead of the sound of *ng* that results when the back of the tongue makes contact with the back of the mouth, contact between the tip of the tongue and the front of the mouth produces an *n*. Mainers often say that they were out *lobsterin'* or *fishin'*, and that something is *gettin' wore out* if it's nearly at the end of its usefulness. If they live in Brewer and are going just across the river to Bangor (pronounced *bang-gore*), they'll say that they're *goin' over town*.

In addition, many Mainers, and especially those living along the coast or on one of the many islands, pronounce the broad *a* of *bath, plant, pass, aunt, half* and *scallops* with the vowel closer to the one used in *father*. When I'm buying halibut at the fish market, I remind myself to ask for *hall-ibut*, not *hail-ibut*, so as not to sound too much like an outsider. After all, locals tend to get the freshest fish.

Also noticeable is the fact that an unstressed syllable in the middle of a polysyllabic word tends to be dropped, so *probably* becomes *prob'ly*, *Saturday* becomes *Sad'dy*, *visitin'* becomes *vis'tin'* and *lobsterin'* becomes *lobst'rin'*.

Almost all Mainers use the same vowel in *cot* and *caught*, producing a vowel that is a little further back in the mouth than the vowel of *father*. More than once I have had to ask whether it was *Dawn* or *Don* we were talking about.

While all of these pronunciations can be heard from Brunswick, just north of Portland, to Millinocket. A couple of hundred miles to the north, and eastward to New Brunswick, they are more prevalent in the towns and on the islands of Mid Coast and Downeast. The name *Downeast* may come from maritime vocabulary. Winds blowing from the northwest took ships sailing from Boston and New York "down" and east, and hence, along the coast of present-day Maine. The Mid Coast stretches from about Brunswick to Mt. Desert (pronounced with the stress on the second syllable, like *dessert*) Island, where Downeast begins at about Bar Harbor and runs eastward all the way to New Brunswick. I say "about" because the exact beginning and ending points for these areas vary depending on who you ask.

In any case, Mainers recognize a dialect division at about Brunswick; to the south these pronunciations are generally not found. In fact, a retired professor and native of the Mid Coast island of Vinalhaven explained that when he first began teaching in the south of Maine, his students had difficulty understanding him and he had to learn to pronounce an *r* where none existed for him. He didn't care for it, and listening to him today you can tell that he stopped doing it once he moved back.

The keen listener will notice that Mainers say *a dight* to mean "a little bit," or a *junk* of wood instead of a "piece" or "chunk." An apartment is *a rent* and a house has *blinds* instead of "shutters." If you go *visitin'*, you will be invited to *set down* and make yourself *to home*. The use of *to* for *at* is a characteristic of some coastal communities that extend well down to the southeastern seaboard of the United States, as well as some rural regions elsewhere. Anything cute, babies included, is *cunnin'*, and a misbehaving child will be told, "Stop your foolishness." In fact, anything annoying or stupid is *foolishness* and can make you *some disgusted*. If you're invited to a *lobstah feed* and your meal is especially tasty, it's *wicked* good.

On Vinalhaven, you might hear someone say *I would be lief* (pronounced *leaf*) *to do something*, which means that they would prefer to, or would just as soon, do it. Downeast, instead of calling someone stupid, they'll say, *He's a plaster*. I'm told that on the islands it can be difficult for an outsider to understand when the locals are speaking with each other, and on the docks one can hear especially "colorful" speech. Some Downeasterners, however, have very creative expressions to express their exasperation – *Gludden on it!* and *Jee-ru-s(a)lem!* – or amazement – *By Thunder!*

English in the St. John Valley

A stretch of some 50 miles of the St. John River in northernmost Maine forms part of the border with New Brunswick. A variety of Acadian French is spoken on both sides of the river but on the US side it is being replaced gradually by English. French-speaking Francos from this area switch back and forth easily between French and English, sometimes within the same sentence, and French has given their English some distinctive features, both in pronunciation and sentence structure.

Franco pronunciation is different in that certain vowels in French are more "closed" than their English counterparts. The vowels in *day* or *date* and *boat* or *vote* are just a couple of those affected. Instead of being pronounced as a two-vowel sequence, or diphthong, as in *da-ee* for *day* or *bo-oot* for *boat*, they are pronounced as a single vowel without the glide – as in French. The influence of French can be heard when words are pronounced with a "pure" vowel, for example *day*, *devastate*, and the name of the town, *Caribou* (pronounced *-boo*, not *-bow*).

When it comes to consonants, one difference is the pronunciation of *p*, *t*, and *k* at the beginning of a word or syllable. They tend to be less aspirated, which means that there is no puff of air immediately after the sound. Most English dialects fully aspirate them, but Francos do not, again from French influence. Occasionally, the cluster of consonants that occurs with the contraction of *not* at the end of a word is reduced to a single consonant, as for example, in the word *didn't*, which is sometimes pronounced *din*.

When listening to Francos, you sometimes hear a different rhythm that stems from the occasional transference of the stress pattern of French. As a result, stress is sometimes indicated by a slight change in pitch rather than with extra force and length, and it might occur at place where it wouldn't occur in English. In the following example, the words receiving a French-type stress appear in bold type: 24 hours a **day**, seven days a **week**.

The transference of French structures can occur in the use of pre-positions, as in *I don't have an opinion on that*, as well as in sentence constructions. You might notice a pronoun such as *me*, *him* or *us* occurring at the beginning or end of a complete sentence, as in *Our generation is weird, us*. This type of structure is common in spoken French.

When it comes to vocabulary and expressions, many of them also come from French. For example, people talk about *ployes* (rhyming with *toy*), a sort of buckwheat pancake that is eaten not for breakfast but in place of bread with dinner or supper. When you have a strand of hair that's sticking up out of place, it's called a *couette*. A colloquial expression to show disbelief, comparable to *Gimme a break!* or *Get out!* is *Voyons voir!* And if an adult says to a child, "Voyons voir!" that child had better "stop the foolishness." Both surprise and anger are quite likely to be expressed by interjections like *Mon doux Jésus!* 'my sweet Jesus!' or the somewhat stronger though still not too offensive *Tabarnak!* 'holy (cow)!'.

The Future of Maine English

Like many rural dialects, those heard in Maine (both English and French) are slowly disappearing due to increased contact with outsiders and various other social changes. At the same time, Maine is a sparsely populated, rural state with relatively small cities, and the climate tends to deter many outsiders from spending more than just the summer months there.

Fortunately, the weather is on the side of dialect preservation. Though dialectologists scoff at the notion that weather has any direct influence on language, it may indirectly aid maintenance by insulating Mainers from outsiders for long periods of the year. Like Maine itself, it may be an exception – and truly exceptional.

Steel Town Speak (Pittsburgh, PA)

Barbara Johnstone and Scott Kiesling

12 Downtown Pittsburgh from the West End overlook. © by Todd Smith.

Many people in Pittsburgh and western Pennsylvania are convinced that a distinctive dialect of English is spoken in the area, which they call "Pittsburghese."

When people talk about Pittsburghese, they often mention words like *yinz* 'you' plural, *slippy* 'slippery', and *nebby* 'nosy', sounds like the vowels in *Stillers* (Steelers) or *dahntahn* (downtown), and expressions like *n'at* (and that, used to mean something like *et cetera*). People in Pittsburgh enjoy talking about Pittsburghese, and they make commercial use of examples of it on T-shirts, postcards, souvenir shot-glasses, and other such items, as well as on the Internet.

But many of the linguistic features considered unique to the Pittsburgh area are found elsewhere in the region. Words like *yinz* are used in other parts of the Appalachian Mountains. Other features are found to the west of Pittsburgh, in the central and south-central parts of the Midwest. Some pronunciations identified with Pittsburghese, such as *still* (steel) are heard throughout the US. Even the features of Pittsburghese that are the most local can be heard in a fairly large area of central and southwestern Pennsylvania.

Although it is not confined to Pittsburgh, many Pittsburghers employ a dialect variety that is known as "North Midland" or "Lower Northern" English.

The earliest English-speaking immigrants to North America brought their native English dialects with them. The people who settled in New England and in the South came mainly from southern England, and they brought elements of southern English dialects. (For example, New Englanders and Southerners alike may drop the *r* sounds in some words.) The Midland dialect area starts in a narrow band in the Mid-Atlantic states (southern New Jersey, southeastern Pennsylvania, and northern Delaware and Maryland) and spreads westward into the Midwest and southward along the Appalachian Mountains. Its boundaries trace the migrations of English-speaking people who came to America by way of Philadelphia and other ports on the Delaware River. These people originated in northern England and Scotland, and they brought some characteristic pronunciations, words, and grammatical structures with them.

The people from northern England, some of whom were Quakers, came to the eastern part of Pennsylvania and moved west into central Pennsylvania. The largest group of early English-speaking immigrants to southwestern Pennsylvania were from Ulster (northern Ireland). These people were largely "Scots-Irish" (also called "Scotch-Irish"), the descendants of Scots who had settled in Ulster at the beginning of the seventeenth century. They spoke a Scottish variety of English (influenced by the Scots Gaelic language) which was then influenced by Irish English and probably also by Irish Gaelic. Many of these Scots-Irish, along with other people from Ulster of native Irish and northern English ancestry, emigrated from northern Ireland to North America at the end of the seventeenth century and during the eighteenth century. Scots-Irish immigrants also settled west and south of Pennsylvania, moving along the Ohio River and the

Appalachian Mountains. Thus many features that can be traced to their way of speaking are found in Midwestern and Appalachian speech as well as in western Pennsylvania. Some of these words and structures are also still in use in Scotland and Northern Ireland.

Among the many words used in southwestern Pennsylvania that are probably Scots-Irish are *redd up* 'clean up, tidy', *nebby*, *slippy*, and *diamond* for a town square. So is the word *jag* in the sense of 'poke' or 'stab', from which come *jagger* 'thorn, burr', *jaggerbush* 'thorny bush', *jag* somebody *off* 'irritate', *jag around* 'fool around, goof off', and *jagoff* 'a derogatory term for someone stupid or inept'. *Yinz*, which is found throughout the Appalachians in various forms (such as *you'uns*), is most likely Scots-Irish as well. So is the grammatical peculiarity found in expressions like *The car needs washed* or *These customers want seated,* where other dialects would have an infinitive (*needs to be washed*) or a present participle (*needs washing*). This is also found in Appalachian English and in the central Midwest.

While it is possible to trace the history of words and structures through written sources, it is much more difficult to tell where regional pronunciations come from. For one thing, our standardized spelling system does not capture the differences between various ways of pronouncing a word (*coffee* is spelled "coffee" no matter whether it's pronounced *cawffee, cahffee, cwaffee,* or some other way). For another thing, large-scale changes in pronunciation are surprisingly common and quick. (Think, for example, of the large differences that now exist between British and North American accents, all of which developed over just a few generations.) But some features of the accent of southwestern Pennsylvania are geographically distributed in the same way – in the Pittsburgh area and to the west and the south – as are words and grammatical structures we know are Scots-Irish in origin. This suggests that these may be older features that spread with the early settlers. One of these is the use of an *r* sound in the word *wash*, so that it sounds something like *warsh*. Another is the tendency to pronounce the long *i* sound in words like *fire* or *tile* as something more like *ah* (*fahr* or *tahl*).

Other pronunciations which people think of as local are shared with other geographic areas. Many people throughout North America use the same vowel sound in *not* and *naught, cot* and *caught, body* and *bawdy*. But unlike many Americans further west (and like many Canadians and some Americans further east), the sound many Pittsburghers use is the *augh* variant, rather than *ah*. Also shared with people elsewhere are the use of the same vowel sound in *steel* and *still* or *meal* and *mill* and the same vowel sound in *pull* and *pool* or *full* and *fool*. These "mergers," or the collapse of two sounds, in some situations, into one, are becoming more common throughout the US. So is the pronunciation of *l* with a *w* or *o* sound in some words, like *skoo* for *school* or *dowar* for *dollar*. There is one pronunciation, however, that seems to be much more restricted geographically. This is the Pittsburghese pronunciation of *down* as *dahn* or *house* as *hahs*. Western Pennsylvanians born before 1900 do not seem to have used this sound, but by the middle of the twentieth century it was quite common. Dialectologists do not yet know how this pronunciation originated.

It is often thought that people in different Pittsburgh neighborhoods and Pittsburgh-area towns have different accents. But if Pittsburgh is like other cities that linguists have studied, this is probably not true. What probably is true is that the same sounds and words are used more in some areas and less in others, depending on things like whether the neighborhood is mainly working-class and whether people stay in the neighborhood to work or commute to work. This is because children learn their accent primarily from their peers, not their parents, and each new group of immigrants to the area learned English from people who were already speaking English. Dialects spread when people pick up features of the speech of people they are like, talk to a lot, or identify with, and the children of immigrants were far more likely to want to emulate the speech of the local people who already spoke English than to emulate their parents' accented speech. Largely because they have always been segregated from other groups in work, education, and housing, the casual speech of African Americans in Pittsburgh, as in other northern cities, continues to preserve more of the southern-sounding features African Americans brought with them, although North Midland features can also be heard in many Pittsburgh African Americans' speech.

Different ethnic groups have introduced new words into the local vocabulary: Germans made up a large part of the earliest European population of western Pennsylvania and words like *gesundheit* and *sauerkraut* are among a number of German terms that are widely used in the US.

Other words that are sometimes associated with "Pittsburghese" have commercial sources. *Jumbo lunchmeat*, *Klondike ice-cream bars*, and *chipped ham* all originated as names for things produced or sold by local companies. The spelling of the Pittsburgh neighborhood name East Liberty as "S'liberty" (which is the way it often sounds when people are talking quickly) was invented in the context of a campaign to promote the neighborhood. *Gumband*, the local term for 'rubber band', may also have been what the first people who sold them in Pittsburgh called them.

Is Pittsburghese going to die out, or is it likely to persist? Some people think that the mass media, together with the fact that we are more mobile than we once were, are making the US increasingly homogeneous. People who think this are likely to suspect that eventually we will all talk the same way. Among the reasons to think that local-sounding speech features may disappear are the facts that many people move around the US more than they once did, and it is easier than it once was for some people to move in different social classes and social circles than the ones they were born into. Furthermore, the media expose us all to the same ways of talking, and new kinds of employment, such as jobs in service industries, often require people to speak in a standardized way.

On the other hand, there are some good reasons to think that local-sounding speech features may persist. People often resist being homogenized, and they may express their resistance by speaking in distinctive ways. Especially when outsiders start to move in, people may need ways to express local pride. When they feel that their local dialect is in danger of dying out, people may want to exaggerate certain features of it to keep it alive. Local ways of talking in Pittsburgh and in many other places are associated in people's minds with the working class. So showing working-class pride may also be a reason for people to use local-sounding language. In addition, words like *yinz*, *dahntahn*, and *Stillers* have become symbols of locale in Pittsburgh. As a result, they can be useful to people who are trying to "sell" the city to tourists or businesses from outside. Linguists still have a lot to learn about the dialects of southwestern Pennsylvania. Like other aspects of local heritage, Pittsburghese is worth understanding and preserving.

Acknowledgment

The authors are grateful for editorial and substantive help with this chapter to Martha Cheng, Peter Gilmore, and Michael Montgomery.

New York Tawk
(New York City, NY)

Michael Newman

13 New York contemplating the Hudson River. © by Emilio Chan.

Back in the early 1970s, all the students in my Manhattan high school were given speech diagnostic exams. I passed, but the boy next to me was told he needed speech class. I was surprised and asked him why, since he sounded perfectly normal to me. "My New York accent," he explained unhappily. Actually, this reason made me less thrilled with my exemption, as if my Detroit-born parents had deprived me of being a complete New Yorker.

As my classmate's predicament shows, my longing for New Yawk sounds was a distinctly minority taste. My school was hardly alone; there was a time when many New York colleges, including my present employer, Queens College, had required voice and diction courses, and their curriculum targeted certain local dialect peculiarities. Furthermore, a person with too many of these features was not allowed to teach in the New York City public schools.

Although these efforts were abandoned decades ago, many New Yorkers still talk of their speech as a problem to be overcome. When I was researching this article, a number of my former schoolmates claimed that their accents weren't "that bad" or boasted that they had overcome "the worst features." As a New York accent fan, I would be more depressed by these claims if they were not actually based almost entirely on denial. Take the case of the *r*, which New York dialect speakers tend to leave out whenever it comes after a vowel sound. Many New Yorkers believe that dropping *r*'s is a serious flaw, but they usually imagine that it is someone else's. An employment agency owner once proclaimed to me that anyone who did not pronounce their *r*'s could not possibly qualify for a professional job – all the while calling them *ahs*.

Perhaps because this man was middle-class, he believed he had to be pronouncing his *r*'s. In fact, he was not altogether wrong; he sometimes put an *r* in where none belonged, a feature called intrusive *r*. It may seem bizarre to pronounce *r*'s that aren't there while skipping over those that are, but in fact, intrusive and missing *r*'s are two sides of the same coin. For *r*-droppers words like *law* and *lore* and *soar* and *saw* are homophones. However, they do not usually drop *r*'s all the time. They sometimes maintain them, particularly when a final *r* sound comes right before another word that begins with a vowel sound. Just as the *r* is sometimes pronounced in *lore and legend*, so it can appear in *law-r-and order*. When they are speaking carefully New Yorkers even occasionally maintain *r*'s when there is no following vowel. You get the idear?

If a little reflection reveals a hidden logic to intrusive *r*'s, a little more shows how baseless New Yorkers' obsession with the whole issue really is. After all, if *r*'s were there to be pronounced, why in England is it considered far better to leave them off? An *r*-pronouncing English person is at best considered rustic and quaint, if not coarse and uneducated. And *r*-less pronunciations have not always been stigmatized in the US. President Franklin Roosevelt was famous for saying that Americans "have nothing to fear [pronounced *fee-uh*] but fear itself." Even today, *r*-lessness can still maintain a tacit prestige in the right context. In the 1980s, former New Jersey Governor Thomas Kean was known for saying, "New Juhsey and you. Puhfect togetheh," and his pronunciation was considered aristocratic. It is only when *r*-lessness combines with other, less obvious New York characteristics that it acquires negative connotations. The *r* really just serves as a symbol for the whole system – a kind of phonological scapegoat.

My colleague Chuck Cairns developed a diagnostic list of 12 features including many of these less obvious characteristics. A particularly important one involves the vowel sound sometimes written as *aw*, as in *all*, *coffee*, *caught*, *talked*, or *saw* and the New York *r*-less *shore*. In New York dialect, this vowel becomes closer to the vowel *u* in *pull* or *put* followed by a slight *uh*. Strong New York dialect speakers say *u-uhl*, for *all* and *cu-uhfee*, for *coffee*, and they don't distinguish between *shore* and *sure*. A similar process applies to the short *a* in *cab*, *pass*, and *avenue*. In this case, the vowel can comes to sound like an *i* or even *ee*, again followed by *uh*. Many New Yorkers try to catch *ki-uhbs* that *pi-uhss* by on Fifth *i-uhvenue*, although not all of us are so extreme.

In our pronunciation of these vowels, we New Yorkers are not unique; related pronunciations can be found from Baltimore to Milwaukee. However, none reproduce exactly the same pattern. Specifically, in New York all the *aws* are affected, but many short *a* words are not – a differentiation called the short *a* split. So in New York, *pass*, *cab*, and *avenue* have different vowels from *pat*, *cap*, and *average*. In most cities between Syracuse and Milwaukee, by contrast, *aw* is nothing like it is in New York, while all the short *a*'s are pronounced like *i-uh*. They not only say *pi-uhss* for *pass* – as in New York – but also *pi-uht* for *pat*, which no New Yorker would ever do. Detective Andy Sipowicz on *NYPD Blue* may seem like the archetypical New York City cop, but his *aw*'s and short *a*'s are obvious clues that Dennis Franz, the actor who plays him, is really from Chicago.

To be fair, it might be hard for Franz to sound like an authentic New Yorker. While there are rules that determine which short *a* words are shifted and which are not in New York, they are quite complicated. For instance, *can* is *key-uhn* in *can of soup* but not in *yes, I can*. The system is so complex that most unfortunate New Yorkers whose parents speak another variety of English never really learn them. We are condemned to not be full New York dialect speakers.

Although these vowel changes are an inherent part of the mix that receives condemnation, New Yorkers seem less concerned about them than they are about *r*'s. Only the most extreme pronunciations receive condemnation. In fact, there is an aspect of their speech that many New Yorkers appear to be actually proud of – the distinctive vocabulary. There are childhood games like *Ring-a-levio*, a kind of street hide-and-seek, *stickball*, baseball played with a broomstick, and *salugi*, the snatching of a kid's bag or hat, which is then thrown from friend to friend, just out of the victim's reach. More widely known are the Yiddishisms, such as *schlep* – to travel or carry something an annoying distance – to pick one out of many. Such terms are used by Jews of Eastern European origin the world over, but in New York they have extended to other communities. A teenage Nuyorican (New Yorker of Puerto Rican heritage) rap artist I know rhymed, "I'm gonna spin you like a dradel," a reference to a top used in Chanukah celebrations. His schoolmate, also Latino, often says, "What the schmuck!" as an expression of surprise, misusing, or perhaps just appropriating, the vulgar Yiddish term for *penis*. Some of these terms may be in decline – I don't hear many young Latinos using *schlep* – but there are recent replacements from other immigrant languages. Besides Nuyorican itself, there is the offensive *guido*, an ignorant Italian American tough guy. More positively, we have *papichulo*, a suave, well-dressed Latino ladies' man.

The appeal of these words lies in their evocation of immigrant roots, and New York dialect, like the city itself, serves as a kind of counterpoint to mainstream Anglo America. The dialect is often called Brooklynese, more because of Brooklyn's status as an icon of urban ethnic life than any real linguistic priority of that borough over other parts of the metropolitan area. The key to understanding the disparagement of New York pronunciations is similarly that they symbolize lack of integration into the American mainstream, and so being stuck in the working class.

Despite the association with immigrant ethnicity, both *r*-lessness and short *a* splits actually originated in England, although they have evolved differently there; in southern England, for instance, *pass* is pronounced with an *ah*, while *pat* is similar to most of the US. Still, immigrant languages have had some influence. They probably led to the New York pronunciation of *d* and *t* with the tongue touching the teeth rather than the alveolar ridge as in most American English, but hardly anyone notices the difference. They may also be behind the famous use of these dental *d*'s and *t*'s in place of *th*, as in *toity-toid and toid*, for *33rd and 3rd*, but you would be hard pressed to hear that anymore among European Americans in New York.

Perhaps this decline, along with others like the notorious *r* for *oy* in words like *oil* and *point* – leaving *earl* and *pernt*, have led some to conclude that New York dialect itself is itself disappearing. Yet a trip to the

European American neighborhoods or suburbs – at least outside of the areas of Manhattan dominated by out-of-towners – will dispel any such concerns. The children of New York dialect speakers continue the linguistic tradition, although, like speakers of all varieties, not exactly as their parents did.

Those, like my high school speech teacher, who wished to cure us of such features as intrusive *r*'s did so because they thought it would be a social and professional handicap. They were mistaken. Many middle- and upper-middle-class New Yorkers of all ethnicities use the dialect, to say nothing of billionaires like Donald Trump. One dialect speaker, former Governor Mario Cuomo, even became nationally famous for his eloquence. Instead, as New York dialect speakers have moved up socially, their speech has lost much of its outsider status. Older speakers may think they speak badly, but they do so almost out of inertia. In fact, many professional Latinos, Asian Americans, Caribbean Americans, and African Americans have adopted their distinctive dialect features, in whole or in good part.

In assuming what has become a common New York middle-class dialect, these speakers either leave behind or alternate with the speech commonly associated with their ethnic communities. Today, this working-class minority speech has taken on the outsider status the classic Brooklynese has left behind. Among young New Yorkers, *r*-lessness is replaced by *aks* for *ask* and *toof* for *tooth* as examples of how one shouldn't speak. Some expressions, such as using *mines* instead of *mine*, in the sentence *That's mines*, occupy a kind of middle ground for these minorities (actually together the majority of the city) of marking roots while still being understood as "incorrect." Again, minority youths often seem proud of their special vocabulary, which expresses their roots in urban life. The speech of minorities is less unified than that of the previous generations of children of European immigrants. But, despite the variation, there is a tendency for some characteristics to be shared widely. Also these forms often extend to other immigrants, particularly Middle Easterners, and even to many European Americans and Asian Americans who associate with rap and hip-hop culture generally.

A good indicator of the linguistic divide can be seen in the way *you* is pluralized. Among most European Americans, like among most other northerners, it is possible to use *you guys* or occasionally *youse* to refer to more than one person. Among New York minorities, by contrast, some form of *you all* is usually used. This can be *y'all*, common among African Americans and Nuyoricans, or something that sounds like *you-ah* or even *you-eh* that I have heard among other Latinos. Another interesting characteristic is the use of *yo*. This has long been used for calling someone as in "Yo, Reggie!" More recently it developed a tendency to go at the end of a sentence as an emphasis marker: "Dat's da bomb, yo!" (That's really great!).

Because New York is a center for the production of rap and other forms of popular culture, some of these characteristics, particularly terms, like *da bomb*, have spread throughout the country, just as young New Yorkers have adopted forms originating in that other major center, California. However, in the end, few New Yorkers, no matter what their race or ethnicity, would really like to be mistaken as coming from anywhere else, and they are constantly developing new words and letting their pronunciations evolve to indicate their origins. *Da bomb* is heard a lot less often than it used to be. So while we may think we speak badly, perhaps in our hearts we don't want to speak the way we think we should. A former Nuyorican student of mine remarked after he got out of the Army, "No matter where I went, people could tell I was from the city." He was obviously pleased by that fact, just as I am when out-of-towners identify me as having a New York accent despite my over-abundant *r*'s and lack of a proper short *a* split. The ultimate resilience and uniqueness of New York dialects lies in our intense local pride, and this is as true for the minority versions as it is for the so-called Brooklynese.

Further Reading

William Labov's mammoth study, *The Social Stratification of English in New York City* (Washington, D.C.: Center for Applied Linguistics, 1966), is still considered to be the authoritative work on English in New York City.

Expressions of Brotherly Love (Philadelphia, PA)

Claudio Salvucci

14 Professionals in Philadelphia. © by Nancy Louie.

One day my linguistics professor singled me out for a question. "What," she asked, "does a Philadelphia accent sound like? How would you describe it?"

I was stumped.

My entire life had been spent in the city and its immediate suburbs. You'd think that describing the way my neighbors spoke would be no different from describing where someone could get a good cheese steak. Who else is supposed to know but the locals?

But this time the local really had no idea. I didn't know how I spoke; I just did. As I would later learn, the Philadelphia dialect is unique in the English-speaking world. Not only does it have a linguistic pattern that is not duplicated in any other major city, but also that pattern had been studied and documented by scholars for over a century.

History of Research

There were incidental accounts of Philadelphia and Pennsylvania speech in the 1800s, but the first true scientific study dates to 1890, with the first transcription of a Philadelphian's speech into the International Phonetic Alphabet (IPA).

During the next century research on the dialect increased dramatically, mostly under larger surveys such as the Linguistic Atlas surveys in 1939; the *Dictionary of American Regional English* surveys in the 1960s, and the *Phonological Atlas* surveys of the 1990s.

Studies specifically devoted to Philadelphia were also published. R. Whitney Tucker contributed two general articles to *American Speech* on the dialect. By far the most extensive research on local vocabulary is Dennis Lebofsky's invaluable doctoral thesis "The Lexicon of the Philadelphia Metropolitan Area" (1970), and William Labov has been in the vanguard of research on Philadelphia pronunciation since the 1970s.

In recent years there have also been numerous books and articles from the mainstream press. Examining all of this data, we can arrive at a good picture of how English is spoken in Philadelphia (or, as we say it, Fulladulfya).

Geography

Philadelphia is the focal point of the Delaware Valley dialect area, which encompasses the Pennsylvania counties of Bucks, Montgomery, Philadelphia, Delaware and Chester, the New Jersey counties of Mercer, southern Ocean, Burlington, Camden, Gloucester, Atlantic, Salem, Cumberland and Cape May, and New Castle County. There are some slight differences even within this generally homogeneous area, such as Norristown *zep* 'submarine sandwich', Trenton *Tick Tack Night* 'Mischief Night', and Jersey shore *shubie* 'summer tourist'.

The Delaware Valley was historically the "hearth" or focal area for all the dialects of the Midland. As settlers moved westward during the 1800s they brought their speech through Pennsylvania and the Lower Midwest. Philadelphia's position along the Eastern seaboard has also greatly influenced its linguistic development. Northern and Southern features have always competed in the city, given its close proximity to both New York City and the Mason–Dixon line.

Pronunciation

At first hearing, Philadelphian sounds quite similar to the New York dialect; I have even been told (by a Long Islander no less!) that I "talk like a New Yorker."

As in most East Coast urban areas, voiced *th* loses it friction, so that it is pronounced like the stop *d* in *dog*; there is a loss of initial *h-* in *yuge* (huge) and *yumid* (humid), and a glottal stop for medial *t* in *sum'n* (something), *nut'n* (nothing). Short *a* exists in two forms, the standard "lax" *a*, and the tense nasal vowel of *yeah*: *maen* (*man*), *baed* (*bad*). New York and Philly both have a contras between the vowels of *cot* and *caught*, with the *aw* distinctively raised: *cawfee* (coffee), *dawg* (dog); both have a typically southern *ow*: *caow* (*cow*), *aout* (*out*), *al* (*owl*), though Philadelphia's is more advanced.

But unlike New York, Philadelphia shares with Baltimore and Pittsburgh a couple of important features: first a very exaggerated fronting of long *o* in words like *home* and *boat*, which sounds something like *eh-oo*; second, retention of all final and pre-consonantal *r*'s (e.g., in *car*, *start*) which are dropped almost everywhere else on the East Coast. An interesting similarity with Canada is the long *i* before unvoiced consonants (*p, t, k, f, s*) which is backed to *uy*, pronounced *uh-ee*: *ruyt* (right), *luyf* (life).

More typically local changes also occur. Short *e* is backed to short *u* or schwa before both *r* and *l*: *vurry* (very), *tull* (tell). Short *i* in medial positions is often lengthened: *attytude* (attitude), *beautyful* (beautiful). Long *a* and *e* are both backed before hard *g*: *vegg* (vague), *beggle* (bagel), *lig* (league), *iggle* (eagle). Initial *s* in *str* clusters becomes *sh*: *shtring* (string).

The Philadelphia *l* is often "vocalized"; that is, the tongue does not make contact with the roof of the mouth, and the back of the tongue is raised instead of the tip. This also tends to weaken the *l* sound so that it almost seems as if the sound is being dropped altogether. Thus the words *pal* and *pow* sound almost the same, as do *balance* and *bounce*.

The *ar* sound is in all cases backed to *aur*: *caur* (*car*), *staur* (*star*). Some may hear these as *core* and *store* – but there is no merger of *ar* and *or* in Philadelphia because *or* raises and merges with *oor*. So *poor* and *pore*, *tore* and *tour* are all pronounced with the long *u* vowel of *tube*. You can get a good overall feel for how this all sounds by listening to television political commentator Chris Matthews, host of CNBC's *Hardball*.

Grammar

Grammatically, Philadelphian does not differ very much from other forms of colloquial American English; but a few regional characteristics can be noted.

Common to many of the cities in the Northeast is the second person plural pronoun *youse*, or an unstressed variant *yuz*, used like the Southern *y'all*: *Aur youse goin'?* (Are you going?).

The positive use of *anymore* to mean "currently" is a Philadelphia usage that has since spread: *Things are so expensive anymore*. Other constructions include: *quarter of* instead of "quarter till" or "quarter to" in telling time: *quooder of five* (quarter till five); omitting the infinitive in *want off* (want to get off) and *want in* (want to get in); and omitting the object of the preposition with: *Here, take it with.*

Vocabulary

Local words characteristic of Philadelphia include *baby coach* 'baby carriage', *bag school* 'skip school', *pavement* 'sidewalk', and *square* 'city block'. A few words with Philadelphia origins have since gone on to more widespread usage: *hoagie* 'submarine sandwich', *yo* 'hey, hello'), and *hot cakes* 'pancakes', and others have become obsolete, such as *coal oil* 'kerosene'.

Ultimately, linguistic research in Philadelphia has had a far wider application than just describing the speech of that city. It has been instrumental in disproving the commonly held notion that within 50 years we will all be speaking a homogenized American English straight out of the evening newscast. In fact, American dialects are now more different from each other than they have ever been, and despite any influence from the national media, in places like Philadelphia they are continuing to evolve along their own lines.

Maple Leaf Rap (Canada)

J. K. Chambers

15.1 Urban life on Toronto's Yonge Street. © by Donald Gruener.

Canada is a nation of immigrants – a fact obvious to anyone visiting Canada's largest cities. In Toronto, almost one in three people (32%) speak a native language other than English or French, Canada's official languages. Immigrant language speakers are also found in Vancouver (27%), Winnipeg (21%), and Montreal (17%).

In New World countries, almost everyone is part of an immigrant group. In Canada, we have groups known as First Nations, the Inuit and the Indians, who have the best claim for being non-immigrants, not because they were always here but because their immigration took place pre-historically. In terms of numbers, there are 207,280 First Nations people (using mother tongue figures), which amounts to about one in every 145,000 Canadians. The other 30 million people are immigrants and the descendants of immigrants.

The language mix in Canada is the result of two distinct immigration waves in the twentieth century that peaked around 1910 and 1960. These waves brought with them thousands of people speaking languages including Chinese, Italian, German, Polish, Spanish, Portuguese, Punjabi, Ukrainian, Arabic, Dutch, Tagalog and Greek – the top 12 immigrant groups in the 2001 census.

Until the twentieth century, Canada's population was formed mostly from two earlier immigration waves. The first began in 1776 and reached its peak in 1793. These immigrants came from the Thirteen Colonies – forerunner of the USA – and are known in Canadian history as Loyalists because they chose to keep their allegiance to England after the American Revolution.

The British government of Canada feared that the colonists might harbor pro-Republican sentiments, because, as Loyalists, they had American ancestry. These fears increased with the American invasion of Canada in the War of 1812 so British and Irish immigrants were encouraged to emigrate to Canada – even though the Canadians showed no sign of defecting to the American side and had defended their borders vigorously. This second wave began around 1815 and reached its peak in 1850, bringing thousands of immigrants from England, Scotland and Ireland.

Both sets of immigrants came principally from English-speaking countries but subsequent immigrants came mainly from central Europe at first and Asia later. These people brought with them more diverse cultural, ethnic, and racial backgrounds. With their arrival, Canada's original Anglo-Celtic hegemony became only one of numerous tiles in a colorful mosaic. The new immigrants spoke their own languages at home and in their communities, but they learned English (or French in Quebec) in order to get along in the workplace, go to school, or read the daily newspaper.

In terms of language, there are the two types of immigrants. Newcomers who arrive speaking languages already intelligible to the home population are "dialect/accent" (DA) immigrants, and those speaking languages unintelligible to the natives are "second-language" (SL) immigrants. Normally, immigration waves bring the two together, but in Canada they arrived in succession, one after the other.

Just as skin color separates people into "visible minorities," SL immigrants are "audible minorities." I can remember, as a youngster, hearing older people in my hometown grumble when they overheard a foreign language on the street. "This is Canada," one old man said. "Why can't they talk like everyone else?" Some people believed that people with foreign accents could not be employed as salespeople, teachers, bank tellers, or the like, simply because they had an accent. Attitudes like these, we now know, were just reflex reactions to what was a fairly sudden social change. People were not used to hearing foreign languages on their streets and reacted to them out of ignorance or fear.

I discovered that these attitudes also affected the DA immigrants arriving in the 1800s. Even though their language was intelligible to the locals, they sounded different – sometimes very different – and those differences in accent and dialect were also portents of social changes. One woman from England wrote a book about her immigrant experience in 1851, and in it, she described the Canadian recruiting officer as speaking with "a drawling vulgar voice." "He spoke with such a twang," she said, "that I could not bear to look at him or listen to him." Predictably, she had a miserable time of it in her adopted country. In this same period, many advertisements for jobs carried the standard line "No Englishman need apply."

One difference between the DA immigrants and the SL immigrants is the literacy gap. Usually, native speakers and DA immigrants have developed their literacy skills from an early age whereas SL immigrants typically arrive in their new country unable to read and write in their home language, or with very limited fluency in it. The extent of this disadvantage for SL immigrants is illustrated by comparative data from the International Adult Literacy Survey, a standardized test applied in 22 nations to determine proficiency rates. The survey is complex and multifaceted, but what is most important here is that it tests both native-born and second-language foreign-born citizens in each country. The discrepancy between the proficiency scores for these two groups constitutes the Literacy Gap.

Figure 15.2 illustrates the Literacy Gap in five English-speaking countries: United Kingdom, United States, New Zealand, Canada and Australia. The percentages are for the median proficiency level (level 3, where 5 is the highest), roughly appropriate for senior high-school students. I selected these five countries because they are all English-language dominant and happen to fall into the middle group among the nations surveyed. The bars indicate the proportion of citizens who attain this

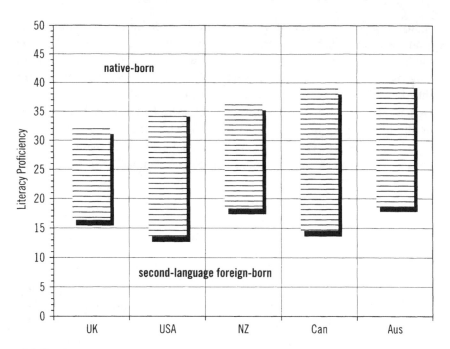

15.2 The literacy gap.

median level of proficiency in the test, and the length of the bar shows the discrepancy between the native-born and the SL immigrants at that level. In Canada, for instance, 39% of native-born people attained this proficiency level but only 14% of SL immigrants achieved it. The figure clearly shows that the Gap exists in every country, and that it is never less than 15%.

SL immigrants clearly find themselves at a disadvantage in terms of literacy compared to both DA immigrants and long-term citizens. As literacy is a vital economic and social tool, minimizing the Literacy Gap should be regarded as a social obligation of governments and educators. In Canada, this obligation is discharged by providing free ESL classes in immigrant communities. But, despite these efforts, the Literacy Gap remains wide – we must continually strive to find new and improved ways to make these classes attractive and to make lessons effective. Of course, the Literacy Gap can never be wiped out entirely because adult learners are not capable of gaining second-language proficiency that matches their first-language competence.

For both DA immigrants and SL immigrants, the English dialect and accent they hear their children speaking is markedly Canadian in many ways. Their children will refer to sneakers as *running shoes*, to obsequious classmates as *browners*, and to colored pencils as *pencil crayons*. When they say that the sun shone, they will rhyme *shone* with *gone* (not with *bone*). They will have the same vowel in both *Don* and *Dawn*, so it is impossible to tell by their pronunciation whether they are talking about a boy or a girl; and they will have the same vowel in pairs like *cot* and *caught*, *knotty* and *naughty*, *stock* and *stalk*, and all similar words.

They will have a long low diphthong in *houses*, but a short, high one in *house*, the phenomenon known as Canadian Raising, and when they say *about the house*, some Americans will think they have said *aboot the hoose*. In other respects, their Canadian accents will share traits with their nearest neighbors, Americans from the inland north and the Upper Midwest. All of them, for instance, refer to shops as *stores*, say they are *sick* not only when they are nauseous but also when they have the measles, and call the front and back end of cars the *hood* and the *trunk* (not the *bonnet* and the *boot*). They all rhyme *can't* with *ant* (not with *want*) and pronounce *r* wherever it is written, as in *car* and *card*.

These similarities with American accents mark Canadian English as one of the branches of North American English. Like most of the accents in the United States, Canadian English descends ultimately from eighteenth-century varieties spoken in England at the time of the early settlers on this continent. The Canadian peculiarities, like Canadian Raising, show that it has been independent long enough to develop some traits of its own, just as varieties in New England, New York City, Texas, and other regions have developed traits of their own.

It should be a source of wonder that the origins of Canadian English remain audible today. After all, its entire history consists of layer after layer of other accents and dialects being imported into its territory and coexisting with it for a while. And here is the final similarity between DA immigrants and SL immigrants. For both of them, when their children go out to play with local kids and go to school with them, the children return home sounding like their playmates and classmates. The Chinese children in 1999 came home sounding like the third-generation Italo-Canadians in their class, whose grandparents in 1949, when they were children, had come home sounding like the third-generation Scottish-Canadians, whose own grandparents had come home sounding like the third-generation Anglo-Canadians, and so on, back to the children of the Loyalists. The linguistic character of the dialect gets established early, starting with the speech of the offspring of the founders, the first native generation. Once it is established, successive generations can exert only mild, and minor, influences. Basically, the next generation always sounds much like the one immediately before it.

The net result is a common linguistic identity linking each generation with the next. And the social purpose of that linguistic identity seems to be to engender the sense of communal belonging in a deep subconscious way.

That sense of belonging apparently hardens in some people into a proprietary feeling, and that sometimes leads them to wonder aloud why the new immigrants can't just talk like the rest of us.

Further Reading

Chambers, J. K. (1993) "Lawless and vulgar innovations": Victorian views on Canadian English. In Sandra Clarke (ed.), *Focus on Canada*. Amsterdam/Philadelphia: John Benjamins, 1–26.

Chambers, J. K. (1998) English: Canadian varieties. In John Edwards (ed.), *Language in Canada*. Cambridge, UK: Cambridge University Press, 252–72.

Chambers, J. K. (2005) "Canadian Dainty": The rise and decline of Briticisms in mainland Canadian English. In Raymond Hickey (ed.), *Legacies of Colonial English: Studies in Transported Dialects*. Cambridge, UK: Cambridge University Press.

Tuijnam, Albert (2001) Benchmarking Adult Literacy in North America. Ottawa: Statistics Canada [Catalogue no. 89–572].

PART III
THE MIDWEST

An Introduction to Midwest English

Timothy C. Frazer

16 Hiding in a wheatfield. © by Viktor Pryymachuk.

One of the grossest misconceptions about the Midwestern United States is that it is home to "General American," a bland, deregionalized variety of English spoken by everyone in the region. Like many generalizations, this is not true.

I live in Macomb, Illinois, located about 200 miles southwest of Chicago and about 150 miles north of St. Louis. My adopted hometown boasts a state university but is otherwise dependent on a rural economy and a rural culture. Recently a colleague of mine originally from Cuba said, "I have lived in this country for more than thirty years and I have been speaking English almost as long, but I can't understand anything they say at the farmers' market." Not long ago, some of my Chinese students observed that they could not understand the vernacular used by African American students on campus. They might also have had trouble with another colleague of mine from Minnesota, who pronounces the contraction *didn't* as *dint*. These Americans the international community could not understand were natives of the Midwest and had lived here most of their lives. So much for the mythical homogeneity of Midwestern English!

So what are the types of Midwest English, and how did they evolve?

African American Vernacular English (AAVE) is a Southern dialect with some relationship to creoles spoken in West Africa and the Caribbean: it is spoken in every major city around the Great Lakes as well as in Cincinnati, Columbus, Indianapolis, St. Louis, Kansas City, Omaha, Minneapolis, and Madison. AAVE came to the Midwest as a result of the "Great Migration" of black people from the South to the (relatively) better economic opportunities in the region. AAVE itself is by no means uniform: an African American student from East St. Louis, Illinois, told me her friends from Chicago made fun of her "Southern accent."

The English of white Midwesterners, however, is even more varied than AAVE, and the reason for this is again migration. After the Revolutionary War, settlers from Virginia, Kentucky, North Carolina, and Tennessee poured into the southern parts of Illinois and Indiana, and to a lesser extent Ohio; in Illinois they moved up the river valleys as far as the sites of Peoria and Burlington, Iowa. More than 200 years later, people living near Macomb tell me that their friends from Minneapolis remark on their "Southern accents." Because these settlement patterns continued into the West, Midwesterners from southern Ohio, Indiana, and Illinois, and from southern Iowa, from Missouri and parts of Kansas, will sometimes pronounce *pin* and *pen* with the same vowel, and will also sometimes merge, for example, *feel* and *fill* as well as *pool* and *pull* and *tire* and *tar*. *Town* will get a fronted vowel so that it sounds like *tay-oon*, while the "long *i*" diphthong occasionally will flatten to where *i* is heard as *ah*. River communities along the Mississippi and Illinois rivers are older and therefore often more Southern, so that I have heard rural whites using perfective *done* (already) as far north as Peoria or Burlington: "Where's my hat?" "I done told you, it's over there!"

Probably a majority of these upland Southern settlers were of Scots-Irish stock. Since later migrants from Pennsylvania and, in later generations, Ohio, were also often of Scots-Irish ancestry, a number of grammatical differences persist which appear to come from Ulster or from Scotland itself. Most prominent are several apparently elliptical verbal constructions in which verbs of desire like *needs, wants,* or *likes* are followed by a past participle, hence *The baby wants fed* or *The car needs washed.* To speakers of Inland Northern or Plantation Southern or British standard English, it sounds as if *to be* needs inserting after the verb. A similar construction uses a preposition as a complement, as in *I want off* or *The cat wants out.*

All of the linguistic features mentioned so far can be identified as either "Midland" or "South Midland." The Midland dialect in the Middle West appears to be due largely to Scots-Irish influence; originally, it included Gaelic words like *clabber* 'sour milk' and *donsie* 'sickly'. Some Midland speakers exhibit a very strong postvocalic *r* and *l* with more velarization, than is used in other dialects of English, and sometimes with the tongue tip raised. Older Midland speakers have an intrusive *r* in *wash* (hence, *warsh*) while others might pronounce *fish* as *feesh*. The low back vowel merger, which makes homophones out of *Don/Dawn* and *cot/caught,* is most noticeable in eastern Ohio (close to its origins in western Pennsylvania). The Midland parts of the Midwest include southern Ohio, most of Indiana, southern Illinois and Iowa, Missouri, Kansas, Nebraska and the western parts of the Dakotas, with some features creeping east into northern Minnesota. Most of the Midland area seems to have as a common part of its settlement history a Scots-Irish predominance.

Another Midwestern dialect, Northern, plays a role in the myth of "General American." Northern became the model for American English dictionaries. Inland Northern is spoken by WASP elites in upstate New York, western New England, and in the urban areas around the southern Great Lakes. The original Northern settlers, the spiritual and intellectual heirs of the New England Puritans, were ambitious, self-righteous people who set out to evangelize the unsettled West during the early nineteenth century. As they came to the Great Lakes states of Ohio, Illinois, Indiana, Wisconsin, and Michigan, they built cities, founded colleges, and established public schools. Believing that salvation lay in the ability to read the Bible, they promoted literacy. By World War II, their dialect had become established in the growing industrial cities that bordered the lower Great Lakes. An Inland Northern-speaking academic, John S. Kenyon (from Hiram College in Northern Ohio) had become the pronunciation authority for *Webster's Second International Dictionary.*

So the Northern dialect became established throughout the Great Lakes cities and adjoining areas, and in colleges, universities, schools, and dictionaries as well. However, the Northern dialect area itself is not monolithic. The Inland Northern dialect, located in the Great Lakes cities, has been for more than half a century the model for dictionaries and pronunciation manuals: this is the variety that is often taught in ESL classes in the United States. But it is in the process of change, so that it is beginning to sound less like examples given in the books. The main shift is in its vowel system. Low central vowels are moving forward, so that to a conservative speaker like myself, a Chicagoan's pronunciation of *sock* or *lock* might sound like *sack* or *lack*.

The rest of the North includes northern Wisconsin, Minnesota, northern Iowa, and most of the Dakotas. Some linguists call this the "North Central" area; others know it as the "Upper Midwest." The southern part of this area is conservative, its pronunciation still close to the dictionary model that originated in the Great Lakes. Farther north and west, especially in western Wisconsin and Minnesota, we find in words like *lutefisk* (fish preserved in brine), evidences of fairly recent settlement by Scandinavians. Farther north, diphthongs in words like *light* and *house* will undergo "Canadian Raising," so that a conservative Northern speaker like myself might hear *loyt* or *hoose*. Here, too, especially around Duluth and Ashland, Wisconsin, we find more evidence of influence by immigrant languages, especially Finnish, German, Swedish and Norwegian. In phonology, *th* consonants become stops, hence *them three* sounds like *dem tree* (this also happens in Chicago). Syntactically, we encounter *I'm going Detroit. You want to go with?*

The Midwest is experiencing an increase in the Spanish-speaking population. The effect a growing influence of Spanish grammar and pronunciation will have on Midwest English is hard to predict. Meanwhile, the large numbers of Spanish-speaking students in ESL classes in the Midwest will continue to be surprised by ways in which the varieties of Midwest English they encounter do not always match those in the classroom.

Further Reading

Cassidy, Frederic G., and Joan Hall (eds.) (1985–) *Dictionary of American Regional English*. Cambridge, MA: Belknap Press of Harvard University Press. (The best authority on dialect words in the USA. Four volumes, A–Sk, are in print.)
Carver, Craig M. (1987) *American Regional Dialects*. Ann Arbor: University of Michigan Press. (A very readable survey of all the dialect areas in the United

States, based on vocabulary found in Cassidy and Hall (eds.), with a fine discussion of settlement history.)

Frazer, Timothy C. (ed.) (1993) *"Heartland" English*. Tuscaloosa: University of Alabama Press. (A collection of papers on the region, including an overview more detailed than the one given here, plus articles on Chicago (3), Missouri German, Oklahoma, AAVE in Iowa, rural adolescent dialect, Wisconsin (2), St. Louis, and others.)

Frazer, Timothy C. (1996) The dialects of the Middle West. In Edgar W. Scheider (ed.), *Focus on the USA* (Varieties of English around the World). Amsterdam/Philadelphia: John Benjamins, 81–102.

Labov, William, Sharon Ash, and Charles Boberg (1996) *Phonological Atlas of North America*. www.ling.upenn.edu/phono_atlas/National Map/National Map.html. (Emphasizes differences in pronunciation, especially those which might confuse a machine scanner.)

Murray, Thomas E. (ed.) (1990) *The Language and Dialect of the Plains*. Special edition of *Kansas Quarterly*, 22(4). (Papers on "Ozarkian English," and on Kansas, Missouri, Wisconsin, Michigan, and Illinois. Back issues are available from the journal at Denison Hall, Kansas State University.)

Murray, Thomas E. (1993) Positive anymore in the Midwest. In Frazer (ed.) (1993).

Murray, Thomas E., Timothy Frazer, and Beth M. Simon (1996) Needs + past participle in American English. *American Speech* 71: 255–71.

Murray, Thomas E., and Beth Simon (1999) Want + past participle in American English. *American Speech* 74: 140–64.

17

Straight Talking from the Heartland (Midwest)

Matthew J. Gordon

17.1 A typical barn in the cornbelt. © by L. R. Kyllo.

Regional stereotypes abound in the US. Most Americans can readily imitate Southerners (*y'all*), New Yorkers (*fuhgeddaboudit*), and Californians (*yo dude*) although these caricatures are usually as inaccurate as they are unflattering.

But if you ask someone to imitate the speech of Midwesterners, you will probably be greeted with silence – even Midwesterners think they speak without an accent.

As a native of eastern Nebraska, I grew up believing that the way I spoke was the norm, not just in my region but for the entire country. Where I lived, teachers did not correct students' everyday pronunciation, and speech therapists did not offer accent-reduction lessons. We may have wrestled at times with a cultural inferiority complex, viewing New Yorkers as more sophisticated or exciting, but we did not covet their accents.

The *cot/caught* Merger

My linguistic illusions were shattered in college. In an introductory phonetics class I discovered that certain words that I had always pronounced the same way were supposed to be distinct. The words included pairs such as *cot* and *caught* and *Don* and *dawn*. The vowel sound in the first member of these pairs was said to be produced with the tongue low and back in the mouth and with the lips spread open, while the vowel of the second member of each pair was said to involve a slightly higher tongue position and a rounding of the lips. For me, all these words had the same vowel, a sound close to that of the former description (i.e., low, back and unrounded). Imagine my Midwestern embarrassment on learning that I was "missing" a vowel!

My vowel system illustrates a phenomenon known as the "low back vowel merger" or simply as the "*cot/caught* merger." A merger is a sound change that involves a loss of phonological contrast as two formerly distinct sounds are merged into a single sound. Mergers have been a fairly common occurrence throughout the history of English, as in other languages. For example, words like *meet* and *meat* used to be pronounced with distinct vowels (*meet* sounded like *mate* and *meat* something like *met*) though today these items have the same sound in most dialects of English. The *cot/caught* merger is a fairly recent development in the Midwest. Dialectologists have for some time known it as a feature of western Pennsylvania (especially Pittsburgh) and of eastern New England, though it has a slightly different form there. It is very widespread across Canada and is also heard throughout the western US. The latter seems to be the source of its introduction into the Midwest as it appears to be spreading eastward. A recent survey directed by William Labov of the University of Pennsylvania has shown that the merger can be found today among younger generations (roughly, people under 40) in Kansas, Nebraska, and the Dakotas. It is also heard across much of Minnesota, Iowa, and Missouri. Similarly, the merger affects central portions of Illinois, Indiana, and Ohio, though its appearance in these areas may represent a westward expansion of the change from Pennsylvania.

Many language changes attract negative attention, particularly when they are associated with young people. It is not uncommon, for example, to hear criticisms of the use of *like* as a discourse marker, a feature common among younger speakers (e.g., *He like just came out of like the store*). The *cot/caught* merger, however, seems not to attract any such stigmatization. In fact, people are largely unaware of it. Nevertheless, it does occasionally lead to misunderstandings. One time, I confused a native of Michigan, where the merger does not occur, by directing him to the "copy room" which he heard as "coffee room." A fellow Nebraskan reports a similar experience in which she was speaking to her grandmother about a friend named Dawn. Apparently interpreting "Dawn" as "Don," the grandmother wanted to know why Dawn's parents had given her a boy's name.

The Northern Cities Shift

In other parts of the "accentless" Midwest another distinctive pronunciation pattern can be heard. This pattern also affects vowel sounds, but unlike the *cot/caught* merger, it does not involve the loss of any distinctions. Instead the affected vowels come to be pronounced with the tongue positioned in a slightly different place in the mouth. As a result, the vowels appear to be shifting around in articulatory space. Since this pattern occurs principally in the large urban centers of the traditional Northern dialect region, it is known as the "Northern Cities Shift" (NCS).

The NCS involves changes to the six vowels illustrated by the words *caught, cot, cat, bit, bet,* and *but.* For people affected by the NCS, the vowel in *caught* comes to be articulated with a more fronted tongue position and with the lips spread. In this way, *caught* takes on a vowel similar to that of *cot* as spoken in other parts of the country. However, these two vowels do not merge into one, as they do with the *cot/caught* merger. The distinction is preserved because the vowel of *cot* also shifts, coming forward in the mouth toward the area in which other speakers pronounce the vowel of *cat*. The *cat* vowel, in turn, is shifted upward from its traditional position in the low, front area of the mouth by raising the tongue. It comes to have a position more like that of *bet* or even *bit*. Often it takes on a diphthongal quality, one that combines two vowel sounds and resembles the second syllable of the word *idea*. For NCS speakers, the vowel of *bit* shifts away from its high, front position toward the center of the mouth, taking on a quality much like that of the second syllable of *roses*. A similar tendency is heard with the vowel of *bet* which can sound more like *but*. The *bet* vowel also sometimes reveals a slightly different tendency toward lowering so that *bet* comes to sound more like *bat*. Finally, there is the vowel of *but* which is traditionally produced with a central tongue position. In the NCS this vowel is shifted backward and may acquire some lip-rounding, making *but* sound like *bought*. The Northern Cities Shift is heard across a broad swath of the Northern US from upstate New York throughout the Great Lakes region and westward into at least Minnesota. As its name suggests, it is most strongly rooted in large cities including Buffalo, Cleveland, Detroit, and Chicago, but it is spreading beyond the urban centers into more rural areas.

For linguists, the NCS represents a significant development. Part of its significance stems from the sounds that are affected. Throughout the history of English, the class of short vowels including those of *bit*, *bet*, and *bat* has remained relatively stable sounding much as they did over a millennium ago. The NCS appears to challenge this longstanding stability. Even more intriguing is the pattern created by the changing vowels. As the earlier description suggested, the NCS consists of a series of changes by which one vowel shifts into the space of a neighboring vowel. The contrast between the vowels is maintained, however, because that neighboring vowel also shifts. For example, *caught* shifts toward *cot*, but *cot* shifts toward *cat*, and *cat* shifts toward *kit* or *keeyat*. In this way, the various components of the NCS appear to be coordinated rather than accidental. Such coordinated patterns of sound change are known as "chain shifts" because the individual elements appear to be linked together. While not as common

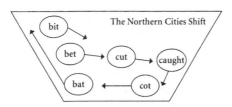

17.2 The pattern of vowel changes known as the Northern Cities Shift.

an occurrence as merger, chain shifts have been documented in a number of languages. In the history of English the changes that occurred between roughly the fifteenth and eighteenth centuries (known as the Great Vowel Shift) are often cited as an example of chain shifting. This historical change rearranged the system of long vowels causing, for example, low vowels to raise to mid positions and mid vowels to raise to high positions.

While people who have NCS in their own speech are generally unaware of it, the shifted pronunciations are noticeable to people from other parts of the country, and occasionally misunderstandings arise as a result of these shifts. For example, John Lawler of the University of Michigan reports that he is sometimes asked why his son, Ian, has a girl's name. Apparently, Michiganders hear the name as "Ann" which, following the NCS, they pronounce as *eeyan*.

The fact that the NCS is well established in Michigan is particularly interesting in light of the dominant beliefs about local speech. As research by Dennis Preston has shown, Michiganders are "blessed" with a high degree of linguistic security; when surveyed, they rate their own speech as more correct and more pleasant than that of even their fellow Midwesterners. By contrast Indianans tend to rate the speech of their state on par with that Illinois, Ohio, and Michigan. Indeed, it is not uncommon to find Michiganders who will claim that the speech of national broadcasters is modeled on their dialect. Even a cursory comparison of the speech of the network news anchors with that of the local news anchors in Detroit will reveal the fallacy of such claims.

Nevertheless, the Michiganders' faith that they speak an accentless variety is just an extreme version of the general stereotype of Midwestern English. The examples of the *cot*/*caught* merger and the Northern Cities Shift serve to contradict the perception that Midwestern speech lacks any distinguishing characteristics. However, both of these developments have been in operation for several decades at least. Why haven't they entered into popular perceptions about Midwestern speech? Perhaps they will come to be recognized as features of the dialect in the same way that dropping of *r* serves to mark Boston speech or ungliding of long *i* (*hahd* for *hide*) marks Southern speech. But, considering the general stereotypes of the Midwest, it seems more likely that they might never be recognized. One thing about linguistic stereotypes is certain: they have less to do with the actual speech of a region than with popular perceptions of the region's people. As long as Midwesterners are viewed as average, boring or otherwise nondescript, their speech will be seen through the same prism.

Resources

Information about the *cot/caught* merger, the Northern Cities Shift, and other active sound changes in American English is available from the website of the TELSUR project (www.ling.upenn.edu/phono_atlas/home.html). The project is directed by William Labov and presents the results of a telephone survey of speech patterns across North America. Labov treats these features as well as historical changes such as the Great Vowel Shift in his *Principles of Linguistic Change* (1994, Malden, MA and Cambridge, UK: Blackwell). For a study of the Northern Cities Shift in rural Michigan, see Matthew J. Gordon, *Small-Town Values and Big-City Vowels* (2001, Durham, NC: Duke University Press). Dennis Preston's research on popular attitudes toward American dialects is reported in his contribution to *Language Myths* (Laurie Bauer and Peter Trudgill (eds.), 1998, London: Penguin).

Words of the Windy City (Chicago, IL)

Richard Cameron

18 Work on a construction project in the Chicago River North area. © by Matthew Dula.

You would think that the city described by Carl Sandburg as the "Hog Butcher for the World" and "the Nation's Freight Handler" would have had many books written about its language. Unfortunately, the Chicago dialect has been neglected by linguists who have preferred to focus on New York City and Boston, although the Midwestern dialect is probably a better indicator of the current state of language in the urban North than its more famous East Coast counterparts.

Early Days

Native Americans – joined later by Europeans – used the portage between Lake Michigan and the Illinois and Mississippi River system for temporary, seasonal settlements. Chicago's first known settlers, the Illiniwek, called the place *Chigagou* or *Chicagoua*, which means something like "wild garlic place." Apart from the Illiniwek, history books recognize Jean Baptiste Pointe Du Sable as Chicago's first year-round settler. Du Sable was Haitian, primarily of African descent, so he spoke Haitian Creole and French as his first languages. French would have been most useful for fur trading at the time, but Du Sable could have used English to speak with the occasional British military visitor. He may also have spoken some Potawatomi, the Native American language of his wife and her family.

There is a lesson to be learned from Du Sable and his wife. English in Chicago has always been spoken by two groups: native speakers of English and non-native speakers of varying abilities in a variety of accents. Currently, Chicago English is spoken natively in two broad dialects: Upper Midwest American English and African American English. Hispanic or Latino English is also on the rise, but it has not been studied in Chicago as extensively as it has been in Los Angeles (see chapter 36, "Talking with mi Gente"). Varieties of Chicago English are also used by native speakers of Mandarin, Cantonese and Hokkien varieties of Chinese, Polish, Spanish, Urdu, Russian, Lithuanian, Romanian, Hindi, Arabic, Italian, Ilocano, Tagalog, Thai, Greek, Korean, Serbo-Croatian, Yiddish, Gujarati, Vietnamese, and Japanese, among others. In fact, a report from the Illinois State Board of Education identifies 107 different languages currently spoken in the Chicago Metropolitan Area. If you add two or three major dialects of English, then Chicago Englishes consist of at least 110 accents used on a daily basis.

One of the earliest of the few publications about Chicago English, "A Sketch of the Linguistic Conditions of Chicago" (1903) by Carl Darling Buck, begins with this pronounced statement: "The linguistic conditions in some of our largest American cities are unique in the history of the world – an unparalleled Babel of foreign tongues." Though Buck's study gives a detailed census report on the "foreign tongues" in Chicago at the beginning of the twentieth century, it says nothing about English except to claim that it had hardly been affected by other languages. At that time, German was the most dominant language in the city, spoken by nearly 500,000 people; next came Polish, still a widely spoken and robust language in Chicago. Then came Swedish, Bohemian, Norwegian and Yiddish, Dutch, Italian, Danish, French, Gaelic, Serbo-Croatian, Slovakian, and Lithuanian – all of which were spoken by 10,000 people or more at home and in the community. Many of these languages – German and Swedish, for example – have all but vanished in Chicago. Today, the second language of the city is Spanish, spoken in various forms by just over one-quarter of the population.

In 1965, the dialectologist Lee Pederson noted that the consonant sounds of metropolitan Chicago were similar to those found in other American English dialects. Of course, people say things like *da Bears*, or *runnin'* instead of *running*, or even *tree* instead of *three* as in *Hey Mack, gimme tree sandwiches*. But people in other US cities do this too, especially when they need three sandwiches and the guy at the counter is called Mack (pronounced more like *Meck* than *Mack*, by the way).

But, in comparison to the consonants, the vowel sounds of Chicago English seemed wild and innovative – at least in the 1960s. Pederson found that Chicagoans of various backgrounds had no fewer than seven different ways of pronouncing the vowel sound in words like *bag*. Some pronounced *bag* somewhat like *beg* – but not exactly – more like *biaeg*. Likewise, the vowel in a word like *touch* had about nine different pronunciations. Pederson recorded the range of pronunciations for Chicago English vowels, but he had trouble finding any consistency and concluded that there was "no clear pattern."

Shifty Chicago Vowels

The vowels are messy but there is a pattern. I first heard it when I thought that a friend was talking about a woman by the name of *Jan* when in fact the woman was a man by the name of *John*. A woman told me she went to "Cully High School" on the South Side of Chicago. When I asked her to spell it, she wrote "Kelly High School."

Like other northern cities such as Detroit, Cleveland, and Buffalo, Upper Midwest American English in Chicago is experiencing a shift in the pronunciation of five or six vowels. Vowels are pronounced by moving the tongue toward certain target areas within the mouth. For the vowel of a word like *Jen*, the target is in the front middle part of the mouth. For the vowel of a word like *Jan*, the target is also in the front of the mouth but lower than the target for *Jen*. For the vowel of a word like *John* it is in the lower middle part of the mouth. The shift involves the vowels in words like *Jan* beginning to sound like *Jen* because the target area for *Jan* has shifted up in the front of the mouth. Remember my confusion of *Cully* for *Kelly*? That's because the vowel of *Jen*, like the first vowel of *Kelly*, is also shifting, but it moves backwards in the mouth where it sounds like the first vowel in *gully*. That's why I heard *Cully* for *Kelly*. In turn, for the vowel in *John*, speakers shift the target area frontward in the mouth toward the spot for *Jan*. Other vowels are also involved in this shift, such as *coffee* sounding more like *cahffee* and *tuck* sounding more like *talk* (see chapter 17, "Straight Talking from the Heartland").

A curious thing about vowel shifts is their pattern of dispersion throughout the region. They spread from the major center of population to neighboring areas by jumping first to towns of intermediate size and then to smaller ones in a pattern that cultural geographers call hierarchical diffusion. Given that Chicago is the biggest city in the Northern cities region, we can deduce that this vowel change began in Chicago.

So how do people use these vowels to position themselves socially when they speak English in Chicago? Though there hasn't been a lot of research, one study (Herndobler 1994) looked at a working-class community on the far South Side that included three generations of speakers and two levels of social classes. For Chicagoans, there is a clear cultural divide between *South Siders* and *North Siders*. The North Siders generally root for the Cubs and, according to some South Siders, try to sound uppity. The South Siders often follow the White Sox and, according to some North Siders, are real "deese and dem kind of people." Not surprisingly, the study showed that the men had higher frequencies of *dat* for *that* and *tree* for *three* than did the women. Also, people who were lower-middle-class more frequently said *dat* and *tree* than did people who were middle-class.

The vowels showed something different. The vowel of *Jan* – the newer pronunciation that is closer to the vowel of *Jen* – was produced more frequently by the women than by the men. And, the newer pronunciation was also produced more frequently by the middle-class than by the lower-middle-class speakers. This is the reverse of what happened for the consonant sounds. It seems that if a speech sound is changing, women will lead the way and that class differences are significant as well.

Things got even more interesting with the vowel of *John*. In the two oldest generations, men produced the newer pronunciation more than women. In the youngest generation, women and men were about equal. In the lower middle class, among the oldest speakers, men produced more of the new pronunciation than women. But in the middle class among the oldest speakers, this pattern was reversed. Women produced more of the new pronunciation than men.

So what's the deal? For a period of time, the little vowel in such words as *John* had two kinds of social meanings. For the elderly lower middle class, it was associated with independent tough men who worked with their hands outside the home in local factories – a vowel used by a man's man. For the elderly middle class, women who also worked outside of the home used the vowel as a sign of independence, education, and competence so it was a self-respecting, forward-looking woman's vowel.

Vocabulary

When I moved to Chicago, three words really confused me – *gangway*, *prairie*, and *parkway*. A *gangway* is a walkway between two buildings. A *prairie* is an empty city lot that may have some stray dogs, but no prairie dogs or coyotes. And a *parkway*, which for me is a highway busy with cars heading into a city, is the grassy strip that separates the sidewalk in front of a house from the street. A *snorkel* or *snorkel truck* is "a large fire truck with master-stream nozzle, boom and bucket." I've noticed *red hots* (an older term for hotdogs), *Italian beef* (because of the Italian spices), *subs* and *hot subs* (not hoagies and grinders), *pop* more than *soda*, and more recently, the *Jíbaro sandwich* (pronounced *HE-bah-row*, with steak and fried plantains instead of bread) invented in the Puerto Rican neighborhoods. To get around you use *the Loop* (downtown), the *El* or the *L* (the elevated train that loops the downtown), and when the *El* crosses over a street, call it a *viaduct* but when one road crosses over another road, call this an *overpass*. Chicagoans say things like *I was by my Mother's house last night* with *by* instead of *at*. Likewise, when you ask for *tree* sandwiches from Mack, he might ask, "Do you wanna take 'em *with*?" instead of *with you*.

What do we know about Chicago Englishes? First, lots of people of many different backgrounds speak them both as their first language and as a learned second language. They do so with many degrees of proficiency and a wide variety of accents. Second, among the first-language speakers born in Chicago, there are at least two major dialects of Chicago English. For some speakers, certain vowels have special meanings. For all speakers, the vocabulary has a few unique features. And if you live here for a while, you begin to take the sentences *with*, even when you're *by* your mother's house watching the *White Sacks* on TV because she has air conditioning in August.

References and Further Reading

Farr, Marcia (ed.) (2004) *Ethnolinguistic Chicago*. Mahwah, NJ: Lawrence Erlbaum.

Herndobler, Robin (1993) Sound change and gender in a working class community. In Timothy Frazer (ed.), *"Heartland" English: Variation and Transition in the American Midwest*. Tuscaloosa: University of Alabama Press, 137–56.

Miller, Michael (1986) Discovering Chicago's dialects: A Field Museum experiment in adult education. *Field Museum of Natural History Bulletin*, September: 5–11.

Pederson, Lee (1965) *The Pronunciation of English in Metropolitan Chicago*. Tuscaloosa: University of Alabama Press for the American Dialect Society.

Pederson, Lee (1971) Chicago words: The regional vocabulary. *American Speech* 46: 163–92.

Different Ways of Talking in the Buckeye State (Ohio)

Beverly Olson Flanigan

19.1 Dusk falls in Dayton, Ohio. © by Stan Rohrer.

When international students come to Ohio University in the town of Athens they are often amazed and puzzled by the speech of the local citizens – but then, so are many Americans. Here, they meet people who tell them their *car needs fixed*, or that the *feesh are bitin' real good*, or that the store has a *spayshul on aigs*. Overseas students are surprised when the local speech doesn't match the books and tapes they've studied as "American English" since Ohio seems like the heartland of America to them. And northern and central Ohioans, not to mention out-of-state students, also wonder how it is that this part of the state sounds so different from Cleveland, Columbus, and even Cincinnati.

Southern Ohioans are less puzzled when they travel north in the state, since they recognize "mainstream" pronunciation and grammar from the media and other sources. But even central Ohioans laugh at the "nasal" speech of Clevelanders and the mountain "twang" of the eastern hills.

In fact, Ohio, like ancient Gaul, can be divided into three parts – dialectally, that is; and those three areas reflect quite accurately three, or perhaps four, major dialect divisions running all through the Eastern United States. Ohio has always been interesting to scholars of language variation because it is a kind of microcosm of dialect differences that can be traced back to the earliest periods of settlement of this country. Although change is always occurring to some degree, especially in the pronunciation of vowels, the three areas remain distinct and recognizable.

Dialect research in the US began in the 1930s with the intention of producing a Linguistic Atlas of the United States and Canada. Regions were sampled according to age and educational levels of selected informants, who were interviewed by fieldworkers to elicit regional lexical items, grammatical structures, and pronunciations. Maps were drawn with isoglosses between major lexical, grammatical, and phonological divisions. Three major areas were distinguished: Northern, Midland, and Southern; the west was, and still is, under study. As the map shows, Ohio, according to this traditional cut, lies in both the Northern and the Midland regions, with a further division into North Midland and South Midland. But there is also considerable overlap with so-called Appalachian speech in the eastern third of the state – 29 of the 88 counties lie in the Appalachian Plateau. On the Ohio River, which forms the southern border of the state, is a mix of South Midland and Southern speech, with Southern ungliding of vowels (*Ah lahk you just fahn*) and shifting of Northern vowels (*feesh, poosh,* and *spayshul*) intruding slowly but surely across the river.

Migration routes from the East and Southeast first brought these distinctive forms into the old Northwest Territory – later to become the

19.2 Traditional dialect boundaries based on the Linguistic Atlas of the United States (Shuy 1967, p. 47).

states of Ohio, Indiana, Illinois, Michigan, and Wisconsin. New England and New York State were the source of settlers in the northern part of Ohio; central Ohio was settled from Pennsylvania and Maryland; and southern Ohio had two sources of migration, one from the Northeast and Pennsylvania via the Ohio River and the National Road (now US 40/70), and the other from Virginia, North Carolina, and Kentucky through the Cumberland Gap and northward on Daniel Boone's Wilderness Road.

Northerners brought with them the transplanted speech forms of southern England, while the midlanders from Pennsylvania were of northern English and Scots-Irish stock. As early as 1878, an anonymous observer commented on the Scots-Irish origins of the English of western Pennsylvania, the Cumberland Valley, and the Alleghenies, noting the use of phrases like *I want out, to wait on* (someone), *to take sick,* and *quarter till* in telling time. Northern equivalents are *I want to go out, wait for someone, get sick,* and *quarter of* or *to*. Furthermore, the low vowel in *want* and *on* would be farther back and more rounded in western Pennsylvania and southern Ohio, as in *wahnt* and *ahn*. An intrusive *r* was noted early in this area, as in *warsh* and *Warshington* – still noticeable but less common are intrusive *t* in *oncet, twicet* and intrusive *l* as in *drawling* for *drawing*. This last is particularly interesting, since the so-called "dark l" in words like *falling* and *call* is disappearing, so that *call* sounds more like the crow's *caw*. A voiced consonant in *greasy,* pronounced *greazy,* is common here too, as it is in much of the South. Even the name of the state is pronounced differently in this region: Ohio sounds like *ahiya*, just as Cincinnati is locally called *Cincinnata*. Southern Ohio shares with the South the pronunciation of *roof* and *creek* with tensed vowels, as in *Rufus* and *creak*, while northern Ohio has *ruhff* and *crick*. Central Ohio uses both pronunciations, with the tensed forms winning out not because of migration origins but because they are becoming the preferred or "prestigious" forms throughout the country.

Central Ohio, the area surrounding Columbus and extending westward to Dayton and Springfield, is often thought of as "bland," speaking a general "Midwestern" or "heartland" English. But it too has distinctive characteristics noticed by outsiders if not by its own residents. Most noteworthy, especially to foreign students accustomed to "book English," is the merger of vowels in words like *cot* and *caught*, or *Don* and *dawn*, or *hock* and *hawk*, in Central Ohio and, indeed, much of the country to the west. The rounded back vowel is essentially lost, so that *caught, dawn,* and *hawk* sound the same as *cot, Don,* and *hock* – with comprehension problems inevitably resulting. Another homophone set becoming more common in this area is that of *fill* and *feel*, both sounding like *fill, sale* and *sell* merging to *sell*, and *pull* and *pool* (and even *pole*), all moving to *pull*. Note that this shift occurs only before *l* and is the opposite of the vowel change occurring in southern Ohio, where the tensed vowels of *feesh, poosh,* and *spayshul* tend to dominate, though the central Ohio pattern is moving southward. A final vowel change in eastern and central Ohio, and much of southern Ohio as well, is the fronting of *o* and *u*, so that *boat* sounds like *ba-oat* and *boot* sounds like *ba-oot*.

Northern Ohio keeps the vowels of *cot* and *caught* distinct, and it also lacks the other vowel changes heard in central and southern Ohio. However, and especially in the large urban centers of Cleveland and Toledo, it exhibits the "nasal" sound so often mocked by other Ohioans. Linguists call this the Northern Cities Shift, a pattern of vowel changes observed from eastern New York State to Wisconsin. The hallmark of this shift is vowel raising, with words like *bad* and *cat* pronounced more like *bed* and *ket*, or even with an inglide to sound like *be-yed* and *ke-yet*. This shift leads to other shifts around the vowel space of the mouth, so that *flesh* sounds like *flush, but* like *bought*, and *locks* like *lacks*.

But pronunciation isn't the whole story of dialect variation in Ohio. Lexical forms like *redd up* 'to clean, make ready', *blinds* for 'window shades on rollers', *sack* instead of Northern *bag, bucket* instead of *pail*, and plural *you'uns*, common in the Pittsburgh area and much of Appalachia, also came into southern Ohio and remain, though less consistently, today. Another second person plural form, *you all*, is increasingly heard, though not in its contracted form *y'all* as it is found in a large region of the South. None of these variants is used outside southern Ohio, but other forms, like northern *pop* for *soda*, *bag*, and *you guys* are now as common in the Ohio Valley as they are throughout the US. But two kinship terms, *mamaw* and *papaw* (for *grandma* and *grandpa*) are not heard in Ohio outside of the southern and southeastern Appalachian areas.

Grammar, too, is variable in the state, though social mobility and education are leveling this variation to some degree. We noted *sick at the stomach* but *He's not to home*, and *He works down to the mill* or *over to [place name]* and the use of participles for past tense (*He done it, I seen him* are still common in the South Midland and in southern Ohio). More sporadic are *hit* for *it*, *used to didn't*, perfective *done* in *He done finished his work*, omission of subject relative pronouns in *He's the man did the work*, personal dative after *get* in *I got me a new car*, and singular nouns of measure as in *ten mile* and *five pound*. A progressive verb construction common in Appalachia is still used occasionally in southern and southeastern Ohio, mainly by older rural people; it prefixes *a-* to the verb as in *They went a-hunting, The house was a-haunted*. The "*need/want/like* + past participle" construction is very common, however: *My car needs fixed*; *The cat wants fed*; *the dog likes petted*. This verb form is spreading all across Ohio, with the exception of the northernmost fringe, as is the so-called "positive anymore" construction. Thus, *It seems like it rains all the time anymore* contrasts with Northern *It never seems to dry out anymore*, where a negative is added.

Ohio has also been influenced by languages other than English, most notably German. Cincinnati had bilingual schooling in English and German for many years and even has a neighborhood called Over-the-Rhine. A dialectal remnant is the use of "Please?" from German "Bitte?" used to ask someone to repeat a phrase not clearly heard. The misnamed Pennsylvania Dutch (really German, from dialectal *Deitsch=Deutsch*) are also in Ohio; in fact, there are more "Deitsch" in Ohio than in any other state, including Pennsylvania. They speak a dialect of German in their homes, churches, and social circles. They are far outnumbered today, however, by Spanish speakers; about 90,000 Hispanic/Latino Americans live in Ohio, and several Spanish dialects are used. Newer immigrants are bringing in Arabic, Somali, and the languages of Southeast Asia. Other heritage languages still used, include Polish, Yiddish, Hungarian, and Greek. With the exception of the rural-based Deitsch, most of these groups are concentrated in the large urban centers, but their English has rapidly taken on various regional characteristics: the Northern Cities vowel shift in Cleveland and Toledo, the *cot/caught* merger in Columbus, and South Midland with a touch of Kentucky in Cincinnati.

Ohio's license plate used to display the motto "Ohio: The Heart of It All." If the Midwest may be said to be "America's Heartland," perhaps Ohio can be called "the heart of the Heartland." In its mix of immigrant languages and English dialects, it is indeed a microcosm of the history of the country – and that isn't likely to change any time soon.

Resources

For more information on the "heartland" of which Ohio is a part, see chapter 17, "Straight Talking from the Heartland." On the adjoining Pittsburgh–Western Pennsylvania dialect, see chapter 12, "Steel Town Speak." The map of American dialect regions is taken from Roger W. Shuy, *Discovering American Dialects* (Champaign, IL: National Council of Teachers of English, 1967). For more recent mapping of pronunciation differences in the United States, see William Labov, Sharon Ash, and Charles Boberg, *Atlas of North American English* (Berlin: Mouton de Gruyter, 2000; preview available at www.ling.upenn.edu/phono_atlas/). A very good introduction to American dialects for ESL learners can be found in *Varieties of English*, by Susan M. Gass and Natalie Lefkowitz (Ann Arbor: University of Michigan Press, 1995).

Spirited Speech (St. Louis, MO)

Thomas E. Murray

20 St. Louis skyline and Gateway Arch. © by Corbis.

Like most dialects in the United States, the one used in St. Louis is distinctive because of a particular combination of features it contains. The combination of features St. Louisans use is especially complex. Linguists have variously characterized it as Northern, Southern, South Midland, or

North Midland/South Midland in its orientation. Such a range of classifications can be confusing, but all the major dialect areas of the central United States have contributed significantly to every aspect of the city's language – its pronunciation, grammar, and lexicon.

For example, St. Louisans typically pronounce an *r* in *wash* and *Washington* (*warsh*, *Warshington*), and routinely use the short *e* vowel of *wet* in *Mary*, *marry*, and *merry*; both of these traits are characteristics that have historically been linked to the North Midland and South Midland regions. Yet they favor the use of an *s* rather than a *z* in *grease* and *greasy* (Inland North/North Midland), and say *which* without an initial *h*, as in *witch* (South/South Midland/North Midland).

In terms of grammar, St. Louisans favor *dove* (Inland North) as the past tense of *dive*, prefer *want off* and *wait on* as in *John wants off the bus* and *Mary's waiting on her husband* (North Midland/South Midland). Lexically, St. Louisans tend to eat *string beans* and *corn on the cob* (Inland North/North Midland), dispose of *pits* from their cherries (Inland North) and *seeds* from their peaches (South/South Midland/North Midland), carry groceries in *bags* (Inland North) and water in *buckets* (South/South Midland).

Large-scale surveys of the language used in St. Louis have identified the city as primarily an Inland North/North Midland speech island that exists in a sea of sharply contrasting Southern and especially South Midland forms. Though speakers living just outside the greater metropolitan area, in rural Missouri and Illinois, tend to sound more Southern/South Midland, those living in the city and its various suburbs usually sound more Inland Northern/North Midland. So, why should the dialect used in St. Louis have such regionally diverse roots? And why should St. Louisans favor the Inland Northern and North Midland dialects?

The answer to the first question is relatively straightforward. The speech system used in the Gateway City is largely the product of the various dialects that settlers have brought to the area. Between 1804, when the transfer of the northern section of the Louisiana Purchase occurred there, and about 1850, most of these people came from states in the South and South Midlands, especially Kentucky, Tennessee, Virginia, the Carolinas, and Maryland. Between the end of the Civil War and about 1900, however, they tended to have their roots in the Inland North and North Midlands, primarily Illinois, Indiana, Ohio, Pennsylvania, and New York. In 1900, a heavy infusion of (mostly African American) settlers came to the city from Mississippi, Alabama, and Georgia as part of the great southern exodus following Reconstruction.

The vast majority of the people who moved to the area represented third-, fourth-, and higher-generation New World families, most of whom had already abandoned their ancestral languages in favor of English.

Of course, thousands of first- and second-generation immigrants also came to St. Louis, beginning with the French, who founded the community in 1764 and named it for their former king, Saint Louis IX, to honor Louis XV. Then came the Spanish, who dominated the area until France sold the Louisiana Purchase, including all of present-day Missouri, to the Americans. The nineteenth century brought the Italians, Czechs, Poles, Scots-Irish, and Pennsylvania Dutch Germans.

It was generally true that immigrants who traveled to the New World before the American Revolution clung to their Old World identities and lifestyles. Only about 1820 did the European newcomers become so swept up in New World nationalism that they willingly abandoned their ethnic identities. For these immigrants, assimilation into the language and other cultural traditions of their new country occurred very quickly, usually within the first or second generation.

Predictably, the two kinds of immigrants who found their way to St. Louis had little linguistic impact: those who were already settled in the country's melting pot simply brought the American dialects of their former regions, and those who retained their ethnic identities tended to segregate themselves.

Thus, the Czechs took up residence in the southern part of the city, the Italians congregated in the southwest, and the Irish, Poles, and Germans lived in various sections of the north. The African Americans in St. Louis have always tended to congregate in the inner city, though since about 1980 they have come to dominate the northern part of the greater metropolitan area as well.

The answer to the second question – why St. Louisans should favor the Inland Northern and North Midland dialects – rests on one of the most basic truisms of linguistics. People most respect those dialects that are used by the groups of speakers they most respect. The dialect has, in short, become the basis of what most Americans consider to be "standard English."

But the complete answer to the question has been reinforced greatly by St. Louisans' strong psychosocial aversion to sounding like a "hoosier" when they speak. *Hoosier*, with the meaning 'hick, hillbilly', is common throughout much of the South and South Midlands; in St. Louis the term is especially pejorative. And "hoosier language," to a St. Louisan, is anything reminiscent of the specific blend of dialect features, especially pronunciations, found in the Ozark Highlands of southern Missouri, southeastern Kansas, and northwestern Arkansas, where South Midland and Southern speech forms prevail. They have also adopted those dialects merely to avoid the stigma of sounding too rustic or uneducated.

When I completed a large-scale survey of the language of St. Louis in the early 1980s, I found that the city's speakers preferred Inland Northern and North Midland speech forms. But another basic truism of linguistics is that living languages change over time to meet the needs of their users. Early in the twenty-first century I replicated the study to determine how the Gateway City dialect had shifted over the previous generation. I wanted to know whether it had become significantly more or less like the Inland North/North Midland standard.

What I found was that certain usages had actually shifted away from that standard (see the box on the *ar* pronunciation of *fork* and other words). The language of St. Louis has become much more Inland Northern and North Midland and less Southern and South Midland in its orientation. For pronunciation, the increase was some 32%; for grammar, 33%; and for the lexicon, 19%. Inland North/North Midland features are being used by more St. Louisans now (and South/South Midland features are being used by fewer St. Louisans) than a generation ago.

St. Louis *Sundae*

One unique feature of the language used in the Gateway City is the pronunciation of *sundae*. Elsewhere in the country, the word rhymes with *Sunday*, with the final vowel sometimes reduced to a long *e* (thus *sundee*). In St. Louis, however, the final vowel is often articulated as *uh*, yielding *sunduh*. This pronunciation is much more frequent among older speakers, and in fact is now heard only rarely among the younger generations (though as recently as 20 years ago, *sunduh* was the standard among young and old alike), suggesting that it will probably be obsolete by the middle of the twenty-first century.

What accounts for *sunduh*? No one knows for sure, though it may be linked to the nearly nationwide ban that occurred in the latter part of the nineteenth century against the sale of soda water, lemonade, pastries, ice cream, and the like on Sundays. (Such items were considered frivolous luxuries, and their sale deemed inappropriate for the Christian sabbath.) Some vendors, unwilling to forfeit the revenue gained from their

Sunday ice cream sales, began topping the ice cream with fruit, marketing the new creation as healthy and nutritious, and – voila! – the ice cream sundae was born. (Why the new treat was called *sundae* is also unclear; the word, dating to 1897, probably derives from *Sunday* and may reflect the irony of the vendors who originated the sundae: What better name for an ice-cream-based dessert sold on Sunday?)

Gateway City folklore relates, however, that many St. Louisans did not accept the sundae as a legitimate exception to the ban, and continued to object to the selling of sundaes on Sundays. Particularly inexcusable, they noted, was that *sundae*, rhyming with *Sunday*, appeared to ridicule the sanctity of the Christian holy day. Enter the early-twentieth-century soda jerks from a particular South St. Louis drugstore, who invented the pronunciation *sunduh* to quell the objections, and the rest, as they say, is history. *Sunduh* spread quickly throughout St. Louis, and began to fade from widespread usage only when its uniqueness finally came to be stigmatized by younger speakers.

Of Forks and Farks: The *ar* Stigma

One feature that occurs in the speech of many St. Louisans is the *ar* pronunciation in words containing an *-or-* spelling. *Lord*, for example, is pronounced *lard*, and *or, born, former, forty, for, sordid, short*, and *fork* are pronounced *ar* (or *are*), *barn, farmer, farty, far, sardid, shart*, and *fark* (the same tendency accounts for *mourning/morning* and *hoarse/horse* being pronounced with non-rhyming vowels, *morning* and *horse* having the *ar*). This pattern is not unique to the Gateway City – it also occurs in central Texas and throughout the Northern and North Midland regions – but many St. Louisans' changing perception of it in recent years is really quite remarkable. As late as the mid-1980s, speakers native to the area routinely pronounced *-or-* as *ar* completely unselfconsciously, with little thought as to any negative social consequences. By the early 1990s, however, the pronunciation had begun to be stigmatized, and was widely stereotyped (at least in St. Louis, by the white middle class) as indicative of working-class status. Columnists for the *St. Louis Post-Dispatch* soon began writing columns in which they wondered about the origins of the "aberrant" pronunciation, and local radio personalities began doing jokes that featured "highway farty-four" and "Farest Park" pronunciations. By the mid-1990s, *ar* was fast receding in popularity, especially among younger, more status-conscious speakers, and today it is widely considered a slip of the tongue when it occurs in words containing *-or-*.

Resources

Reliable non-technical descriptions of the language of St. Louis do not exist, but see Thomas E. Murray's essay on the subject in Timothy C. Frazer (ed.), "Heartland" English (Tuscaloosa: University of Alabama Press, 1993, chapter 8). Chapter 20 in William Labov, Sharon Ash, and Charles Boberg, *Atlas of North American English* (Berlin: Mouton de Gruyter, 2005) also contains a thorough account of the city's pronunciation system. For more on the sociocultural and historical development of the Inland Northern dialect as "standard English," see the essays by Thomas S. Donahue and Timothy C. Frazer in Frazer's book cited above (chapters 3 and 4, respectively). And additional information on the dramatic shift of the language of St. Louis over the past 20 years toward the Inland Northern/North Midland standard can be found in Thomas E. Murray's article, "Language variation and change in the urban midwest: The case of St. Louis," in *Language Variation and Change* 14.3 (2002), 347–61.

Saying Ya to the Yoopers (Michigan's Upper Peninsula)

Beth Simon

21 Ice fishing is a popular pastime among the "Yoopers" of Michigan's Upper Peninsula.
© by Ronda Oliver.

In Wisconsin, it begins north of Rhinelander. In Michigan, somewhere after Ludington. Bumper stickers appear urging people to "Say Ya to the UP," tourist gear emblazoned with "Uf Da", and Finglish epigrams decorating restaurant placemats. These linguistic signs indicate that one is leaving the land of trolls (south of the Mackinaw Bridge) and entering Michigan's Upper Peninsula (or UP).

Upper Peninsula speech, especially that of the western UP, is an excellent example of a "focused" dialect – perceived as a distinct entity by its speakers and by those who come into contact with it. The English spoken on the western side of Michigan's UP, and especially on the Keweenaw Peninsula, is a dialect replete with evidence of multifaceted social interactions, economic change, and cultural complexity.

The Development of the Peninsula

The Keweenaw Peninsula is an isolated, copper-rich area, which was lightly populated by Menominee-nation Ojibwa when French missionaries and French Canadian trappers first arrived there in 1621. In 1840, while surveying for the state, Douglas Houghton reported to the Michigan legislature that veins of almost pure copper ran under the entire peninsula. Between 1846, when the first commercial mine opened, and 1968 when the last productive mine closed, over 10.5 billion tons of copper were brought to the surface. The population of "Copper Country" (as it is still called today) rose from approximately 25,000 in 1880 to over 90,000 in 1910 when more than two-thirds of residents were born either outside the US or to foreign-born or non-citizen parents. The English spoken on the Keweenaw was English English, Cornish English, Irish English, and the English of the Scottish Lowlands. "It was English," said one descendant of Cornish immigrants, "but not the King's English. Not the Queen's English."

Cornish miners were especially sought after because of their experience of innovative mining methods in England's southwest peninsula. After the Civil War, mine-owners recruited workers from Europe, because, as the General Manager of the Keweenaw's largest mining conglomerate wrote, they preferred men who had "just arrived in this country . . . We would rather make American citizens of these people in our own way than have anyone else do it." Copper Country residents understood the cultural complexities of the UP. "My father used to say, forty nationalities, a church for every one and every church full . . . In school there were Polish, Italian, Irish, Finnish, English, Cornish," recalls a Keweenaw native.

The end of profitable mining on the Keweenaw coincided with the opening of mines in the American West and Southwest, the availability of hourly wage jobs in the northern cities, and the Great Depression. By 1930, the local population was less than 60,000. Of those who remained, most were Finns, who continued to use Finnish (usually alongside English) at home and in social organizations. Other residents were native English speakers and other immigrant groups who no longer maintained their first language. Because they were able to maintain their ancestral language, the speech of people of Finnish background has had the strongest influence on the English dialect of the western UP.

Dialect Features of Yoopers

Of all UP identified pronunciations, the one most remarked, imitated and parodied is occurrence of the stop *d* and sometimes *t* where most American English speakers expect or produce the fricatives spelled *th*. First-generation Finnish immigrants would have substituted *t*, and later *d*, in words such as *these*, *them* and *the*. Certainly *d* for *th* is common in the ethnic-identified urban dialects of American English found from Milwaukee to the east coast. Nonetheless it is this sound that is often perceived as definitive of UP speech (see box). A related phonetic feature also from Finnish is *t* for the final *th* in *with*, producing *wit*.

Michigan Technological University Professor Victoria Bergvall, originally from eastern Montana, notes that outsiders identify UP vowels as "Canadian," especially the *o* vowel, which, on the UP, is produced with the lips tightly rounded. This, Bergvall points out, is also heard in local Ojibwa speech and elsewhere across the north. Also noticeable is the

---

Da Yooper Creation Story

In da beginning dere was nuttin, see.

Den on da first day God created da UP, eh?

On da second day He created da partridge, da deer, da bear, da fish, an da ducks ya know.

On da third day He said, "Let dere be YOOPERS to roam da UP."

On da fourth day He created da udder world down below and on da fifth day He said, "Let dere be TROLLS to live in da world down below."

On da sixth day He created DA BRIDGE so da TROLLS would have a way to get to Heaven, see.

God saw it was good and on da seventh day He went huntin!!

---

centralization of the diphthongs *i* (*pie, I*) and *ou* (*house, about*), with the tongue starting the sound in the mid center of the mouth, and lack of offglide on diphthongs, also typical of Scandinavian settlement in Minnesota, Wisconsin and northern Iowa. UP speakers often mention that they say *in'* for *ing* in participial forms (*Youse guys goin'?*), and while this usage is common across regions, social groups and style levels, some UP speakers have a heightened awareness of what they regard as an informality.

There are grammatical items typical of UP speech – or that speakers believe to be. One is the construction *The car needs washing* (*need* + present participle) which is, in fact, part of the American North dialect, contrasting with *The car needs washed* (*need* + past participle) used in the American Midland dialect. But UP residents claim it as specifically "Yooper," so much so, that the logo for an Upper Peninsula parts catalog combines the visual image of a woodsy-looking handyman with the question "Something need fixing?" Finnish influence is seen in noun phrase constructions, where two situations in the Finnish have affected the UP grammar: the loss of positional indicators on Finnish nouns (which functioned like prepositions in English) and the lack of definite articles. The result is that UP speakers will say *Let's go camp* where others have *Let's go to the camp*. The in-joke title of the song "Guess Who's Coming to Sauna" (by UP reggae band Conga Se Menee) assumes community recognition while cleverly commenting on the sudden arrival of outsiders in the hallmark recreational activity of white Finnish America.

A plural second person pronoun form, *yous(e)* is commonly used by many speakers, but perhaps the most characteristic grammatical feature of the UP speech is the tag *hey*, as in *You're coming to dinner, hey*, added to the end of a statement to indicate or invite agreement or understanding. This is comparable to the sentence-ending Canadian *eh*.

The UP's multiethnic legacy is most noticeable in the vocabulary, where words for objects, actions, locations and psychological states are drawn from a number of languages. Finnish foods best known in the community are mostly bakery such as the sweet bread *nisu* or the custard pancake, *pannukakku*. People eat *bakery*, an item of baked goods, in the German settlement areas of Milwaukee and Cleveland, but UP speakers claim it as theirs. The *pasty*, a meat-and-root-vegetable-filled pastry, was introduced by Cornish mining families although Finns may claim it as their own.

Mention must be made of the Finnish word *sauna* which is pronounced with three vowels, *sa-u-na*, amongst older speakers of Finnish background, a diphthong and a vowel, *sou-na*, for a generation influenced by speakers of Finnish background, and two vowels, *sa-na*, for the rest of us.

Da Yooper Glossary

This parody of the most salient (often Finnish-based) features of UP speech and culture can be found at www.ring.com/yooper/glossary.htm.

Choppers A deer skin mitten with a wool mitten insert. What Yoopers wear to keep their hands warm.

Chuke What the Trolls call a stocking cap. A knitted hat usually with a tassel and usually hand-knit by your grandmother.

Da Yoopers Not only means the inhabitants of Michigan's UP, but also the name of one of the most popular bands in da UP.

Eh A word that ends practically every sentence in the UP (example: "Say ya to da UP, Eh!").

Eino Half of famous Finnish duo Toivo and Eino. Many, many Yooper jokes feature Toivo and Eino!

Finglish The official language of Da UP. Examples: Dese, Dem Dose, and De Udders (and De Udders ain't on De Cow!).

Flatlander A person from the lower peninsula (see also **Loper** and **Troll**).

Going Shop-ko (or Co-op) Yooper phrase meaning "Going to the store."

Holyowha Yooper expletive meaning, roughly "Holy ————!"

Loper Native of the Lower Peninsula of Michigan (see also **Troll** and **Flatlander**).

Pasty Finnish (or Cornish, depending on who you want to believe!) meat pie made with onions, beef, and potatoes.

Quill Pig The native UP porcupine.

Sisu The quality possessed by Yoopers which enables them to endure and even enjoy Yooperland winters.

Snow Cow Moose (or mother-in-law).

Suomi Kutsu The longest running Finnish-American television show in America. Hosted by Carl Pellonpaa, it airs on WLUC-TV 6, on Sunday mornings. Suomi Kutsu is Finnish for "Finland Calling."

Swampers Rubber boots worn by Yoopers in the spring during the muddy season. (Not a winter boot.)

Terrorist People from Detroit or Ohio who visit the UP every November.

Troll Refers to a native of the Lower Peninsula of Michigan (see also **Loper** and **Flatlander**).

Tweener Someone who is constantly running between home and da camp!

Wha! An exclamation used only by Yoopers. Used in place of "WOW!"

Contemporary UP speech includes sounds, grammatical constructions and vocabulary reflecting a complex history of interaction with the original Ojibwa inhabitants, European immigration, and increasingly, the intrusion of the outside into the formerly insulated area. Members of the Ojibwa of the Baraga reservation host "Reggae on the Rez," where UP-identified performers entertain an ethnically mixed audience. The name of the popular performing band, Conga Se Menee, mixes the conga of Caribbean and South American musical traditions with Finnish *se menee*, a reflexive third person singular, that means "it/that goes," but which, in modern Finnish, occurs only in such colloquial phrases as *kuinka se menee?*, "how's it going?" Conga Se Menee is a linguistic creation exemplifying how language changes as different kinds of speakers come into contact, bringing with them new sets of experiences and new linguistic possibilities.

Although the financial good times of the last two decades have brought more visitors to the UP, some of whom have built vacation homes with views of Lake Superior, the permanent population has not increased dramatically. While seasonal migrants generally do not exert much direct influence on a local dialect, the influx of non-local speakers, whose dialects more closely match the notion of a standard, may have contributed to the unease that some locals have about their own speech (an issue investigated by Kate Remlinger of Grand Valley State), and may perhaps lead to change in some of the more salient or commercialized features associated with UP dialect.

PART IV
THE WEST

Getting Real in the Golden State (California)

Penelope Eckert and Norma Mendoza-Denton

22 Soaking up the rays in southern California. © by Jason Stitt.

When people think of California English, they often recall stereotypes like those made famous by Frank and Moon Unit Zappa in their song "Valley Girl," circa 1982. "Like, totally! Gag me with a spoon!" intoned Moon Unit, instantly cementing a stereotype of California English as being primarily the province of Valley Girls and Surfer Dudes.

But California is not just the land of beaches and blonds. While Hollywood images crowd our consciousness, the real California, with a population of nearly 34 million, is only 46.7% white (most of whom are not blond and don't live anywhere near the beach). For generations, California has been home to a large Latino population that today accounts for 32.4% of the state's total numbers. It has also been home to a large Chinese American and Japanese American population and, with the influx in recent years of immigrants from other parts of Asia, the state now boasts a large and diverse Asian American population (11.2%). Most of the sizable African American population (16.4%) in California speaks a form of African American Vernacular English, with few traces of surfer dude or valley girl.

Each of these groups speaks in a distinctive style providing a rich set of linguistic resources for all inhabitants of the state. Ways of speaking are the outcome of stylistic activities that people engage in collaboratively as they carve out a distinctive place for themselves in the social landscape. In fact, linguistic style is inseparable from clothing style, hairstyle, and lifestyle. No style is made from scratch, but is built on the creative use of elements from other styles, and California's rich diversity makes the state a goldmine of stylistic activity.

In 1941, linguist David DeCamp proclaimed that California English was no different from the English of the East Coast. But, over the decades since the 1940s, a distinctive accent has developed among much of the population of the state. Some of the features of this accent were highlighted in Moon Unit's parody of California speech.

It is important to remember that California is a new state. It takes time and a community to develop common ways of speaking, and English speakers have not been settled in California long enough to develop the kind of dialect depth that is apparent in the East Coast and the Midwest. In a study of three generations of families living in the Sunset neighborhood of San Francisco, linguist Birch Moonwomon discovered that what was a fairly diffuse dialect at the beginning of the twentieth century became quite homogeneous by the end of the 1990s. While the oldest speakers born in the Sunset district pronounced their vowels in a variety of ways, their grandchildren pronounced them in a more uniform way.

So what are these features that constitute the stereotypical California accent? A group of linguists led by Leanne Hinton at the University of California at Berkeley studied the accents of a range of speakers in Northern California. In the speech of white people in California, as in many parts of the West, the vowels of *hock* and *hawk*, *cot* and *caught* are pronounced the same – so *awesome* rhymes with *possum*. Also notable is the movement of the vowels in *boot* and *boat* (called back vowels because they are pronounced in the back of the mouth). These vowels all have a tendency to move forward in the mouth, so that the vowel in *dude* or *spoon* (as in *gag me with a . . .*) sounds a little like the word *you*, or the vowel in *pure* or *cute*. Also, *boat* and *loan* often sound like *bewt* and *lewn* – or *eeeeuuw*. Finally, the vowel in *but* and *cut* is also moving forward so that these words sound more like *bet* and *ket*. These are all part of the commonly imitated California surfer speech. But there are also a few vowel shifts that go by almost unnoticed: the vowel of *black* often sounds more like the vowel in *block*, the vowel of *bet* is moving into the place of *bat*, and the vowel of *bit* is moving into the place of *bet*. Some linguists refer to these coordinated changes as chain shifts – one can think of them as a game of musical chairs played by the vowels in the mouth. It is different configurations of these games of musical chairs, as it were, in progress in different parts of the country that create regional accents. The chain shift occurring in California, although relatively early in its progress, will have a lasting effect on the system, eventually resulting in significant differences from other dialects.

Of course, the prototypical California white speech variety is not just a matter of vowels. A single feature like this does not make a style, marking someone as a Californian. Rather it is the coordination of both linguistic and paralinguistic features in time, organized according to topic and differentially highlighted according to audience that characterizes the speech of any dialect. The extreme versions of the pronunciations that are described above are primarily found among young white Californians. Innovative developments in the stereotypical California linguistic system may be so new as to be restricted to certain speech settings, with the most extreme pronunciations evident only in peer-group youth interactions. It is precisely these interactions that are the crux of stylistic development, and that is why linguists in California are spending considerable energy studying young people. One of the innovative developments in white English of Californians is the use of the discourse marker *I'm like*, or *she's like* to introduce quoted speech, as in *I'm like, "where have you been?"* This quotative is particularly useful because it does not require the quote to be of actual speech (as *she said* would, for instance). A shrug, a sigh, or any of a number of other expressive sounds as well as speech can follow it. Lately in California, *I'm all* or *she's all* has also become a contender for this function. We know that the quotative *be all* is not common in the speech of young New Yorkers, for example, while *be like* is. This allows us to infer that *be all* might be a newer development and that it may also be native to, or at least most advanced in, California.

With its diverse population, California's communities bring together adolescents from a wide variety of backgrounds, and their styles play off of each other. Hostility may cause people to differentiate their styles, while curiosity or admiration may cause people to pick up elements from other styles. So the real story of California dialects is a story of influx and contact, evident demographically in migration patterns and evident linguistically in the flux of styles and their accompanying features.

One important group in California is the Mexican American population or Chicanos. Some Chicanos exhibit a distinctive variety of English, which we will call California Chicano English. (For a discussion of Chicano English see chapter 36, "Talking with mi Gente.") This variety is the result of speakers socializing in networks in which other Mexican Americans participate, innovating and reinforcing a historically distinctive speech variety. Much of California was ceded from Mexico to the United States in 1848, so the indigenous and Mexican populations have had the longest continuous linguistic history in the state. Pervasive Spanish/English bilingualism among Mexican Americans has had a tremendous impact upon Chicano English. Spanish has influenced the development of Spanish-like vowels among native speakers of English. In Northern California, the vowel in the second syllable of *nothing*, for instance, has come to sound more like *ee* among some subgroups of Chicano English speakers, differentiating them from other minority groups where *nothing* sounds more like *not'n*. In this case, Spanish is drawn on as a distinctive stylistic resource. This does not mean, however, that all innovations in Chicano English necessarily derive from Spanish. Sometimes innovations develop independently and in the opposite direction from what one would expect if one were to assume Spanish influence. One of the most salient innovations in Los Angeles is the lowering of the vowel in the first syllable of *elevator* so that it rhymes with the first syllable of *alligator* – not Spanish-sounding at all. Carmen Fought has shown that in LA, young Mexican Americans participate in other changes that are characteristic of whites as well – such as the fronting of *boat* and the backing of *black* mentioned earlier. However, they do so in distinctively patterned ways that mark communities and subcommunities, social networks and personal histories.

The turbulent history of migration and ethnic relations in California is another lens through which we must view past and current developments in California English. If dialects reflect the history and meaningful activity of subpopulations within the body politic, why is it that some groups have ethnic linguistic varieties (such as Chicanos) and others do not? With a historically large population of Japanese Americans and close proximity to the Pacific Rim, why do we find very little contemporary evidence of an ethnic variety of English among Japanese Americans in California? Research by Melissa Iwai and Norma Mendoza-Denton into generational differences among Japanese Americans indicates that the oldest generation of Japanese American native speakers of English, the *nisei*, do exhibit a distinct patterning of vocalic and consonantal phenomena, while the *yonsei*, or fourth generation (now in their twenties and thirties), are indistinguishable from their white counterparts. Detailed interviews with nisei residents revealed that, when they were detained in internment camps in California and Arizona during World War II, torn from their families and subjected to ostracism, they felt it was a distinct disadvantage to sound Japanese American or be distinguished as being Japanese in any way. Furthermore, Franklin Delano Roosevelt's policy of dispersal in resettlement prevented the reconstitution of the original communities, fatally rupturing established social networks and preventing the entrenchment of their nascent variety of English. In this example of the death of a California dialect we can see how stereotypes and discrimination about people and their language (what linguists call "language ideology") can have dramatic effects on a community's linguistic development. For Japanese Americans, assimilating to the speech of the white majority of the time was a linguistic consequence of the catastrophic events in their community.

California English is a reflection of the politics, history, and various intersecting communities of the state. Sixty years after DeCamp's original investigation, we can confidently say that Californians have developed distinctive ways of speaking. As the real California continues to show an even greater degree of linguistic and ethnic contact, we hope that stereotypical images of California English will be changed to include some of the linguistic realities that we have described above.

Desert Dialect (Utah)

David Bowie and Wendy Morkel

23 The chapel at Temple Square, Salt Lake City, Utah. © by Sathis VJ.

Up until the 2002 Winter Olympics, Utah didn't really get much attention from the rest of the world. Sure, some people knew that Mormons live there, and a few even knew that Utah is home to some fabulous skiing, but it wasn't at the forefront of most people's minds. Over the past few years, though, not only has the world learned a bit more about Utah's scenery and culture through the Olympics, but even a bit of Utah English managed to get noticed – the "Oh my heck!" of *Survivor: Marquesas* contestant and Layton, Utah, native Neleh Dennis.

What Is "Utahn" English?

What is now Utah had been visited by English speakers in the early 1800s, but the first permanent English-speaking settlement began in 1847. That's the year that members of The Church of Jesus Christ of Latter-day Saints (the LDS Church), having been forced from their religious colony in Nauvoo, Illinois, began arriving in the Salt Lake Valley to establish a new colony. By the 1850 census, 11,380 people, excluding Native Americans, had settled in the Territory of Utah. The population continued to rise through the nineteenth century at rates similar to the surrounding territories, and the 1900 census showed 276,749 residents of Utah. The vast majority of nineteenth-century "Utahns," the common label for residents, lived in a line of cities less than 100 miles long sandwiched between the Wasatch Mountains on the east and the Great Salt Lake and Utah Lake on the west.

So what makes Utah English? If you were to ask Utahns this question, you would find some widely held stereotypes – one of the strongest being that they change their vowels when they come before *l*. The most widely recognized of these is where short *i* becomes short *e*, so that *milk* gets pronounced as *melk* and *pillow* gets pronounced as *pellow*, but there are others. For example, long *e* can become short *i* and long *a* can become short *e*, so that *steel mill* gets pronounced *still mill* and *house for sale* gets pronounced *house for sell*. (It isn't even that unusual to see that last one in classified ads.) These examples appear in other parts of the US, but Utahns tend to be aware of them as "Utah English." Utahns often associate these features with rural areas of the state, but a dialect survey conducted by linguist Diane Lillie in the 1990s found that they are most strongly present in the urban corridor along the Wasatch Front.

There is another change in vowels before *l* heard in Utah English – although it is not seemingly recognized by Utahns themselves – where long *u* changes before *l*, so that *pool* and *fool* are pronounced like *pull* and *full*. Linguists Marianna Di Paolo and Alice Faber have investigated the ways all of these vowels before *l* are produced in Utah English, and have concluded that it is undergoing changes in its vowel system analogous to those occurring in the United States South.

Possibly the most interesting stereotype Utahns hold about their own variety, however, is that they pronounce the vowels in words like *card* and *cord* the same (a feature linguists have called the *card/cord* merger). In Utah English, instances of *or* can be pronounced as *ar*, so that (to take one widely used example) the name of the town of Spanish Fork is pronounced like Spanish *Fark*. This is a highly stigmatized form in Utah, although it is fairly geographically widespread in the state. This feature has also had an interesting history. With only a few exceptions, linguists tracking linguistic changes have found that if a change starts in a particular area and it starts to gain traction, its momentum builds and builds until it finally "succeeds" – that is, the changed form completely replaces the original one. Utah's *card/cord* merger, however, hasn't followed this pattern quite so cleanly.

In the middle of the twentieth century, linguists Val Helquist and Stanley Cook found that the *card/cord* merger was very strongly present in the Salt Lake City metropolitan area. In fact, it was so strongly present that you could have probably said that pronouncing *born* like *barn* and *corn* like *carn* was completely ordinary there. By the end of the century, however, Diane Lillie found that the merger was only occurring at very low levels, and there were signs that it was actually disappearing. Going back to the nineteenth century (which you can do indirectly by listening to audio recordings of Utahns who lived at that time), you would find that the *card/cord* merger occurred at very low levels mid-century (when English speakers first settled in Utah), and that it increased later. So there was a linguistic change in Utah when the state was first settled: *ar* and *or* were generally pronounced differently, but the trend of pronouncing them the same took hold and gained momentum over the next hundred years. For some reason, though, during the following fifty years the trend suddenly shifted into reverse.

There is another feature of Utah English that has followed the same trajectory: the pronunciation of the long *i* in words like *time* and *bye*. This trait often gets brought up in descriptions of Southern American English – the change of a long *i* to something like *ah*, so that the question *What time is it?* gets pronounced more like *What tahm is it?* This feature isn't really thought of as being part of Utah English, and Utahns themselves seem to be pretty much unaware of it, but it can be found at low levels throughout the state. This feature seems to have followed the same path as the *card/cord* merger and it is clear that this pronunciation of the long *i* was increasing from the beginning of Utah's English-speaking settlement through the rest of the nineteenth century, but it has been in decline from the middle of the twentieth century.

The pronunciation of *time* as *tahm* is generally thought of as a Southern feature, but discussions of Utah – linguistic or otherwise – have emphasized Utah's links to the Northern United States (also, to a lesser extent, with northern England and parts of Canada). The tradition of emphasizing these links goes back at least to the 1930s, when dramatist and historian T. Earle Pardoe drew connections between words (particularly place names) used in Utah and New England. Later studies confirmed the linguistic links between Utah and the United States North for most of Utah. More recent studies by linguists in Utah have found strong links between Utah English and Southern varieties of American English. So why have different analyses come to different conclusions regarding whether Utah English is, at core, a Southern or a Northern variety? And which analysis is correct?

The answer to the first question makes the second one easier to answer. If you look at the studies that have connected Utah English to Northern varieties of English, you'll notice that they all deal with issues of lexical choice: that is, they find that the words Utahns use are generally Northern in origin. (For example, Utahns use the Northern *husk* to describe the leafy covering of an ear of corn rather than the Southern *shuck*, and they use the historically Northern *moo* for the sound a cow makes rather than the Southern *low*.) The studies that draw connections between Utah English and Southern American English, on the other hand, all look at issues of phonetics: they find that the sounds of Utah English are, to a great extent, Southern. A close look at the data reveals that these claims are both based on solid footing, so that depending on whether you focus on words or sounds, you can reach different conclusions about Utah English. And that gives us the answer to the second question: Utah English is, at core, both Southern and Northern. But how did this mixed variety come about?

In order to understand present-day occurrences in the language variety of certain areas, we have to look at the group that first brought the language there. Utah is unique among the Western states in that it was founded as a religious colony by members of the LDS Church; this history is reflected in the historical majority of LDS Church members in the state. As mentioned earlier, these first English speakers in Utah settled there after having been forced out from Nauvoo in west-central Illinois. Before they left Illinois, the group had settled for some years in and around Independence, Missouri, and before that in Kirtland, Ohio (near Cleveland). The church itself had been officially founded in Fayette, New York, and most of its members lived in western New York and northern Pennsylvania.

If this list of places represents the history of the group of individuals who planted English in what was to become Utah, a possible reason for the mix of Northern and Southern features becomes apparent. The early members of this group were largely from areas where Northern varieties of English are spoken: New York, northern Pennsylvania, northern Ohio and a sizable number from Massachusetts. Many of their children, however, were born in areas that have had a notable amount of Southern linguistic influences: western Missouri and southern/western Illinois. As a result, Utah's initial English-speaking settlers were themselves linguistically mixed, with largely Northern-speaking adults and Southern-speaking children. The result of this mixing at the outset, then, seems to be that the adults had greater influence on Utah English words, while the children had more influence on Utah English sounds.

So what is Utah English? It is a mixed system, with some Northern features and some Southern features – and together they make up a system all its own.

Dialects in the Mist
(Portland, OR)

Jeff Conn

24 Fishing on the banks of the Willamette River, Portland, Oregon. © by Norman Eder.

Like many people from Portland, Oregon, I grew up thinking that an accent was something that other people had. It wasn't until I began studying linguistics that I realized that my "General American" accent was, in fact, not. The first shock came in an introductory phonetics class, where I was determined to produce all the sounds of the world's languages. Much to my dismay, I did not have a distinct pronunciation for the word *caught*, but pronounced it the same as *cot*. Not only was my accent deficient of a vowel, but I was also unable to produce or perceive the difference between this phantom vowel and the vowel of *cot*. This merger of the vowels in *cot* and *caught* was the first sign of my accented speech.

Since then, I have been able to identify other characteristics of my accent. However, my narcissistic search for a description of my own dialect has led to the realization that there are practically no descriptions of this dialect. Furthermore, the reliable *Linguistic Atlas* projects, a series of exploratory projects designed to investigate North American dialects, did not collect data from Oregon before the project was prematurely abandoned. Like other dialect areas of the American West, descriptions are lacking, contributing to the myth that there are no distinctive dialects in the United States west of the Mississippi River.

There has been a lot of work on various North American dialects, in traditional dialectology as well as in contemporary sociolinguistics. The traditional dialectology approach uses word choices as a primary way to categorize dialects, while the sociolinguistic approach typically organizes North American dialects according to changes in pronunciation of vowel phonemes. The dialects of the Pacific Northwest, however, have been virtually ignored in both lines of research.

Besides the *Linguistic Atlas* projects, another traditional dialect project that investigates North American varieties of English is the *Dictionary of American Regional English* (*DARE*). The analysis of the data from *DARE* suggests that there is a unique dialect region in the Pacific Northwest, and Portland may be the center of it. Culturally, Portland and Seattle continue to grow as independent urban centers, while at the same time, they are bound together, creating a larger Northwestern identity. Dialect-wise, this may indicate subtle dialect differences emerging from a common variety of English.

In a sociolinguistic approach, Portland is considered part of the West. This large dialect area stretches from the Pacific Coast states east, and includes Washington, Oregon, California, Idaho, Montana, Utah, Nevada, Wyoming, Colorado, Arizona, and New Mexico. One project adopting this framework is the *Atlas of North American English* (*ANAE*), a survey of

North American English pronunciation conducted by William Labov, Sharon Ash and Charles Boberg at the University of Pennsylvania. In order to understand this project's organization of dialects, including Portland as part of the West, it is necessary to briefly outline their approach to describing dialects. While traditional dialect studies examine different words used by different communities for the same thing, e.g. *bucket* vs. *pail*, and characterize dialects by these vocabulary differences, modern dialectology and sociolinguistics organize North American English dialects by pronunciation of vowels using a language change approach. Dialects are grouped by speakers' participation in a handful of identified vowel shifts. These shifts indicate a change in pronunciation of vowels, using a historical organization of these vowels as a starting point. This historically based phonemic inventory represents the pronunciation of Modern English vowels in North America during the seventeenth century. From this set of vowels, historical word classes are established, which group words together that contained the same vowel. For example, the short-*a* word class includes words such as *dad*, *bat*, *pan*. This framework was established in order to preserve original contrasts in vowel production between two sets of historical word classes that may have lost the distinction and merged. An example of a merger for many North Americans is what is known as the *horse/hoarse* merger, where the vowels in both word classes are identically produced for many, but not all, speakers.

Over time, the way a vowel is produced can change, which in turn may cause a chain reaction of modifications in other vowel pronunciations. One of the prominent vowel chain shifts is the Northern Cities Shift, so called because it was first discovered in the inland metropolitan areas of the United States, such as Chicago, Detroit, Cleveland, and Buffalo. Figure 17.2 on p. 109 shows how a change in vowel production of one vowel can trigger changes in other vowels in order to maintain distinctions between them and in order to fill voids in phonetic space – the space located in a speaker's mouth where the tongue changes position in order to produce vocalic sounds.

According to the Northern Cities Shift, a speaker from Detroit says *cat* like *kee-at* and *cot* more like *cat*. Some advanced speakers of the Northern Cities Shift produce vowels in *bet* that sound to many speakers like *but*. Dialects follow different shifts over time and become distinct, which is why American English differs from British and Australian English, for example. Although different dialects can share some of the same vowel changes, it is a combination of different changes that make a dialect unique. For example, Southern British English, Southern American English, and

Australian and New Zealand English all have front pronunciations of the vowels in *boot* and *boat* (sounding like *biwt* and *bewt*), as well as low and more central pronunciation of the vowels in *key* and *bay* (sounding like *Kay* and *buy*), but the pronunciation of the front short vowels (*bit, bet* and *bat*) is what makes each dialect unique. Therefore, a dialect is defined by its participation in a combination of vowel changes.

The Inland North region of the United States is following one series of vowel changes, while the American South is following a different one. In addition to these two large dialect areas, there are smaller dialects that can be identified by a combination of vowel changes that may or may not be organized into a comprehensive vowel shift. While *ANAE* describes in detail much of the English spoken in North America, the dialect area classified as the West is still largely undefined. One characteristic of this area is the *cot*/*caught* merger. This is the identical production of the vowel in the words *cot, Don, collar* and the vowel in *caught, Dawn, caller*. This merger is not limited to the West, and is a characteristic of many other dialects, such as Pittsburgh, parts of New England and the Midwest, as well as Canada. In addition to this merger, Canadian English is participating in the Canadian Shift, which is the lowering and centralization of the front short vowels *bit* and *bet* (sounding something like *bet* and *bat*), similar to the Northern Cities Shift shown above. However, unlike the raising of the vowel in *bat* in the Northern Cities Shift (to *bee-at*), Canadians are lowering and centralizing (retracting) this vowel (sounding something like *bot* or *baht*). This shift is also reported to be operating in Californian English, and is stereotyped in the speech of Valley Girls, as in *gahg me to the mahx*. Another aspect of Californian English is the fronting of the back vowels in the words *boot, book,* and *boat*, similar to Southern American English. This can be heard in the words *totally* and *dude* (sounding like *tewtally* and *diwd*). Since Portland, Oregon is located half-way between California and Canada, it is not surprising that a Portland dialect would contain some of these features.

With regard to a Portland dialect, it seems unlikely for two people to meet and for one of them to say to the other, "You have such a strong Portland accent." This may be due to the very young age of the West in general. The dialect has not had time to unify, emerge and become recognized as either a unique dialect, or part of a larger dialect. Like the California dialect, the Portland dialect is rather diffuse in older speakers, but seems to be becoming a unified and focused among the younger speakers. Furthermore, a small group of researchers at Portland State University have begun to describe characteristics of the dialect, and data collected so far have shown that Portlanders are beginning to participate in a shift similar to its neighbors to the north and south.

The *cot/caught* Merger

One of the characteristics that Portland shares with Canada and with other Western cities is the *cot/caught* merger discussed above. Nearly all Portland speakers, especially those under the age of 60, have a merged low back vowel. This merger, however, is not present in some older speakers (over 80), which indicates that this merger is relatively recent in Portland.

The *cat* Vowel

While Canada and California seem to be a bit more advanced in the backing of this vowel toward the vowel of *cot*, the speech of younger Portlanders suggests that Portland is also changing. Before nasal consonants, however, this backing does not happen and Portlanders produce a higher vowel in this environment. So, *Anne* does not have the same vowel as *add*, but sounds very like *Ian*. Another Portland pronunciation is in words with this vowel before *g*, such as *bag*, *tag*, and *gag*. Instead of a simple *bat* sound, many speakers produce a vowel with a *y*-like glide. In addition, a similar glide quality is produced in *e* before *g*, making *beg* and *bag* sound nearly identical, and sounding like the vowel in *bake*. Although this has not quite reached a merged stage, there is an increase in these productions in younger speakers. Another Canadian/Californian quality is a more open and lower realization of the vowel in *bet* words, sounding almost like *bat*. This lowering is evident in a few Portland speakers, and this may be a change that Portland will participate in in the near future.

Back Vowel Fronting

In addition to the front short vowels, Portlanders share another characteristic with Californians. This is the fronting of the back vowels in words like *boot, book,* and *boat.* This change, although not characteristic of the Inland North, is characteristic of many other North American dialects. The fronting of the vowels in *boot* and *book* is more common, and Portlanders, like their Californian neighbors, are producing very fronted *boot* vowels, where *boot* and *beet* differ mostly in the glide part of the vowel (sounding like *bi-wt* and *bi-yt*). While the *book* vowel is not quite as front, many young speakers can be heard saying *gid* for *good,* and are often misunderstood when saying *look,* which sounds to others like *lick.* The fronting of the *boat* vowel is not as common, and is one measure that the *Atlas of North American English* uses to categorize dialects. Therefore, *boat* fronting is an important quality to identify in order to accurately describe and classify a dialect. Younger Portlanders can be heard saying *boat* vowels with a fairly central nucleus, sounding like the vowel in *but.* The more extreme examples sound almost like *ge-ow* for *go,* but these extremes are not the most common, although Portlanders will probably continue to front this vowel over time. In addition, research also shows that fronting is strongly disfavored in the production of the *boot* and *boat* vowels before *l* (as in *pool* and *pole*). Also, there is some evidence that *pool* and *pole* vowels are moving toward a merger in the future. Another characteristic of the back vowels is the *boat* vowel before nasal sounds, like *home* and *bone,* where some speakers produce words such as *home* with a vowel closer to a *cot/caught* vowel than to a *boat* vowel.

Intonation Patterns

Another aspect of the Portland dialect that may be noticed is the use of a particular intonation pattern. This intonation pattern is known as "up-speak," or high rising terminal contours. Basically, this is the use of a rising question intonation on a declarative sentence, so that a statement like *Then we went to the store* may sound like a question rather than a statement. While this intonation pattern has been found in many different dialects (Australian English, for example), it is usually associated with teenage girls. This is the case in Portland, but research also shows that the use of this intonation contour is not limited to women, and not limited to teenagers. The functions behind the use of this intonation contour are still under investigation, but its use may become more and more a part of the Portland dialect as it spreads outside the teenage female realm.

Vocabulary

Though there are many other aspects of the Portland dialect that remain to be investigated, Portlanders show signs that they are following a similar pattern to one that is found in Canada and California. The distinctiveness of a Portland dialect may remain in its way of life, where *granola* is more than a breakfast food; it's an appropriate adjective to describe clothing, beliefs and attitudes. Or in lexical choices, terms such as *full on* and *rad* indicate coolness. As Portlanders continue to front their back vowels, they will continue to *go to the coast* (*geow to the ceowst*), not the *beach* or the *shore*, as well as to *microbrews*, used clothing stores (where the clothes are not too *spendy* 'expensive'), *bookstores* (*bik-stores*), and *coffee shops* (both words pronounced with the same vowel). Also, the existence of *buckaroos* (Oregonian cowboys) may continue a Southern connection that may play out linguistically. What lies in store for the Portland dialect is the emergence of a dialect from the mist (or the rain, or the drizzle, or the spitting, or the pouring, etc.). Dialect regions of the Pacific Northwest may just be emerging, but it is clear that they now are carving out a unique niche among the varieties of American English.

Acknowledgment

A special thank you to Dr. G. Tucker Childs, Rebecca Wolff and Mike Ward for all their work on the Portland Dialect Study at Portland State University.

Resources

Information about the *Atlas of North American English* can be found at www.ling. upenn.edu/phonoatlas/ and more information about the principles of language change can be found in Labov's two volumes *Principles of Linguistic Change* (1994, 2001). For more information about *DARE* and a dialectology approach to American dialects, see Craig Carver's 1987 book *American Regional Dialects: A Word Geography* or visit the *DARE* web page at http://polyglot.lss.wisc.edu/ dare/dare.html. For more information about the *Linguistic Atlas* projects, visit http://hyde.park.uga.edu/index.html.

Arizona's not so Standard English

Lauren Hall-Lew

25 Monument Valley, Arizona. © by Kenneth C. Zirkel.

To the outside world, Arizona might be "cowboys and Indians," Route 66, or the O.K. Corral. It's known for the SUVs of Scottsdale and the Sun City golf carts, or its picturesque sunsets and its prickly green cacti. If you ask any Arizonan what makes the state unique, they might agree with some of these judgments from the outside world, but they certainly won't claim that it's the way that they speak. In fact, most white Arizonans will vehemently deny that they have an accent, calling their English standard, unaccented, general, or even bland, blah, or boring. Even linguists of the past have passively agreed with these folk perceptions, and there is a near void of dialect data from Arizona or even most of the Southwestern US. Like other states in the West, the settlement populations have just been too young and too new to study any one established regional speech variety. Consequently, until the past couple of years, no one had looked at the speech of Arizona English. But most Arizonans will still insist that a local Arizonan accent doesn't exist.

So then why study Arizona English, anyway? Even proud Arizonans will be the first to proclaim how boring their speech is. Well, I am one proud Arizonan who disagrees. Everyone in the world has an accent when compared to their neighbor, and Arizona is sure to be linguistically interesting because it has some very interesting neighbors. The Southwestern states are flanked on either side by California and Texas, and this location is important both for how Arizonans identify themselves and for understanding the web of European American migration patterns into the Southwest. Arizona has been hanging out at the pawn shop lately, trading in some well-worn boots and stirrups in exchange for a new cellular phone – at least, as far as language is concerned.

A Brief Arizona History

Well before white migration, the linguistic landscape of Arizona was complex. The borders of current-day Arizona enclose the homes of the Hopi people, the Navajo people, the Hualapai people, the Gila River people, the White Mountain-, Yavapai-, and Tonto Apache peoples, the Yavapai people, the Pascua Yaqui people, the Ak-Chin people, the Tohono O'odham people, and at least 11 more separate native communities, all totaling over 256,000 people. Five percent of the state's population is Native American, the third highest percentage in the country after California and Oklahoma. Arizona was home to countless other established and transient native peoples who may or may not appear in the mainstream recorded history. Although good linguistics work has been done on many of these native languages, linguists haven't systematically studied the accents of English spoken by any of these particular indigenous nations in Arizona.

Spanish was the first European language to reach what is now Arizona, and the influence of Mexican Spanish continues to thrive with healthy zeal and to assert a tremendous influence on the diversity of English spoken throughout the Southwest (see chapter 36, "Talking with mi Gente"). The influence of Mexican Spanish of course bears on both the words and the speech sounds used by Arizona's monolingual Chicano English speakers, but it also shows up in English of the general mainstream population. The words *corral*, *ranch*, *canyon*, and *adobe* are just a few of the well-established Spanish derivatives in the vocabulary of today's white Arizonans. One of the defining characteristics of the Southwest is the place names based on Spanish, including Arizona towns like *Casa Grande*, streets like *Tanqueverde*, features of the landscape such as the *Rio de Flag River*, and of course the little mountain with the redundant title, *Table Mesa*.

The official state of Arizona began in the late 1800s with railroad builders, lumberjacks, farmers, cattle ranchers, and copper miners who migrated in from the Southern and Midwestern states. These laborers settled the land and some stuck around for good, with some types of these lifestyles still active today. Arizona's big urban boom began in the mid-1900s when industrial manufacturing became more profitable than mining and farming, continuing to the present day with the growth of high-tech industry. Many of these later migrants came and still come to Arizona to escape the congestion of urban California. Arizona residents often blame these Californians for the state's all-too rapid urban expansion, although current migrants also come from places like Colorado, Illinois, Texas, and Oregon. Today the state's total population is about 5.5 million people, of whom about 80 percent are European American. Arizona is a Sun Belt state, boasting 1000 percent population increase since the 1940s. These migration patterns have changed the face of the population and, consequently, the way that English is spoken.

Arizona's geographical and social place ultimately affects how people speak and how people identify themselves. For example, when the Californian business person meets the Oklahoman rancher, there is a meeting of two contrastive English dialects – urban and rural, West and South. The amazing fact is that their grandchildren, who have all become native Arizonans, will retain measurable traces of these dialect differences. What's more, if the grandchild of the rancher likes the urban California lifestyle, her speech may be perceived as Californian, but if the grandchild of the businessman grows to admire and emulate the historic Arizona cowboy, he may articulate a form of the rural dialect. This is what makes the Southwest a complex and fascinating area of dialect study.

Contemporary Urban Dialect

Arizona is best understood by looking at dialect research from the Western states (including California, Oregon, and Utah) and from research on rural Texas or Oklahoma. In American English, different dialects are often based on how the speakers say their vowels; studies of how consonants vary don't seem to correlate as well or as frequently with US regional differences of English, although they're quite useful for looking at an individual's style of speech, class, ethnicity, and dialect variation in languages other than English. Urban-oriented speakers of Arizona and the other Western states are differentiated from the rest of the US by a particular way of pronouncing certain vowels. One of the most salient vowel shifts relates to the vowels of words like *so* and *dude*. Though usually pronounced in the back of the mouth, these are often pronounced more to the front of the mouth, so that *so* is pronounced more like *seh-ow* and *dude* more like *diwd*. Vowels of the second type, *iw* vowels, move more often and more to the front than the *ow* vowels. Another well-established vowel difference is that the words *caught* and *cot* are pronounced the same, while they're differentiated in the South, the Northeast, and most of the East Coast. The words *filled* and *field* might also sound the same when some Arizonans speak, but this is less frequent and it happens only before an *l*-type sound.

Finally, like other speakers in the West, most urban Arizonans say the vowel in *Anne* with their tongue high in the mouth so that it sounds almost like *Ian*. But unlike the vowels of Michigan, for example, this is only true when the vowel is before the nasal sounds *n*, *m*, and *ng*. An Arizonan might take you to visit the *Greeand Keeanyon*, but you would also stop for lunch in the town of *Flagstaff*. A young person might even tell you that you're lunching in *Flahgstahff*, if they've tuned into a more recent California vowel change where young people pronounce the *cat* vowel with their tongue toward the back of the mouth. Together, these vowel changes comprise just one part of a speech style that typifies Arizona English.

The Rancher Accent

Arizona ranchers are distinguished by a different set of vowels, although there is some overlap with the Californians. For example, the vowel change that makes *dude* pronounced as *diwd* is very common for many accents of English, and is characteristic of speakers from Oklahoma, Texas, and the South, as well as of speakers from California. It's no surprise that it's found for both the urban vowels and the rural vowels in Arizona. What's different, though, is that the ranchers distinguish a *field* from a *filled* thing and a *cot* from a *caught* thing, and they don't say *Greeand Keeanyon*. Another prominent rural feature is that the vowel in *my* doesn't glide from *ah* to *ee*, as it does in urban speech. For rural speakers *my* and *fine* sound more like *mah* and *fahn*, although not quite as strongly as they would in the South or in Appalachia. And sometimes, vowels in unstressed syllables may be lost completely, so that *every day* might be pronounced just as *ever' day*.

Unlike the urbanites, the Arizona ranchers also have noticeable variation in their English grammar. The *-s* of verbs with third person subjects (e.g. *she goes*) may attach to verbs with other subject forms as well, as in *you's* for *you've*, including somewhat novel conjugations such as *we's gots*. Finally, rural Arizonans use a common yet socially stigmatized speech pattern found in many other varieties of English: the double negative, as in *We didn't have none*. Double negatives have been used in English for centuries and across many dialects. These are simply another linguistic resource that rural Arizonans use to distinguish themselves from urban Arizonans.

Along the lines of double negatives is the use of *ain't*, that very handy contraction that has no good equivalent in the urban dialect. In fact, even if you can't tell a rancher by his vowels or his syntax, you can probably tell him by the words he uses. Besides living on a *ranch*, something that doesn't even exist in many parts of the country, a rancher's children probably raise animals for the county fair and compete in *barrel racing*, if they're girls, or *bull riding*, if they're boys. Participation in such pastimes is one of the only ways to tell which kids in the urban schools come from a rancher background. Finally, if your conversation partner is quite elderly, they may even talk about taking the *covered wagon* to visit Phoenix last week – that's certainly an object you won't hear about all that often in urban places!

Just how the rural Arizona dialect compares to other rural dialects in the United States is still a big question for linguists. In any case, it's evident that many speakers who were born and raised in Arizona still speak with the dialect that their parents or grandparents brought with them from Oklahoma and Texas. This formed the basis for white Arizona English, and can still be found in some urban speakers who identify with or emulate the ranching lifestyle.

The Big Picture

Present-day Arizona English is a mixture of the rural South and the urban West. Given its location, this dialect complexity is really no surprise, and in fact is found in other parts of the Southwest, such as in Utah (see chapter 23, "Desert Dialect"), where the choice of words tends to be Northern but some pronunciation features are Southern. A similar situation is true for Arizona, but with the pronunciation traits matching up to the West for the urban speakers, and the grammar and some words derived from the Oklahoma/Texas area for rural speakers.

Describing Arizona English doesn't stop with understanding this dialect mixture or even with seeing the impact of an individual's identity on the way they speak. The exciting fact of Arizona English is that we can see it changing *right now*. The future of Arizona English is fairly predictable; as ranches become less profitable, the younger generations move into the cities, and the use of the rural accent diminishes. This trend is not a new one, as changes in international trade policies have been affecting domestic ranching for several decades now. Consequently, the large majority of Arizonans are sounding more and more like our Californian neighbors and less and less like our Oklahoman predecessors. Arizonans who are in their twenties today are already using more of the shifted California vowels than are Arizonans in their fifties. As migration into Arizona from California increases, it's likely that this change will follow suit. It's not just a matter of vowels, but a matter of the person's identity: as an Arizonan, as a young person, or as a member of urban society. The only other foreseeable influence on Arizona English, at this point, is the linguistic pressure from the growing Mexican and Chicano populations, as well as the growing numbers of immigrants from all corners of the globe. Such changing demographics are sure to impact the future dialects of Arizona and the rest of the United States.

Further Reading

Arizona Commission of Indian Affairs. www.indianaffairs.state.az.us/tribes/index. html.

Craig, Beth (1991) American Indian English. *English World-Wide* 12: 25–61.

Labov, William, Sharon Ash, and Charles Boberg (2000) *The Atlas of North American English*. Berlin: Mouton de Gruyter. www.ling.upenn.edu/phono_atlas/.

See also chapters 22, 23 and 26 of this volume.

PART V
ISLANDS

26

Topics from the Tropics (Hawai'i)

Miriam Meyerhoff

The young woman behind the photo counter at Long's drugstore in Mo'ili'ili wasn't taking especially long with my order, and it was actually quite nice to escape the mid-August sun pounding down outdoors. But for some reason, my three-month-old, Sam, wasn't happy. As his face scrunched up to let rip with a full-blown howl, the woman serving us leaned over to him: "Sorry, baby, sorry," she crooned, drawing out each "sooory" in a singsong. Two things about this epitomized Hawai'i. One was her orientation to and inclusion of even very little babies in day-to-day conversation; the other was the way she used *sorry* as an expression of empathy, instead of as an apology. It was one of those moments when you are reminded that you really are in the Pacific when you are in Hawai'i. Many things are different from the mainland, not least of which is the way people talk.

Like most things that are ubiquitous in Hawai'i today, English is a recent introduction. And also like most of the things that have been introduced – plants, birds, mammals – it has had a devastating effect on what was originally there. Despite the strength of Hawaiian right up until the end of the nineteenth century, and despite the subsequent introduction of other languages, English has taken over.

English didn't become particularly widespread until after the overthrow of the Hawaiian monarchy and the annexation of Hawai'i by the United States in the last decade of the nineteenth century. In fact, the poet and naturalist, Adelbert von Chamisso, writing about his travels in 1815–18, reported that, "Many Hawaiians understand a little English, but none of them have good command of the language, not even those who have worked on American ships (as many have)." As contact with English speakers increased, so did its use in the Islands. In the 1840s and 1850s, there are some initial reports of mixed or "broken" English being spoken in various places, but at that time Hawaiian (a Polynesian language closely related to Maori, which was simultaneously being squeezed out of most public domains by English in New Zealand) was still remarkably vital. The Islands were then an independent and internationally recognized country; Hawaiians were highly literate and had a rich oral tradition, so throughout the nineteenth century the pressure on newcomers to the Islands was to learn Hawaiian.

But as the plantation and grazing economies became more important, the demographics of the Islands began to change. More English speakers took up permanent residence, and migrant workers with other native languages began to arrive. The first to arrive came from China; subsequent migrations saw large numbers of Portuguese, Japanese, and Filipinos come for work, and many Haoles, or whites, also prospered from the economic development of Hawai'i. In 1893 a group led by a number of US businessmen staged a coup and took the head of the Hawai'i nation, Queen Lili'uokalani, hostage and in 1898 they formally annexed Hawai'i to the United States.

Indigenous Hawaiians, who today are fighting to hold onto their tenuous language and economic rights, are now far outnumbered by migrant ethnic groups. There have been some modest successes in revitalizing and providing institutional support for the language in recent years, and the Pünana Leo or "language nests" are helping speakers of Hawaiian pass on their language to a new generation. There are some Hawaiian-medium schools which enable children to keep up their Hawaiian throughout their education, but fluent speakers of Hawaiian remain a small minority of the state's population, even within the ethnic Hawaiian community.

The English spoken by Locals today in Hawai'i is distinctive on many levels. Naturally, borrowings from Hawaiian make it stand apart. At least a couple of hundred borrowings are known and used in colloquial speech. They include words like *hula* and *ukulele* which would be familiar anywhere in the United States, and words like *'a'a* and *pahoehoe* (types of lava) which are part of the international vocabulary of geology. Some Hawaiian words used on a day-to-day basis only in Hawai'i are *keiki* 'child', *kuleana* 'responsibility', *akamai* 'clever', *äina* 'land', *kökua* 'care for, support', *tütü* 'grandmother', and *hulihuli* 'barbecue'. A good many relate to food – *liliko'i 'poi* 'pounded taro', *limu* 'seaweed', and *poke*, a Local style of ceviche – this reflects the importance food has virtually anywhere as a way of defining and identifying with local culture. Even to say something tastes good, Locals use a borrowing from Hawaiian, *'ono* meaning "delicious, tasty."

However, even though these words all have a Hawaiian source, it's debatable whether you would want to say that these are borrowings from Hawaiian into English. That's because most of them have made it into Hawai'i English via Pidgin. This can be seen in some subtle changes of meaning. In Hawaiian, your *tütü* is either your grandmother or your grandfather, but in Pidgin and in general use in Hawai'i English its meaning has specialized to mainly refer to a grandmother.

Pidgin is the language spoken by most of the people who were born and grew up in Hawai'i. These are the people who think of themselves and are called Locals (which is why I have been using the capital L; people are only called "Hawaiian" on the Islands if they actually have Hawaiian ancestry). Pidgin is a creole that is based on English, but only in the sense that most of the vocabulary was taken from English. It's a language that took its shape in the mouths and interactions between members of the ethnic and linguistic mix that came together to work the nineteenth-century forms of agri-business. This means that even though Pidgin superficially looks like Standard English, the grammar of the language is very different. Unfortunately for many Pidgin speakers, this superficial similarity fosters misconceptions that can disadvantage them at all stages of the education system.

There are a number of levels on which Pidgin differs from English. For one thing, there is a fairly distinctive Local accent. Locals use comparatively full vowels where mainlanders would have a reduced vowel, a schwa, or no vowel at all. For example, the word *button* has a full *o* sound in the final syllable, and you will hear pronunciations like this even in relatively formal contexts, like when a computer programmer is explaining features of new web-based software to a journalist. This lack of reduced vowels in unstressed syllables often leads to differences in how words are stressed and changes the rhythm of Hawai'i English. For many Locals, the main stress in *ceremony* falls on the third syllable – *seraMOni*, and there are different rules for stressing compounds like *volley BALL*.

In addition, the *o* sound whether stressed or unstressed is more likely to be an unglided vowel than it is on the mainland. In other words, instead of *boat* sounding like *bowt*, or *so* sounding like *sow*, in Hawai'i English, you get a long, steady *o*, *soo*. This is also true for the long *e* diphthong in words like *wait* and *fate*. There is marked lip-rounding with the vowel in words like *shoot* or *rude* and Pidgin is one of the *r*-less varieties of US English. And syllable-final *l* is almost invariably vocalized: you see signs advertising *Loco* (i.e. local) food and the name Russell is often spelled *Russo* in Pidgin writing.

Mike Forman, who teaches linguistics at the University of Hawai'i at Mānoa, has suggested that another important accent feature of Pidgin is that Locals put their tongue right on the edge of their teeth when they say *n* and *l*. You can get some idea of how this sounds if you try almost biting your tongue when you say *Nanakuli* (the name of a town on O'ahu). People often say Pidgin sounds "softer" than other accents of American English and I suspect that this perception has something to do with these dental consonants, the *l*-vocalization and the *r*-lessness of Pidgin.

But pronunciation differences alone don't make a different language. Many of these pronunciation features typify Pidgin but they also occur when Locals are speaking Standard English. What makes Pidgin clearly a different language from Standard English are more fundamental properties of its grammar. Clear examples of this can be seen in the way Pidgin expresses time and manner relations with verbs.[1] A particularly striking difference is how the two languages use the base form of the verb. In Pidgin, the base form may be used to refer to present events, generic events, or even past events. Here is a good example of the last option from a story told to the linguist Viveka Velupillai by a man from Maui:

> *Dis spri wen jamp intu dis wan gai, fal awntu da graun eriting*
> This spirit had jumped into this one guy, he [=the guy] fell onto the ground and everything

Here, Pidgin uses the base verb *fal* (fall) where Standard English would use the form marked for past tense.

The example also shows a unique feature of the way Pidgin marks the manner of an event. Velupillai found that *wen* forms (like *wen jamp*) are used when the event being discussed has some limit that's crucial to what's being discussed. In other words, the meaning of *wen* V forms is different from any single verb inflection or helping verb in Standard English.

Another feature of the verb phrase that is considered highly stereotypical of Pidgin (both by Locals and outsiders) is the use of *stei* 'stay' as a helping or auxiliary verb. *Stei*, too, means something very different from any single verbal form in Standard English. Moreover, its meaning varies depending on what form of the verb it combines with. When *stei* occurs with the base form, as in *hi stei wak araun* 'he walks around', the meaning overlaps with the habitual and the continuous in Standard English. But when it combines with the *-in(g)* form of the verb, as in *da sista stio stei stanin bai da fon bu* 'the girl is still standing at the phone booth' or *hi stei reikin da livs* 'he was raking the leaves' there is a superficial similarity to the Standard English progressive. But the resemblance ends there. The way *stei* V-*in* forms are used in discourse shows that Pidgin *stei* V-*in* requires a greater focus on some idea of "now" than the progressive does in Standard English.

Pidgin also allows more subjects to be left out than Standard English does. This is particularly noticeable with existential sentences where Standard English requires a dummy subject, *there* (in this respect Standard English differs from many of the world's languages), e.g., *There are still some places on the left*, *There's more than one way to skin a cat*. However Pidgin doesn't need a dummy subject here and instead you get sentences like, *At lis, —— get kompetishin* 'At least, [there] was a competition'. As the example with *fal awntu da graun* showed, Pidgin also allows speakers to leave out the subject when it refers to a person, and the constraints on when you can and can't do this are rather different from the constraints in Standard English (where it is really only acceptable with the same subject across coordination, e.g. *Yves Klein liked blue a lot and —— painted mesmerizing work in it*).

Finally, negation is expressed according to different rules. As with the dummy *there* subjects, Pidgin negation manages without the material required in Standard English, specifically, the auxiliary verb *do*. Pidgin can simply negate a verb by prefixing it with *no* (or *neva* in the past). So standard English *We didn't like to play with him anymore*, is *wi neva laik plei wit him no moa* in Pidgin.

This rough sketch gives you some sense of what Pidgin is like as a language, but as I draw it to a close I find myself wrestling with some dissatisfaction. I feel like I have ended up further away from the reality of Pidgin than I was with the anecdote at the start. A real problem with brief outlines like this is that they give a pretty disembodied picture of a living and changing language. The ideal palliative to this, of course, would be for every reader to go to Hawai'i and find out first-hand what English is like there. But since for most people that's not an option, perhaps the best way to really savor how Pidgin sounds and differs from Standard US English is by reading some of the Local writers – search out names like Lois-Ann Yamanaka, R. Zamora Linmark, Darrell Lum, and Lee Tonouchi.

Some of them make concessions to their wider audience and tailor the syntax of their Pidgin accordingly, but even so, this literature will open your eyes to a Hawai'i that transcends the mass-marketed fantasies of swaying palms on beaches, swaying hips on hula dancers, and endless sunny days reflected in sunny smiles. To be sure, there are aspects of that in Hawai'i, but it is also a place where real people live real lives, quietly and defiantly defining themselves as different from the rest of the United States. It is also a place where an entrenched history of multilingualism and the oppression of the indigenous language Hawaiian mean that language openly functions as both a resource and a commodity.

But the best reason for reading the Local literature is that not only does it give you an idea of what Pidgin actually is, it also gives you an idea of the more evanescent aspects of language use that are impossible to cover in an article like this – What do people talk story about in Hawai'i? What attitudes to others come out in everyday discourse? How do you tease your little brother? How do you fight with your parents or school mates? How do you make love to the person you want to grow old with?

More than palm trees in the wind, more than waves on the shore, more than ukuleles and falsetto singing, those are the sounds of Hawai'i for me. Go read, listen, and see what you hear.

Note

1 What follows here is necessarily a simplification of a very rich grammatical system and it draws heavily on work by the linguist Viveka Velupillai and Alison Tonaki, a native speaker of Pidgin who worked with me in Honolulu. My thanks to both of them.

Further Reading

Tonouchi, Lee (2001) *Da Word.* Honolulu: Bamboo Ridge. (Fiction).
Tonouchi, Lee, Normie Salvador, and Carrie Takahata (eds.) *Hybolics.* (Literary magazine.)
Velupillai, Viveka (2002) *The Tense-Mood-Aspect System of Hawaii Creole English.* Munich: Max-Planck-Gesellschaft zur Förderung der Wissenschaften. (This book is written for a linguistics audience.)
Yamanaka, Lois-Ann (1997) *Blu's Hanging.* New York: Avon. (Fiction.)
Yamanaka, Lois-Ann (1999) *Heads by Harry.* New York: Avon. (Fiction.)
Zamora Linmark, R. (1996) *Rolling the R's.* New York: Kaya. (Fiction.)
There is also a vibrant Local recording industry. You can get a lot of comedy in Pidgin and a lot of music in Hawaiian (some singing is also in Pidgin). Music by Israel Kamakawiwo'ole, Hapa, and Sudden Rush are reasonably widely available. Classic comedy is by Rap Reiplinger. Somewhere between the two is Bu La'ia. On the Internet: www.aloha-hawaii.com/pidgin/pidgin.html; www.extreme-hawaii.com/pidgin/vocab; www.une.edu.au/langnet/hce.htm.

Speaking Strictly Roots (West Indies)

Renee Blake

27 Women preparing crayfish, Jamaica. © by Tony Arruza/Corbis.

Global appreciation of music originating from the West Indies has contributed greatly to the world's familiarity with Caribbean English. This
recognition began in the 1950s, with Harry Belafonte and his calypso hit
"The Banana Boat Song" and extended in the 1970s with the explosion of
Bob Marley's reggae tunes onto the pop scene. In 2001, the best-selling
CD in the US was the mellifluous "Hotshot," by the Jamaican American
artist Shaggy, who refers to his artistic style, in which he combines his

Jamaican-accented voice with a fusion of reggae, jazz, rhythm and blues, and pop music, as "dog-a-muffin."

The spoken word of the West Indians is a clear example of how language is used to mark or identify a people. In the US, their rhythmic and lilting singsong accents connote an easy-going and luminous charm. This was no more evident than at the opening of the 2002 Winter Olympics in Utah when newscaster Katie Couric introduced the Jamaican delegation with an exuberant "Yes mon!" reminding viewers of the motion picture hit *Cool Runnings*, which endeared the Jamaican bobsled team to American audiences.

The West Indies are comprised of highly oral societies. Many oral traditions are found on the islands with ritualized speech styles and linguistic performances, be it at the church pulpit, in literary dialogue, everyday conversation and songs or at entertainment venues. A combination of creativity, eloquent diction, originality, quick wit, and elaborate grammar

Angel (by Shaggy with Rayvon)

Now, dis one dedicated to all a you dem who out dere,
An' wan' fi say nice tings to dem girls.
Treat (h)er like diamonds an' pearls.
Dedicated to all de girls aroun' de worl'.
An' dis is Rayvon an' Shaggy wid de combination whi(ch) cyan' miss
Flip dis one 'pon yah musical disk, well

Chorus
Girl, you're my angel, you're my darling angel.
Closer than my peeps you are to me, baby [Tell (h)er]
Shorty, you're my angel, you're my darling angel
Girl you're my frien' when I'm in need, lady

Life is one big party when you're still young
But who's gonna have yah back when it's all done
It's all good when yah little, you have p(y)ure fun
Can't be a fool, son, what about de long run
Lookin' back Shorty always a mention
Say me not givin' (h)er much attention
She was dere through my incarceration
I wanna show de nation my appreciation

rewards speakers with "But yah talkin' gud," "Oh gawd nah mon, soundin' sweet," "Tell it!" or "Teach!" and "Sweet talking" (i.e., using flattering words to persuade or pacify). Extemporaneous oratory is steeped in folkloric tradition as it exploits the local vernacular language. This is evident in the Shaggy hit, "Angel."

Caribbean English: A Little History

While the predominant present-day stereotype of West Indians in the US may be one of laid-back, fun-loving people, this view hides the multiple dimensions that exist within the people and their language. The disquieting history of the Caribbean is reflected in the languages spoken by the inheritors of a colonial past. Five hundred years ago Columbus arrived at Caribbean shores, most of them populated with societies of Carib and Arawak Indians. His encounters marked the beginning of European exploitation of indigenous, enslaved, and indentured peoples. Following the Spanish conquistadors were the British, Dutch, French, and Portuguese in the sixteenth century.

Under colonization, the social and political structures of the Caribbean evolved around the plantation system, in which a sharp stratification existed between the owners or administrators of the land and those exploited to work it. The plantation was the breeding-ground for the process of creolization, i.e., the mixing of a variety of people, their cultures and languages. Creoles arise among individuals and groups who do not share common tongues and yet need to communicate. Out of the framework of colonization in the West Indies an amalgamation arose of the language spoken by the colonialists with those who were colonized. While a creole may sound like the European language from which it derived, it also contains many linguistic elements from the original languages of the subordinate populations. As a creole becomes the mother tongue or native linguistic system for succeeding generations, it stabilizes into a full-fledged language.

In the Anglophone Caribbean, West Indian Creole has the status of the local vernacular, or the language of the masses, co-existing with a form of English similar to British English, its European lexifier language. As national identities emerge in a post-colonial West Indies, the vernacular variety, also referred to as "dialect," "patois," "slang," or "broken English", gains in linguistic, cultural and political currency although Standard English carries institutional prestige.

Features of Creole English

As a group, the creoles spoken in the West Indies are referred to as Caribbean English Creole (CEC). While there is variation found among the CECs, they share many linguistic features. The most salient difference between the Standard English spoken in the Caribbean and standard British English or American English is the sound system. The distinctive Caribbean accent gives the impression of having a singsong sort of rhythm or intonation, which results from each syllable receiving approximately the same amount of time and stress. These languages, produced with syllable timing, stand in contrast to American and British varieties of English, which are produced with stress timing. In stress timing, stress is prominent in different places and each syllable does not receive an equal amount of time.

Three vowels in the CEC sound system help outsiders to distinguish a Caribbean accent – the sound in the standard American English pronunciation of the vowel in *box*, the sound in the pronunciation of *a* in *scale*, and the sound in *phone*. CEC, like some varieties of British English, does not have the sound found in the American English pronunciation of *man*; in CEC, *man* is pronounced so that it has the same vowel as *Tom*. Furthermore, in many of the CECs, the *a* and *o* sounds are pronounced in their "pure" state rather than in combination with another vowel in the same syllable (making a diphthong). In CEC, for instance, the *a* in *cake* is pronounced as a pure vowel, not as the diphthong found in non-West Indian Englishes. In some CECs, if a diphthong is present, it is in reverse to the non-West Indian varieties. Thus, in some varieties of Jamaican CEC, the *a* in *cake* would be pronounced as *eeuh* rather than *a*, and the *o* of *vote* as *uo* rather than *o*.

The most prominent consonant trait is the production of the voiced *th* sound in *that* and the voiceless *th* sound in *thing* as *d* and *t*, respectively. In "Angel," we see many examples of the voiced *th* as *d* in words like *dis* (this), *dere* (there), *dem* (them), and *de* (the). Another consonantal feature is the pronunciation of *ing* as *in* in words like *lookin'* and *givin'*. Consonant clusters at the ends of words are also reduced to one consonant; in "Angel" this is apparent in *an'* (and), *aroun'* (around), and *worl'* (world). Another noticeable feature of the CEC varieties is the *y* sound after *k* and *g*, e.g., *kyan* (can), *gyarden* (garden). A feature specific to Jamaican Creole is the loss of *h*, such that you can get *it* for *hit*.

Prominent grammatical features include generalization of the pronominal system where the same form of the pronoun can be used for the subject, object and possessive, as seen in the "Angel" lyric "Me not givin' (h)er attention." In this same sentence, there is another key feature of CEC, the uninflected verb, or absence of the verb *be*. Unmarking is also extended to past tense (*we eat* 'we ate'), as well as to third person singular verbs (*she like it so* 'she likes it so'). In CEC, *dem* is used instead of a plural marking on a noun, even in cases where it may not be marked in English ("Dis one dedicated to all a you dem who out dere"). Finally, CEC has an elaborate verbal system and uses particles to mark the verb ("Lookin' back Shorty always a mention").

While much of the CEC vocabulary is attributed to English, other influences are present depending upon the colonial history of a given island. On all of the islands, there are imprints on the lexicon from West African languages like Yoruba and Twi, including *eye-water* 'tears', *susu* 'cooperative savings plan', and *obeah* 'sorcery'. Other influences can be found on various islands from French, Spanish, and Indic, as well as often overlooked Amerindian survivals (such as *canoe*, *papaya*, and *mauby*). Across the CECs a variety of words are used for the same referent (e.g., a *susu* in Dominica, Grenada, St. Lucia, St. Vincent, and Trinidad is a *box* in Guyana, a *pardner* in Jamaica, and a *syndicate* in Belize).

West Indians in the US

Since the 1900s, New York City has been the magnet for the majority of West Indians coming to the US in search of a "better life." Today, West Indians as a whole are the largest immigrant group in the city, comprising approximately eight percent of the population. With the largest groups coming from Jamaica, Guyana, Barbados and Trinidad, there is a growing pan-Caribbean influence on US politics and economic structure, as well as its cultural and linguistic constitution. West Indian communities are largely transnational in nature, with continuous movement between the US and native Caribbean homelands. As a result, there has been a strong American impact on the "home" societies.

The West Indies and the United States share colonial trajectories. Therefore, it should be no surprise that overlap exists between Caribbean English Creole and African American Vernacular English. Nonetheless, just as there are sociocultural distinctions between blacks in the Caribbean and blacks in the US, there are also linguistic differences. The superficial similarities between CEC and English may lead educators to place West

Indian immigrant schoolchildren in mainstream classes. While children who are highly educated and adept at standard English (albeit with Creole pronunciation) excel in mainstream classes, most are CEC speakers needing some degree of educational assistance. This is an area of growing concern for educators in the US – sensitivity is needed as these students believe that they are speakers of something close to standard English.

If past and present are any indication, the trend toward mass West Indian migration to this country will continue for years to come. It is clear that contact between West Indians and others in the US fosters multi-directional influences. We may also safely assume that such exchanges will continue to add colorful details to the nation's language mosaic.

Further Reading

Allsopp, Richard (1996) *Dictionary of Caribbean English Usage.* Oxford: Oxford University Press.

Foner, Nancy (ed.) (2001) *Islands in the City: West Indian Migration to New York.* Berkeley: University of California Press.

Henke, Holger (2001) *The West Indian Americans.* Westport, CT: Greenwood Press.

Kasinitz, Philip (1992) *Caribbean New York: Black Immigrants and the Politics of Race.* Ithaca: Cornell University Press.

Roberts, Peter A. (1988) *West Indians and Their Language.* Cambridge, UK: Cambridge University Press.

Winer, Lise, and Lona Jack (1997) East Caribbean Creole in New York. In O. Garcia and J. A. Fishman (eds.), *The Multilingual Apple: Languages in New York City.* Berlin: Mouton de Gruyter, 301–40.

Gullah Gullah Islands (Sea Island, SC, GA)

Tracey L. Weldon

28 South Carolina river basin. © by Index Stock/Alamy.

Anyone who has traveled to the coast and Sea Islands of South Carolina and Georgia is likely to have heard the distinctive sounds of Gullah being spoken by African Americans native to the area. While it is difficult to capture the true rhythm and sounds of Gullah on paper, the following excerpt from the tale "Ber Rabbit and the Lord," as recounted by a resident of Wadmalaw Island, South Carolina, is illustrative of its character.

Ber Rabbit jump on Ber Gator head. When Ber Gator get cross to other shore, Ber Rabbit knock the Ber Gator in e head and knock all he teeth out, and carry em to the Lord.

As this passage from Patricia Jones-Jackson's *When Roots Die* illustrates, the vocabulary of Gullah is primarily English (described in linguistic circles as "English-based") but its distinctive nature derives from the African languages that contributed to its development.

Creoles are language varieties that emerge among speakers who do not share a common language. The term is also applied to these varieties as they develop into the native tongues of later generations of speakers. As the only English-based creole spoken in the United States today, Gullah (also known as Geechee or Sea Island Creole) traces its roots back to the days of slavery. Gullah developed during the Atlantic slave trade era among Africans who spoke a variety of mutually unintelligible languages. They had to communicate not only with each other but also with their owners who spoke English. Thus Gullah, like the English-based creoles of the Caribbean, grew out of contact between English and a number of West African languages spoken during this era. The structure of Gullah reflects these multiple influences.

Gullah Features

In the Ber Rabbit example cited above, one can observe some of the distinctive grammatical features that are characteristic of the variety. One such feature is the variable marking of tense on verbs. Though taken out of context, this excerpt describes an event that occurred in the past. However, past time reference is not marked on the verbs themselves in this passage. Instead, past time reference is established at the beginning of the tale by the adverbial expression *once upon a time*. Gullah speakers also occasionally indicate past time reference through the variable use of the preverbal marker *been*. The sentences in table 28.1 illustrate the use of this preverbal marker and others used for marking time distinctions in Gullah.

As well as its verbal system, the pronominal system of Gullah also exhibits some distinctive characteristics. In the passage above, the use of the pronoun *e* for *his* in the sentence *Ber Rabbit knock the Ber Gator in e head* represents one such feature. In Gullah, the pronoun *e* may be used in instances in which English would require the subject pronoun *he, she,*

Table 28.1 The use of preverbal markers for marking time distinctions in Gullah

Time reference	Gullah	English
Past	I been work	I worked
Continuous	I da work(ing)	I am working
Completed	I done work	I have worked
Habitual	I does work	I usually work

or *it*, or the possessive pronoun *his*, *her*, or *its*. In addition, one might find the use of the pronoun *um* used in Gullah where English would have the object pronoun *him*, *her*, or *it*.

Other grammatical features that characterize Gullah include the verb *say*, which may be used to introduce a quotation, as in *(H)e tell me, say, "I ain't got no car right now."* And the word *for* may be used in place of *to* in Gullah to form infinitival expressions, as in *He come for get the car washed.* Many of these distinctive features may be attributed either directly or indirectly to influences from the West African languages that contributed to Gullah's development. Such influences are also found in the vocabulary of Gullah, with words such as *buckra* 'white man', *gumbo* 'okra', and *tote* 'carry'.

Gullah's Origins

Linguists have attempted to reconstruct the course of events that led to the formation of Gullah. A number of competing theories have emerged from these efforts. Early descriptions of Gullah were non-linguistic, and often racist, accounts that attributed the distinctive features of the variety to laziness or to physical or mental limitations on the part of its speakers. Dialectologists, who primarily study regional dialects, later debunked these myths by showing the systematic nature of the variety and arguing that Gullah was an English dialect whose distinctive features were retentions from earlier varieties of British English. This theory was later challenged by Lorenzo Dow Turner, whose book *Africanisms in the Gullah Dialect* led several scholars to argue that the Gullah system was primarily African.

In the 1960s and early 1970s, a theory developed that linked the origins of all Atlantic creoles to a putative sixteenth-century Portuguese-based pidgin spoken along the West African coast during the Portuguese monopoly of the African slave trade. Like creoles, pidgin varieties emerge in situations of contact among speakers who share no common language among them. Unlike creoles, however, pidgins typically are not spoken natively by any group of speakers, but are instead very simplified systems used as second-language varieties among speakers in contact situations. The belief was that as other Europeans entered the Atlantic slave trade, they relexified the Portuguese pidgin with their own native vocabularies, while preserving the basic grammatical structure of the original pidgin. Some scholars, therefore, argued that a seventeenth-century West African Pidgin English emerged out of the English trade and was transported by the slaves to the North American plantations, where it was passed on to succeeding generations of slaves, eventually creolizing into Gullah. Others questioned, however, whether the process of creolization took place on the American plantations themselves or whether the slaves arrived on the plantations already speaking a creole. Proponents of the latter view argued that the creole developed either on the West African coast itself or on the island of Barbados before slaves were transported to North America.

An alternative theory suggests that Gullah emerged independently in the Carolina region between 1720 and 1750, as the growth of the rice industry, institutionalized segregation, and an African majority on the plantations created the need for communication in the form of a creole. In this case, Gullah would have been preceded in its development not by a pidgin, as proposed by earlier scholars, but by Africans in the colony speaking closer approximations to English. This theory is based on the observation that Africans would have had greater access to English during the early years of the colony's development, when Europeans formed a majority. It is not clear whether the variety of Gullah spoken in Georgia emerged under similar but independent conditions or whether the creole was directly transported to the Georgia coast by slaves relocated from South Carolina.

Gullah Today

Following the end of the plantation era, the distinctiveness of Gullah was preserved for many years by the isolation of the Sea Islands and limited travel to and from the mainland. Those who believed that a Gullah-like creole was fairly widespread on the plantations of the Southeast hypothesized that mainland varieties of the creole became more English-like following the breakdown of the plantation system as blacks and whites began to interact with one another on a more regular basis. This process, known as decreolization, has been said by some to have resulted in what is now recognized on the mainland as African American English. In this sense, Gullah is believed to represent not only a modern-day descendant of the early plantation creole, but also a key element in the search for clues about the history and development of mainland African American English.

Today, however, the building of bridges and the growth of the tourism industry have resulted in a significant increase in mobility to and from the Sea Islands, which many believe has also contributed to the merging of Gullah with mainland dialects. It has led many, in fact, to argue that Gullah is in the process of dying. In addition, negative stereotypes and misconceptions about the variety have discouraged some locals from speaking Gullah or passing it on to their children for fear that they will be ridiculed by outsiders. Still Gullah serves an important function in the communities where it is spoken as a marker of culture, history, and identity. And while outsiders may not always be aware of the extent to which Gullah is used, it appears that both young and old Gullah speakers are at least subconsciously aware of its importance in their communities. This awareness alone may be enough to preserve the dialect for many years to come.

References and Further Reading

Jones-Jackson, Patricia (1987) *When Roots Die: Endangered Traditions on the Sea Islands*. Athens: University of Georgia Press.

Mufwene, Salikoko (1993) Gullah's development: Myth and sociohistorical evidence. In Cynthia Bernstein, Thomas Nunnally, and Robin Sabino (eds.), *Language Variety in the South Revisited*. Tuscaloosa and London: University of Alabama Press, 113–22.

Nichols, Patricia C. (1983) "Linguistic options and choices for black women in the rural south." In Barrie Thorne, Cheris Kramerae, and Nancy Henley (eds.), *Language, Gender, and Society*. Cambridge: Newbury House Publishers, 54–69.

Turner, Lorenzo D. (1949) *Africanisms in the Gullah Dialect*. Chicago: University of Chicago.

Wood, Peter H. (1974) *Black Majority: Negroes in Colonial South Carolina from 1670 through the Stono Rebellion*. New York: Knopf.

Islands of Diversity (Bahamas)

Walt Wolfram, Becky Childs,
Jeffrey Reaser, and Benjamin Torbert

29 Governor's Island, Bahamas. © by Harry Thomas.

While Caribbean English is certainly one of the most readily identifiable English accents in the world, there is also great diversity based on cultural background, regional location, and language contact history. No set of islands represents this variation better than the Commonwealth of the Bahamas.

The Bahamas consist of more than 700 sprawling islands. They extend from Grand Bahama in the north, located about 60 miles off the Florida coast, to Inagua to the south, located approximately 50 miles from Cuba and Haiti. The 30 inhabited islands are home to almost 300,000 permanent residents. Many Afro-Bahamians, who comprise 85 percent of the population, originally came from the Gullah-speaking area of South Carolina, while many early Anglo-Bahamian settlers were British loyalists from North America who came to the Bahamas after the American Revolutionary War.

A Distinct History

The first known inhabitants of the Bahamas were the Lucayan Indians who migrated to the Bahamas from South America as early as 600 AD and inhabited the islands until the Spanish invasion led by Christopher Columbus at the end of the fifteenth century. The Spanish conquest managed to destroy the indigenous population. Its lasting contribution is the name *Bahamas*, taken from the Spanish words *baja* and *mar*, meaning "shallow sea."

In 1648 the first English settlers in the Bahamas arrived from Bermuda and established a colony on the island of Eleuthera. Limited natural resources and disease caused many of the settlers to return to Bermuda. During this time, the first colony, New Providence Island, was established on the site that is now the Bahamian capital city of Nassau.

After the American Revolutionary War, in the 1780s, many British loyalists fled the newly formed United States and settled on the major and outlying islands of the Bahamas, coming from ports in New York and Florida. There is an apparent connection between a historically isolated group of Anglo-Bahamians located in the out-island community of Cherokee Sound on Abaco Island and the speech of coastal North Carolina. Approximately 5,000 to 8,000 loyalists remained in the Bahamas after an extensive immigration during the years following the American Revolutionary War.

The abolition of slavery in 1833 changed the social structure of the islands to some extent. In the 1950s, the Bahamas established long-term economic stability through the tourist industry. In 1973 the Commonwealth of the Bahamas became independent. The unique cultural history, the ethnic demographics, and the past and present social dynamics of the islands have helped create and maintain distinct varieties of English in this vast chain of islands.

Sounds of Bahamian English

Some of the most distinctive traits of Bahamian English are found in its pronunciation. A sentence like *Ve 'ope you like honion* highlights a couple of distinctively Bahamian pronunciation features. The pronunciation of *v* and *w* in the same way, usually more like a *v* than a *w*, as in *vatch* for *watch* or *vin* for *win*, is a notable feature of Bahamian English. This pattern was found in some earlier English regional dialects in England, in Gullah, the Southeastern US creole, and even in some dialects spoken by white loyalists from the Carolinas, but it is not common in other Caribbean creoles or in most present-day native English dialects in the US or England. Another distinctive trait of Bahamian English is *h*-dropping as in *'ope* for *hope*, as well as the insertion of *h* before a vowel as in *honions* for *onions*. Most people attribute this to earlier Cockney influence, one of the primary British influences on Bahamian speech, but *h*-dropping is a naturally developing trait in a number of English dialects.

The vowels of Bahamian English illustrate its diversity and complexity, as they blend aspects of British English, American English, and Caribbean English. The vowel of *trap* is pronounced like the vowel of *father*, as it is in some other Caribbean dialects. The diphthong of words like *prize* and *time* shows both ethnic distinction and regional distribution. For Anglo-Bahamians living on out-islands like Abaco, this vowel sounds like *proize* or *toime*, similar to its pronunciation on the Outer Banks of North Carolina and much of the Southern Hemisphere, including Australian and New Zealand English. Afro-Bahamians, however, tend to align their pronunciation of these vowels with African American speech in the Southern US, so that *prize* is pronounced as *prahz* and *time* is pronounced as *tahm*. The cadence of Bahamian speech, like other Caribbean varieties, is syllable-timed so that each syllable gets approximately the same beat, and vowels in unstressed syllables are not reduced as they are in American English. The intonation of affirmative sentences makes them sound more like questions than statements to the ears of most North Americans, who may interpret a statement with rising intonation such as *We're going now* as a question instead of a statement.

Sentence Structure

The sentence structure of Bahamian speech ranges from the use of creole forms to a style that closely approximates standard English. The most creole-like version, which linguists refer to as the "basilect," may be difficult for outside listeners to understand when it is spoken among friends in a casual context, whereas the more standard-like variety, the "acrolect," doesn't seem very different from varieties of English spoken elsewhere. Some speakers shift their speech when talking to different people in different circumstances. Code-switching, ethnic variation, social distinction, and regional distribution within the Bahamas all contribute to the complexity – and the intrigue – of Bahamian language use.

The basilectal version of Bahamian English spoken by Afro-Bahamians in Nassau and other Bahamian locales reveals creole-like features that include the lack of past tense marking for past tense events and the marking of aspect with verbal particles. We hear sentences like *When he get money yesterday he buy a present* for an activity that occurred in the past. Completed action is indicated with *done* as in *She done go straight to bed after she eat*. The verb *be* may be absent in sentences like *She nice* or *They actin' nice*, linking it with other creoles such as Gullah as well as with English varieties with historical creole connections that include African American English in the US. Isolated out-island Afro-Bahamian communities are particularly noted for their use of these remnant forms of English.

Words and Sayings

Some of the most engaging differences of Bahamian speech are found in vocabulary items and phrases. Though the vast majority of words are shared with other English dialects, there are also words that would likely confuse the first-time visitor to the Bahamas, such as *obeah* for 'witchcraft' or a 'hex'. Many words are identifiable because of their association with common English words, but they are used with different meanings: *reach* for 'arrive' in *Have they reached yet?* and *back-back* for 'reverse'. There are also a number of words used by Afro-Bahamians that suggest a connection with other Caribbean English varieties, Gullah, and even African American Vernacular English. For example, *day-clean* is used for 'sunrise' as it is in other varieties of Caribbean English and in Gullah. *Cut eye* in *Don't cut your eyes at me!* refers to a type of disdainful rolling of the eyes.

Finally, a visitor to the Bahamas can be treated to a rich assortment of proverbs and sayings that describe universal kinds of social relations and conditions. For example, *you can't hold two cow tail the same* refers to the biblical admonition "you can't serve two masters." These are just a few of the dialect treasures found in Bahamian speech that link language and

A Sample of Bahamian English Words

biggity uppity, self-important
big eye greedy, selfish
big up pregnant
bridle dry saliva
burying place cemetery
camolly big bump on the head
creek narrow inlet
crocus bag coarse woven material used for packaging material
cutlass machete
eye winker eyelash
fetch in, fetch up come ashore
fix put a hex on someone
gapseed gossip
gussy mae heavy woman
haint ghost
hoe cake unsweetened cornmeal cake
kitty corner crooked
long out pout
manjack, mainjack special male friend
one-one scattered
peanut cake peanut brittle
parrot toe pigeon-toed, feet turn inward when walking
pick somebody's mouth get gossip from someone
pone baked pudding
potcake hybrid dog, mongrel
puckertery confused, in a quandary
quarm walk in an affected manner
sometimey inconsistent, moody
souse boil meat with onions and seasoned water
stench to be stubborn about something
switcher a lime drink
tarpree short fence
yuck jerk

culture. There is little doubt that the English language in all its variations is one of most attractive cultural resources of the Bahamas.

Further Reading

Details about pronunciation and grammar come from Becky Childs and Walt Wolfram, "Bahamian English: phonology" (Vol. I, 435–49) and Jeffrey Reaser and Benjamin Torbert, "Bahamian English: morphology and syntax" (Vol. II, 391–406) in *A Handbook of Varieties of English* (Berlin: Mouton de Gruyter, 2005). Information on the words of Bahamian English can be found in John Holm and Alison Shilling, *Dictionary of Bahamian English* (Cold Spring, NY: Lexik House, 1982). More lighthearted phrase books by Patricia Glinton-Meicholas, such as *Talkin' Bahamian* (1994) and *More Talkin' Bahamian* (1995), are published by Guanima Press in Nassau.

Dialects in Danger (Outer Banks, NC)

Walt Wolfram

30 Ocracoke Island. © by Ann Eringhaus.

As the public argues about the status of well-known dialects such as Southern American English and Ebonics, a unique dialect heritage along the Southeastern coast is quietly eroding. For a couple of centuries, the dialect spoken on the barrier islands and the adjacent coastal mainland of North Carolina has been one of the most distinctive varieties of English in the US.

Small, isolated communities dotting the Outer Banks once nurtured the so-called Outer Banks brogue, a borrowed word from Irish meaning "twisted tongue." In the last half century, however, the Outer Banks has been transformed into a tourist mecca flooded by outsiders, or *dingbatters*, for up to nine months of the year. In the process, a longstanding, unique dialect of American English has become an "endangered dialect."

Traits of the Outer Banks Brogue

The most distinguishing traits of the Outer Banks "brogue" are the pronunciation of several vowel sounds, although there are more subtle differences as well. The pronunciation of long *i* in words like *tide* and *high*, which sounds like the *oy* vowel of *boy* or *toy* to listeners, is the most noticeable trait, and the reason that these speakers are sometimes referred to as *hoi toiders*. (The actual production is more like the combination of the *uh* sound of *but* and the *ee* sound of *beet*, so that *tide* really sounds something like *t-uh-ee-d*.) This region is not the only place where this sound is found; it is characteristic of particular regions in the British Isles and in the English of Australia and New Zealand as well. But in the American South, including mainland North Carolina, the pronunciation contrasts sharply with the pronunciation of *tahm* for *time* or *tahd* for *tide*.

The Outer Banks production of the vowel in *brown* and *found* is also very distinctive. The vowel actually sounds closer to the vowel of *brain* and *feigned*, and outsiders often confuse words like *brown* and *brain*. In fact, when we play the pronunciation of the word *brown* to listeners from different areas and ask them what word it is, they typically say "brain."

Another pronunciation trait, the *augh* sound in words like *caught* and *bought* is produced closer to the vowel sound in words like *put* or *book*, a pronunciation that is quite distinctive among the dialects of American English. The pronunciation of this vowel is actually more like its pronunciation in many British dialects of English and one of the reasons that Outer Bankers are sometimes thought to sound British or Australian. As it turns out, North Americans are not the only ones who think that Outer Banks English sounds more like British dialects than it does American dialects. At one point in our study of Outer Banks English, the well-known British dialectologist Peter Trudgill visited the Outer Banks to hear the dialect for himself. He took back with him a sample of Outer Banks speech and played it to a group of 15 native speakers of British English in East Anglia. The listeners were unanimous in attributing a British Isles origin to the Outer Banks speech sample; most listeners identified its place of origin in the "West Country" – that is, southwestern England.

Most people focus on the pronunciation of the Outer Banks brogue, but there are also vocabulary and grammatical dialect traits. Although we have found only a couple of dozen uniquely Outer Banks words out of the thousands of dialect words used in this area, they point to some important differences.

Words like *dingbatter*, and in some locations *dit dot*, are widely known terms for outsiders, whereas a term like *O'cocker* (*OH-cock-er*) is reserved exclusively for an ancestral islander of Ocracoke – that is, a person whose family genealogy is firmly rooted on the Outer Banks. There are also some meaning nuances of dialect words. The use of the word *mommuck*, an older English word found in the works of Shakespeare and in some more isolated dialect areas such as Appalachia, has developed a meaning on the Outer Banks that sets it apart from both its original meaning and its current meaning in other regions. In the works of William Shakespeare it is used to mean 'tearing apart' in a literal sense (e.g., *They mommucked the curtain*), whereas on the Outer Banks its meaning has been extended to refer to mental or physical harassment (e.g., *The young 'uns were mommucking me*).

Dialect words also reinforce an important point about Outer Banks dialects: it is the combination of the old with the new that defines its current state.

For example, words like *mommuck, quamish*, meaning 'upset', as in *quamished in the gut*, and *token of death*, meaning 'an unusual sign of impending death', such as a rooster crowing in the middle of the day, have been in the English language for centuries. On the other hand, words like *dingbatter* for 'outsiders', and *scud* for 'riding around the island' are relatively new. In fact, our research on the term *dingbatter* shows that it was adopted from the popular 1970s television sitcom "All in the Family." In this show, Archie Bunker regularly calls his wife Edith a "dingbat" when she displays a lack of common sense. Prior to that time, terms like *foreigner* and *stranger* were used for outsiders.

A few grammatical differences also distinguish the dialect. The use of *weren't* where other dialects use *wasn't*, as in *I weren't there* or *It weren't in the house*, is only found in the Mid-Atlantic coastal region, although its use extends from the coastal areas of Virginia and Maryland to the north down to the southern areas of coastal North Carolina. The use of the preposition *to* for *at*, as in *She's to the house tonight* is also fairly limited, though it is found in some other coastal areas of the mid-Atlantic coastal region.

The use of an -s on verbs in sentences such as *The dogs barks every night* is characteristic of the Outer Banks brogue, but it is also found in other historically isolated dialects as well, such as those in Appalachia, as is the use of the *uh* sound with verbs, as in *The dogs was a-huntin' the possum*.

The grammar of the Outer Banks does not add many unique dialect features to the make-up of the dialect, but it is certainly part of the overall mix that makes Outer Banks English what it is.

The History of the Brogue

Most of the early residents of the Outer Banks came south from Tidewater Virginia and from the eastern shores of Maryland, starting in the first decades of the 1700s. The early migration south along the coast was by boat, as the complicated network of rivers, estuaries, and inlets and the expansive marshlands made overland travel impossible. Although residents of the tidewater area did not come from a single location in the British Isles, southwestern England was well represented in the early population, although there were people from East Anglia and other areas as well, including some Scots-Irish. Some dialect traits can be traced to prominent features of southwestern English, but there are also some features that can be traced to Irish English that make Outer Banks English similar to the dialects of Appalachia, where the Scots-Irish English effect is well established.

The dialect resulted from a selective molding of various traits from the British Isles that took on a regional dimension along the coastal areas and islands of the Mid-Atlantic, concentrated in the islands running from the Chesapeake Bay to the Outer Banks. Although we can only speculate about the time of its emergence, the examination of some of the written documents, including the logs kept by lighthouse pilots, letters, and memoirs, shows that the dialect was well in place by the early and mid-1800s and flourished well into the mid-twentieth century.

The Future of the Brogue

What will happen to the brogue as the Outer Banks is flooded by the ever-increasing wave of dingbatters who transformed the barrier islands from a self-contained, marine-based economy into a service-based tourist industry during the past half century? The classification of the brogue as an "endangered dialect" has sometimes caught the fancy of the media, but the threat to the brogue in communities up and down coastal Carolina is very real. If we compare just three generations within the same family, we can see how quickly a unique language can die. In some families, the grandparents may still retain many traditional speech characteristics of the dialect, including the traditional pronunciation, vocabulary, and grammar; the children, however, show a significant reduction in the use of the forms, and the grandchildren have virtually none of these traits. We have documented this pattern of dialect erosion in a number of families we have interviewed over the past decade, so we know that the traditional dialect could, in fact, vanish in a couple of generations.

Dialectologists and linguists worry about the disappearance of the brogue, and liken language loss to the extinction of biological species, arguing that science, culture, and history are lost when a language or dialect of a language dies. In our quest to understand the general nature of language, we learn from diversity, just as we learn about the general nature of life from biological diversity. When a language or dialect dies, there is an essential and unique part of a human knowledge and culture that dies with it. The Outer Banks would certainly still be the Outer Banks if the dialect were to disappear completely, but a part of the traditional culture of the island surely will be lost if it does. I personally find it hard to imagine certain stories being told without the resonating sounds of the brogue.

One thing seems to be certain about the brogue. It has been an essential part of the traditional Outer Banks culture, and people in the community and students in the schools need to know about it if they have any desire of staying in touch with the legacy that has made the Outer Banks such a unique place. The dialect heritage deserves to be indelibly documented and preserved – for *hoi toiders*, for new residents, and for tourists who wish to understand why it is such a special place. To this end, our activities on the Outer Banks have included recording interviews with islanders of all ages, producing video documentaries and audio compact disks and cassettes that preserve the brogue, and developing a school-based curriculum for students to learn about their dialect heritage.

Ocracoke Dialect Vocabulary Quiz: How to Tell an O'Cocker from a Dingbatter

Word List

across the beach	buck	dingbatter	doast	good-some
call the mail over	meehonkey	mommuck	quamish	goaty
miserable in the wind	Russian rat	say a word	scud	O'cocker
up the beach	slick cam	smidget	to	young 'uns

1. They went _____ to Hatteras to do some shopping.
2. That _____ is from New Jersey.
3. That place sure was smelling _____.
4. Elizabeth is _____ the restaurant right now.
5. I put a _____ of salt on my apple.
6. We took a _____ around the island in the car.
7. They're always together because he's his _____.
8. Back in the old days they used to call hide and seek _____.
9. The ocean was so rough today I felt _____ in my gut.
10. Last night she came down with a _____.
11. I saw a big _____ in the road.
12. That meal last night was _____.
13. When Rex and James Barrie get together they sure can _____.
14. You can't be an _____ unless you were born on the island.
15. The sea was real rough today, it was _____ out there.
16. When they _____ I hope I get my letter.
17. She used to _____ him when he was a child.
18. There was no wind at all today and it was a _____ out there on the sound.
19. There was a big, dead shark that they found _____.
20. _____ don't act like they used to back then.

Answers

1. up the beach 2. dingbatter 3. goaty 4. to 5. smidget 6. scud 7. buck 8. meehonkey 9. quamished 10. doast 11. Russian rat 12. good-some 13. say a word 14. O'cocker 15. miserable in the wind 16. call the mail over 17. mommuck 18. slick cam 19. across the beach 20. young 'uns

An Ocracoke Lexicon

Following is a sample of some of the vocabulary items used on the Outer Banks Island of Ocracoke, taken from Wolfram and Schilling-Estes, 1997.

buck friend (male). *He's my buck.*
breakwater Set up a barrier to stop the flow of water. *They breakwatered the inlet.*
dingbatter A non-native resident or tourist. *Dingbatters now outnumber O'cockers.*
goaty Foul-smelling. *It sure does smell goaty there.*
meehonkey Hide and seek. *The kids used to play meehonkey a lot.*
mommuck Harass, bother. *They sure were mommucking the young 'uns.*
O'cocker A native of Ocracoke. *There are about 300 O'cockers on the Island.*
quamish sick to the stomach. *They were quamished in the gut from the rough sea.*
say a word Talk a lot. *Some folks sure can say a word.*
slick cam Smooth water. *The sound is slick cam today.*

Resources

A popular description of Ocracoke speech is found in Walt Wolfram and Natalie Schilling-Estes, *Hoi Toide on the Outer Banks: The Story of the Ocracoke Brogue* (Chapel Hill: University of North Carolina Press, 1997); a more technical description is provided in Walt Wolfram, Kirk Hazen, and Natalie Schilling-Estes, *Dialect Change and Maintenance on the Outer Banks* (Publication of the American Dialect Society 81, Tuscaloosa: University of Alabama Press, 1999). A video, *The Ocracoke Brogue*, and a CD/cassette, "Ocracoke Speaks," which gives the stories of Ocracoke in the voice of the residents themselves, can be purchased from the Ocracoke Preservation Society (www.ocracoke-museum.org). Speech samples can also be found on the web at www.ncsu.edu/linguistics and www.ocracoke-museum.org.

Fighting the Tide (Smith Island, MD)

Natalie Schilling-Estes

31 Fisherman, Smith Island, Maryland. © Nathan Benn/Corbis.

There is a widespread belief that dialect differences in the English language are fading away, as speakers of localized varieties come into more contact with prescribed standards. But linguists who study American English dialects have discovered that the situation is more complex. Dialect differences do survive in some measure, even as older, localized dialect words, pronunciations and sentence structures are disappearing.

One place in which dialect differences have not only persisted but have actually become more pronounced over several generations is Smith Island, Maryland. Smith Island is located in the Chesapeake Bay, about 10 miles from the mainland Delmarva Peninsula. It is actually a small group of islands, extending about eight miles north and south and four miles east and west. The current population is about 360. Smith Island has been accessible only by boat since its first English-speaking inhabitants took up permanent residence there, in the late 1600s. Many of these early settlers came from southwest England, particularly Cornwall (usually via Maryland or Virginia). Over the centuries, a unique dialect has developed on the island, fostered in part by the island's geographic isolation from the mainland, and in part by the islanders' longstanding sense of cultural distinctiveness.

The Island Dialect: Preserving Older Ways of Speaking

Like many small dialects in isolated places, the Smith Island variety is often characterized as "Elizabethan English," "Shakespearean English," or even "Old English." Perhaps this is because isolated dialects like this one often retain vestiges of older usages, long since faded from more mainstream varieties. Some examples of older lexical items found on Smith island are *drudging*, meaning 'catching oysters by pulling them up with a net attached to a metal frame' (this dates back to at least 1709; the activity is also called *dredging*); *jag* 'big load of oysters' (late 1500s); *mudlarking* 'picking up oysters or crabs in the shallows' (dates back to at least 1796); and *progging* 'collecting arrowheads and other artifacts from the marshland' (early 1600s). Pronunciations that represent older usages include saying *zink* for *sink* (which dates back to Middle English) and adding an extra *g* sound to the ends of *ng* clusters, as in *hung up* or *long island*. (Think of how some New Yorkers pronounce "Long Island.")

Islanders' pronunciation of the long *i* sound in words like *night* and *nine* is also reminiscent of the way *i* was pronounced in Elizabethan times, when it sounded something like *uh* (as in *but*) and *ee* (as in *beet*) pronounced in rapid succession. However, the fact that older speakers on Smith Island (and in other areas where this feature occurs) actually use this pronunciation less frequently than younger speakers strongly suggests that today's pronunciation is a comparatively recent innovation that happens to sound like an older usage, rather than a holdover from Elizabethan days. Older sentence constructions found in Smith Island English include adding an *uh* sound before verbs ending in *-ing*, as in *The men went a-huntin'*, using the word *it* for *there* to indicate the existence of someone or something, as in *It was a lot of wind* for *There was a lot of* *wind*, and using phrases like *of a night* or *of a winter* instead of *at night* or *in the winter*, as in *We used to visit our neighbors of a night* (meaning *We used to visit our neighbors at night*) or *We go ice skating of a winter* (meaning *We go ice skating in the winter*).

Something Old, Something New

Despite the persistence of all these older features in the Smith Island dialect, it is not correct to classify it as "Elizabethan." Like all dialects, even the most isolated, Smith Island English has undergone considerable change over the centuries, and it includes many words, pronunciations, and sentence constructions that originated in the Americas rather than in the British Isles. For example, of all their unusual pronunciations, islanders are most noted for their pronunciation of the *ow* sound in words like *house* and *down* as more of an *ey* (as in *hey*) or *i* (as in *my*) sound, so that *house* sounds something like *hace* or *hice*, and *down* sounds like *dane*.

However, this pronunciation does not date back to Elizabethan days; in fact, it seems to have sprung up on the island itself, and it did not attain widespread usage until the mid-twentieth century.

Similarly, the lexical feature for which the island (and surrounding coastal areas) is best known is their rich stock of terms having to do with the intricacies of the crabbing industry, which did not become the chief way of making a living on the island until the latter half of the 1800s. (The original settlers were farmers; following this, most families supported themselves through oystering.) Among the many terms associated with crabbing, we find dozens that refer to the crabs themselves, including terms for various sizes of soft crab (ranging from *mediums* to *hotels* to *primes* to *jumbos* to *whales*) and crabs in various stages of their molting cycle. For example, *greens* are crabs that are two weeks or less from shedding their shells, *peelers* are hours away from shedding, *busters* have started to shed or bust, and *soft crabs* have shed their old shell but not yet grown a new one. Soft crabs are highly prized as a delicacy, and so it is important for islanders to recognize how long it will be before a crab reaches this short-lived stage, and to have the words to be able to talk about it. Other terms associated with crabbing include *scraping* and *potting* (two methods of catching crabs), *crab floats* (wooden boxes where peelers are kept until they shed), *shanties* (the small buildings that house crab floats), *jimmies* (male crabs), and *sooks* (sexually mature female crabs).

Perhaps the best-known dialect feature of Smith Island, and also of neighboring Tangier Island, Virginia, is "backwards talk." Backwards talk is similar to irony, in that it involves saying the opposite of what you mean (for example, saying *It sure is nice out* when it's raining cats and dogs). It is also similar to what linguists refer to as "semantic inversion," or using a word to mean its opposite. However, on Smith and Tangier, backwards talk is ubiquitous, not just occasional, and is highly creative, not just confined to one or two conventionalized words or phrases. For example, among more commonplace usages like *She's pretty* for *She's ugly* and *She ain't pretty none* for *She's very pretty*, we also find such creative constructions as *He ain't headin' it none* (He's going too fast – that is, making too much headway), *That weren't no common trick* (That was a low-down trick), and *He's barefoot* (He's wearing a great-looking pair of shoes). Clearly, backwards talk can be confusing or even downright incomprehensible to an outsider, but islanders always know whether they're talking backwards or "frontwards," probably through a combination of intonation, facial expression, gesture, general context, and close relationships with their neighbors. And just like the *ow* sound and the crabbing vocabulary for which the Smith Island dialect is so well known, backwards talk doesn't seem to have become common until at least the mid-1800s, two centuries after English speakers first began emigrating from the British Isles to Tidewater Virginia and surrounding regions.

Population Loss and Dialect Increase

In recent history, Smith Island has undergone a number of changes. With the rise in large-scale seafood harvesting and processing plants and the seeming decline of crab and fish populations in the Chesapeake Bay, it has become increasingly difficult for small-scale crabbers to make a living. The island population has been steadily declining over the past half-century or so, and even those who remain are often forced to seek employment on the mainland, sometimes commuting back and forth on the ferry every day, sometimes returning home only on the weekends. In addition, the island suffers from massive erosion problems and may even be sinking into the Bay (as has happened with several other inhabited islands before it), and large portions of habitable land mass have been lost over the years.

The seeming doom of the traditional island community, coupled with increasing contact with mainlanders among those who remain on the island, seems like a recipe for the decline and eventual death of the Smith Island dialect. Interestingly, though, just the opposite is occurring. The dialect has actually become more – rather than less – distinct from surrounding varieties over the course of several generations, and it is holding its own today, even among its youngest speakers. For example, pronunciation features like the long *i* and *ow* sounds mentioned above have increased dramatically in frequency in the past half century or so, as have such grammatical features as using *it* for *there*.

Also on the rise is another interesting grammatical feature – the use of *weren't* for past tense *to be* in negative sentences, regardless of subject person and number (as in *It weren't me, She weren't home, They weren't there*). The use of the *were* stem for all subjects does not extend to affirmative contexts, where things are fairly standard: we are far more likely to hear *I was, you were,* and *he was* than *I were* or *he were*. It is not at all uncommon in vernacular dialects for speakers to regularize irregular verbs like *to be* by using one form for all persons and numbers, even though standard English might dictate the use of two or more forms. (For example, constructions like *you was* and *they was* are commonplace, as is *ain't* for all forms of negative present *to be*.) However, using *weren't* for all subjects is rare in American English and has been found in only a handful of mid-Atlantic and Southern dialects to date. Despite its rarity, its usage has increased dramatically on the island in the past couple generations, further contributing to the heightening distinctiveness of the dialect.

Because the dialect is becoming stronger as fewer and fewer people speak it, we classify it as a case of "dialect concentration," as contrasted with the "dialect dissipation" that usually occurs when formerly isolated communities come into contact with the wider world. Although it is not uncommon for speakers in such communities to heighten their usage levels of one or two distinguishing dialect features as they relinquish traditional ways of speaking, cases of the increasing distinctiveness of an entire dialect are rare. In fact, none has been conclusively documented for any other English language dialect.

Why Concentration and not Dissipation?

How has Smith Island retained – and even enhanced – its dialectal character despite the loss of its speakers and their distinctive culture? There are several factors involved. First, although islanders are indeed coming into more contact with mainlanders in some ways, in other crucial ways they are not. For example, the island school only goes through eighth grade, and teenagers must attend high school on the mainland. In previous generations, transportation was available to them only on a weekly basis, and they had to board with mainland families during the school week, bringing them into sustained contact with mainland ways of speaking. In recent decades, however, a daily school began operating, and today's teenagers now come home every afternoon, which restricts their contacts with mainlanders and solidifies their relationships with fellow islanders. Secondly, we have to consider not only amount but also type of contact. For Smith Islanders, most contact with mainlanders takes place off-island and not in their home community, since few tourists or other outsiders visit the island. In other formerly isolated communities, insiders often reach out, but outsiders also come in; and this close contact on one's home territory is probably more conducive to dialect diffusion. Thirdly, it is likely that Smith Island's small population concentrated in a restricted geographic area allows the community to heighten its dialectal distinctiveness to a level that is impossible to attain in larger, more diffuse communities, where there is necessarily more intercommunication with outsiders. Finally, Smith Islanders have always considered themselves a highly independent, distinctive people, and they consider their dialect to be an important symbol of their cultural uniqueness. Thus, no matter how often they encounter other language varieties, they are not likely to assimilate to them, since they value their own unique ways of living – and talking – so highly.

The importance of the Smith Island dialect has been heightened in recent decades as islanders have come face to face with the possible demise of their environment and their traditional ways of life. It makes sense that they would heighten their dialectal distinctiveness even as they fight to maintain their cultural uniqueness. And there is hope in sight: Jetties are being put into place to stem the island's erosion, and islanders are experimenting with new ways of making a living without leaving their island home, even as they work persistently, and hopefully, to hold on to their traditional water-based livelihoods. If the islanders' ability to maintain – and enhance – their dialect is any indication of how successful they will be at preserving their way of life, then their culture is sure to persist, just as the tides continue to rise and fall, and the crabs to shed and re-form their shells, in the waters surrounding this small island community.

A Smith Island glossary

bail (n.) lunch, as in "When it was time for a break, the men took out their bails and chatted while they ate."

carry (v.) take or escort, as in "He carried her out on a date."

edge of dark (n.) twilight

fly flap (n.) flyswatter

fuzz cod (n.) gale or storm

gut (n.) marshy creek

hide and switch (n.) hide 'n' seek

kofered (adj.) warped or bent, as in "The pier was old and kofered by the wind and tide." This word may derive from "coffer," an obsolete verb meaning "to curb up, twist, warp."

noogs (n.) sweets or desserts, as in "She baked us some really good noogs for Thanksgiving dinner."

Pancake Day (n.) St. Patrick's Day

pop (n.) soda

right smart (n.) a lot, as in "She puts right smart of pepper in her crab cakes."

rinch (v.) rinse

skiff (n.) small boat

sun dog (n.) reflection of the sun that may appear next to the sun; brings an easterly wind, cooler temperatures, and fewer crabs

yarney (n.) what Smith Islanders call people from Tangier and vice versa. Comes from the common practice on both islands of yarnin', or telling yarns

Further reading

Dize, Frances W. (1990) *Smith Island: Chesapeake Bay.* Centreville, MD: Tidewater Publishers.

Horton, Tom (1996) *An Island Out of Time: A Memoir of Smith Island in the Chesapeake.* New York/London: W. W. Norton & Co.

Shores, David L. (2000) *Tangier Island: People, Places, and Talk.* Newark: University of Delaware Press/London: Associated University Presses.

From Cod to Cool
(Newfoundland, Canada)

Sandra Clarke

32 Excavations have proven that the Vikings were the earliest European visitors to Newfoundland. © by Cindy England.

In 1949, the island of Newfoundland – along with its mainland and more northerly portion, Labrador – became the tenth and newest province of Canada. Of all regions of the country, Newfoundland/Labrador is linguistically the most homogeneous: approximately 98% of the province's total population of just over half a million speak English as their sole mother tongue. Yet the English spoken by the majority of Newfoundlanders represents a highly distinctive variety, one that exhibits many differences from standard Canadian English.

Historical Background

A British colony until 1949, Newfoundland has always maintained close ties with Great Britain. Indeed, the island boasts the designation "Britain's oldest colony," having been formally claimed by the British crown in 1583, to ensure control of the rich cod-fishing grounds of the Grand Banks. Although settlement was sparse until the end of the eighteenth century, it has been continuous since the first decade of the seventeenth century. Up to the middle of the twentieth century (when the government imposed a resettlement program that reduced the number of communities by about a quarter), Newfoundland's small population was scattered in approximately 1300 tiny "outport" fishing communities on the island's long coastline, many of them accessible only by boat. Since the collapse of the inshore cod fishery at the beginning of the 1990s, small outport communities are once again in danger. The loss of their principal source of livelihood has resulted in considerable out-migration – not only to the provincial capital of St. John's, but also to the more prosperous provinces of the Canadian mainland. Lack of a secure economic base has resulted in very little in-migration to the island for well over a century.

Much of the English-speaking founder population of mainland Canada consisted of Americans who moved north around the end of the eighteenth century, after the American War of Independence. Newfoundland experienced none of this wave of settlement, however. From the seventeenth to the mid-nineteenth centuries, its European founder populations came directly from two narrowly defined geographic areas: the southwest or West Country of England, and the southeast counties of Ireland. The relative geographical isolation of the island, along with the lack of in-migration from diverse sources, are among the factors that have resulted in a very distinctive speech variety in present-day Newfoundland.

Characteristics of Newfoundland English

Many features of Newfoundland English can be traced directly to the linguistic heritage brought to the island by its earliest settlers from southwestern England and southern Ireland. Some characteristics are echoed in speech patterns found in various Eastern seaboard dialect enclaves with similar settlement histories, from North Carolina to the Caribbean. A number of features of Newfoundland English (particularly grammatical ones) display obvious parallels to conservative African American English (AAE) and Gullah. This suggests the preservation in all these varieties of certain features, which were more widespread in earlier English.

A resident of mainland North America (in local parlance, a CFA, or "Come from away") would immediately be struck by the distinctiveness of Newfoundland English. To the mainland Canadian ear, though perhaps not to Midwestern Americans, the low vowels (those typically spelled with *a* or *o* in words such as *cat/trap*, *start/park*, *cot/caught* or *Don/dawn*) sound very fronted or "broad." Residents of Ontario have been known to (mis)interpret Newfoundlanders' pronunciation of *John* as *Jan*. Most Newfoundlanders do not make a distinction between the pre-*r* vowels in such words as *beer*, *bear* and *bare*, whereas many varieties of North American English make a two-way distinction. The same is true for such pairs of words as *pour* and *pore*, or *lure* and *lore*. Those Newfoundlanders who grew up in the heavily Irish-settled southeastern portion of the island, including the city of St. John's, do not exhibit "Canadian Raising" for the *ou* vowel in words like *mouth* (*mooth*) and *house* (*hoose*). In this part of the island, however, the vowel in words like *mug* or *tough* is often pronounced with lip-rounding, as in Irish English. In addition, throughout Newfoundland, words like *side* and *time* are pronounced much like *soid* and *toim*, resembling the *oi* vowel articulation displayed by "Hoi Toiders" on North Carolina's Outer Banks. For traditional Newfoundland speakers, whether of Irish or southwest English ancestry, the vowel written with *o* in the sequences *oi* and *or* may be unrounded, so that *toy* sounds like standard English *tie*, and *north* sounds like *narth*. For these speakers as well, the vowel sound in words like *gate/day* and *go/though* may be long and steady, pronounced (as it was in earlier standard English) as a single vowel rather than as the present-day standard diphthong, or dual-vowel sound.

The pronunciation of certain consonants is equally striking to visitors from "away." Newfoundlanders in the southeastern portion of the island often display two obvious Irish-like pronunciations of the consonants *l* and *t* after a vowel: the former (as in *feel* or *pull*) is fronted and "clear"; the latter (as in *put* or *Saturday*) has a distinct *h*-like quality. In those parts of the island settled by the southwest English, however, the most noticeable consonant feature is word- and syllable-initial *h*, which may be deleted (e.g. *home* pronounced *ome*), yet at the same time may be inserted in words that in standard English begin with a vowel (as in *egg* pronounced *hegg*). The chief factor that conditions this *h*-patterning is syllable stress, as stressed syllables are more likely to insert the *h*. In all areas of the province, *th* is often pronounced in casual speech as *t* or *d* (e.g. *thing* as *ting*, and *those* as *dose*). In a few areas, when *th* is not syllable-initial, it may be articulated, as is also the case in AAE, as *f* or *v* (so that *bath* sounds like *baf*, and *breathe* is pronounced *breave*).

Many of the grammatical features of vernacular Newfoundland speech, while inherited from English and Irish source varieties, are not found in the standard English of today, and hence are often stigmatized. A number of these features have become obsolescent, in that they were last regularly used by speakers born by 1900. Some examples are *dee* (=*thee*) for *you* (sg.), and initial *a-* on past participles of verbs (e.g. *abeen*, *adrinked*). Many features, however, remain very vibrant. These include the use of *-s* as a generalized present-tense suffix for lexical verbs (*they runs every day*, *we wants three of 'em*) – a feature not confined of course to Newfoundland English, but also found in such varieties as AAE. Another robust feature is the use of the "after perfect," which was brought to the island by the settlers from Ireland, and which is regularly used as an alternative to the more usual "have perfect" (as in *I'm already after doin' that* for *I've already done that*). Table 32.1 lists a number of non-standard grammatical features which have been preserved in Newfoundland. Most of these are still quite current, at least among more traditional speakers in rural communities. A number bear obvious similarities to features found in dialects of AAE, and even Gullah.

The traditional vocabulary of Newfoundland is typically described as "colorful" by outsiders. The *Dictionary of Newfoundland English* stands as a testament to the multitude of terms that are in some way unique to the province. Many local lexical items have been preserved from their British and Irish sources, yet have taken on new meanings and forms. These include a host of items relating to the fishery, the weather, and local flora, fauna, games and activities. Over the years, many of these terms have been lost, as a result of a combination of factors including technological change, the decline of the fishing industry and loss of rural populations. While

Table 32.1 Some grammatical features of Newfoundland English

Feature	Example
Pronoun exchange: subject-like forms used as stressed objects; more rarely, object forms as unstressed subjects	*Give the book to she, not he.* *They want it, don't 'em?*
do be (pronounced *duh be*) instead of *is* to express a regularly occurring (habitual) event (more common in Irish-settled areas of Newfoundland)	*They do be sick a lot.* *He don't be here very often.*
Habitual *bees* instead of *is* (more common in southwest-English-settled areas)	*It bees some cold here in the winter.*
For . . . to (pronounced *fer duh*) complementizer Stative preposition *to* (rather than *at*, etc.)	*She come (=came) for to talk to us.* *Can we stay to the table?* *She knocked to the door.*
He/she used as a third singular pronoun for inanimate nouns, rather than *it*	*He's an ol' fork.*

lads in outports may still describe a favorite springtime activity, jumping from pan to pan of ice in the harbor, in terms which differ depending on their region of the province (e.g., *copying, flip(s)ying, tabbying, jumping clumpers/clampers, tippying, ballycattering*), most traditional terms are no longer part of the active vocabularies of younger Newfoundlanders.

The Future

Most Newfoundlanders are ambivalent about the future of their speech. Quite a number profess pride in their dialect as a symbol of their cultural and ethnic identity. Yet many Newfoundlanders also harbor somewhat negative attitudes toward their speech variety, perceiving it to be of limited value in terms of socioeconomic mobility. Throughout the history of the island, Newfoundland speech has been identified with the low socioeconomic status of the vast majority of the island's residents, and as such has often been subject to negative appraisal by outsiders. In the

Table 32.2 Some Newfoundland words in common use today

Word	Meaning	Origin
fousty	moldy-smelling	Southwest England
glitter (also known as *silver thaw*)	ice coating (e.g. on trees, roofs) that results from freezing rain	Southwest England
horse-stinger	dragonfly	Southwest England
yaffle	armful (e.g. of wood, fish)	Southwest England
sleeveen	rascal	Irish Gaelic
streel	untidy or dirty person, esp. a woman	Irish Gaelic
toutin/touton	piece of bread-dough fried in fat	unclear
moldow (often stressed on second syllable)	Spanish moss	unclear
emmet/immit	ant	common in earlier English

words of one early nineteenth-century visitor (Lt. Edward Chappell, 1813), "a stranger must not be surprised to observe a constant violation of the most ordinary rules of speech." Recent language attitude studies reveal that mainland Canadians view Newfoundland speech as the least "correct" and "pleasant" in the country. Inevitably, many Newfoundlanders have been affected by this negative stance, and would no doubt agree with the editor of a local newspaper, the *Gander Beacon*, who in 1982 wrote, "the dialect as handed down to us . . . is misspelled, illiterate, and sloppy." Such attitudes undoubtedly were at the root of the failure to adopt the dialect reading programs advocated by a handful of linguists and educators in the 1970s, when Newfoundland experienced its own "mini-Ebonics controversy." The idea that incorporating local dialect features into early-grade reading programs would ultimately enhance children's reading skills, as well as self-esteem, was met with an outcry from local parents, and the plan was put to rest.

Over the past decades, a fairly rapid linguistic change has been observed among younger generations of Newfoundland speakers. This typically takes the form of a greater tendency to incorporate more standard or supralocal speech features, to the detriment of local ones. For younger upwardly mobile urban residents of such cities as St. John's, this may mean the adoption of features of pronunciation that more resemble the North American norm, such as the loss of fronted *l* in words like *pill* and *pull*, and even the retraction of low vowels in words like *dog* and *start*. The inevitable result is a degree of dialect erosion among younger speakers. Yet the embracing of norms from outside the community does not in itself entail that local dialects are destined to disappear. Many younger Newfoundlanders do not abandon their home speech variety, but continue to use it on a regular basis with members of their in-group. The result is recent generations of bidialectal younger speakers, who possess greater style-switching abilities than did previous generations.

Newfoundland English, though in large measure stigmatized, will undoubtedly remain vibrant for some time to come. Already there are the beginnings of an attitude change: oil revenues are bringing some measure of prosperity; Newfoundland's cultural brokers (musicians, entertainers, writers) are making their presence felt on the national and international stage. St. John's has recently been touted as a "cool" travel destination by several national publications. Perhaps some day soon, Newfoundlanders may also become, as we say locally, some proud of their distinctive linguistic heritage.

Resources

A bibliography of over 200 publications and papers on Newfoundland English can be found online at www.mun.ca/linguistics. The *Dictionary of Newfoundland English*, by G. M. Story, W. J. Kirwin and J. D. A. Widdowson (2nd edn., 1990, University of Toronto Press), is an invaluable resource for local lexicon. An online version of the dictionary can be found at www.heritage.nf.ca/dictionary. The Newfoundland Heritage website, which houses the dictionary, also provides a good source of information on the history and culture of the province.

The World's Loneliest Dialect (Tristan da Cunha)

Daniel Schreier

33 Edinburgh, Tristan da Cunha. © by Robert Harding Picture Library/Corbis.

What would happen if a dialect of English were isolated on one of the most remote places on Earth? Would the dialect stop developing in the absence of outside influences, or would it become more and more distinctive? Few places are better suited to provide answers to these questions than the island of Tristan da Cunha in the South Atlantic Ocean, more than 1400 miles from anywhere.

Tristan da Cunha is situated almost exactly in the middle of the South Atlantic, about half-way between Cape Town, South Africa and Uruguay in South America. Its geophysical isolation is unparalleled: the Guinness Book of Records credits Tristan with being "the remotest inhabited island in the world." Even today it is difficult to travel to the island. There is no airfield, and the sea is the only way to get there. Only about eight or ten ships go to Tristan each year, an 1800-mile voyage that lasts between five and twelve days, depending on the weather.

Geographic remoteness has had a deep impact on the island's history. The Portuguese discovered it in 1506, but there was no permanent population until American whalers settled there at the end of the eighteenth century. The British colonized Tristan in 1816, when the community consisted mainly of shipwrecked sailors and castaways from the British Isles, America, Holland and Denmark. Several women emigrated from St. Helena in 1827, but from the 1850s on, the American whale trade declined and the community became increasingly isolated. In 1882 only two ships stopped at Tristan da Cunha. The dwindling number of ships meant that fewer new settlers came to the island: only two newcomers settled in Tristan in the second half of the nineteenth century.

The social and cultural isolation of Tristan da Cunha peaked around World War I. The community received no mail for more than ten years, and a minister reported in the mid-1920s that the children had never seen a football. This changed in April, 1942 when the British installed a naval station on the island. The abrupt exposure to the outside world led to far-reaching economic changes. A South African company established a permanent fishing industry on the island, and the resulting economic development led to a rapid transformation of the traditional Tristanian way of life. These changes were further reinforced when a volcano erupted near the settlement in 1961. The entire community had to be evacuated and was forced to spend two years in England. The Tristanians quickly adapted to modern life, and brought a taste for modern dress, dances and entertainment when they returned to the island. A new fishing company provided all the households with electricity, and the 1970s and 1980s were a period of economic prosperity. The late 1990s saw further modernization as electronic mail, Internet access and satellite television became available.

Today there are about 280 people residing on the island, all of whom live in Edinburgh of the Seven Seas, the only settlement on Tristan. The community has more contacts with the outside world than ever, and many islanders go abroad for secondary education, job training and vacations. Out-migration is limited, though. The Tristanians have a strong local identity; most of them are happy where they are and would not want to live anywhere else.

Tristan da Cunha English

Tristan da Cunha English has been influenced by the several dialects of British and American English that were transplanted to the island, along with St. Helenian English. Some of the earliest settlers were native speakers of Dutch, Danish, Italian, and Afrikaans, but their linguistic contribution was fairly limited. The community was reported to be entirely English-speaking in the mid-1850s. Dutch and Afrikaans-speaking settlers did leave an imprint in the form of a number of loanwords, mainly in the areas of fishing terminology (*snoek, steenbrass*), everyday life (*kappie* 'knitted hat', *lekker* 'good, delicious', *kraal* 'sheep pen', perhaps *kiki* 'ear'), and food (*gurken* 'cucumbers'). Moreover, recently imported goods led to the borrowing of loanwords from Afrikaans (such as *braaj* 'barbecue', *boerewors* 'sausage' and *bakkie* 'pickup truck'). Tristanians also picked up a few words from American English, mainly from the settlers who arrived from New England and the American whalers who frequented the area in the 1840s and 1850s. An English minister wrote in 1885 that "all the people here speak English slightly Yankeefied as they do a good deal of trade with Yankee whalers." The American impact is found in words like *gulch, bluefish*, the contracted form *tater* 'potato' or in the second person plural pronoun *y'all* and the frequent usage of the phrase *your own self*.

Today, however, the islanders believe that they speak British English. As former Chief Islander Harold Green puts it: "we got this slang on Tristan, the 'Tristan slang' we call it, it's not really number one English, but it's British."

Tristan da Cunha English resembles British English in a number of ways. For instance, Tristanians do not produce *r* in words like *car* or *park*.

The grammar and sounds of Tristan English also were influenced by settlers from St. Helena. The women from St. Helena had an especially strong impact, as the men were frequently employed on whaling ships and left the island for lengthy periods of time. Consequently, a number of grammatical features were directly transplanted from St. Helena to Tristan da Cunha, such as the absence of *-s* on verbs (*that's what make us so cross*), *is* with all persons (*I's a lot happier than a lot people is*) and a distinctive usage of *done* (*they's done kill that black bull*). (Interestingly, this usage of *done* bears a certain resemblance to Southern-based vernacular American English, such as White Appalachian or African American English *the paper done jammed.*)

The legacy of British and American English manifests itself in double modals such as *might could* or *may should* (*she might could check it out for you*), the usage of *for to* (*he tell us for to steer west*) and *be* instead of *have* (*I'm checked the parcels already*).

While Tristan da Cunha English has many borrowed features, it has a number of other features that are found almost nowhere else. The dialect has preserved features that were once widespread in British English and are now virtually extinct, such as the usage of *be* for *have* in perfect structures (*she must be got no work to do*) or hypercorrect *h* (in words like *egg*, pronounced *hegg*, or *expedition*, *hexpedition*). Its speakers have independently developed new forms as well; for example, they use the past tense in sentences like *we never used to kept records in them days* and *we used to went Nightingale Island all the time*. They also have unique pronunciations for certain words, such as *sink* for *think* and *srow* for *throw*.

Tristan da Cunha English in the Twenty-first Century

It would be wrong to assume that the Tristan dialect stopped changing because of its relative isolation. Even though Tristan English developed in the 1820s and 1830s, and its speakers had little contact with the outside world for long periods of time, it is not a relic of the early nineteenth century. It is a mix of sounds, words and grammatical structures that reflect virtually all of the diverse people who have settled and traded there. From the early colonial period to the present day, the island has had intermittent contact with the outside world, resulting in a number of linguistic adaptations and community-based innovations.

Tristan has undergone abrupt transformation since the middle of the twentieth century. Tristanians are now spending more time than ever in the outside world, and their accents are often noticed and commented on in South Africa and England. As a result, the Tristanians are very aware of their linguistic distinctiveness. The question, then, is what the future holds for Tristan da Cunha English. Is the dialect going to erode as the community emerges from insularity and adapts to the modern world?

It is not easy to answer this question, and it may be too early to tell. Younger Tristanians speak somewhat differently, but they continue to use typical Tristan features, albeit less often than their parents and grandparents. Perhaps this trend will continue and the traditional features will die out within a couple of generations. On the other hand, members of the community may continue to speak Tristan da Cunha English with their families and friends but switch when communicating with outsiders, speaking a dialect that resembles British or South African English. The best we can do is to pursue our studies and to monitor language changes in the generations to come. What is certain, though, is that Tristanians are aware that their dialect reflects their rich and unique history and would feel a sense of loss if "Tristan slang" disappeared.

Resources

A more technical description of Tristan da Cunha English is Daniel Schreier, "Terra incognita in the Anglophone world: Tristan da Cunha, South Atlantic Ocean," *English World-Wide* 23: 1–29 (2002). More information about Tristan and the "Tristan slang" can be found on the website of the North Carolina Language and Life Project at www.ncsu.edu/linguistics/. An excellent account of Tristan from its discovery until the beginning of the twentieth century is Jan Brander's *Tristan da Cunha 1506–1902* (London: Allen and Unwin, 1940). For additional information on all aspects of life on Tristan da Cunha, visit websites at http://website.lineone.net/~sthelena/tristaninfo.htm and www.btinternet.com/~sa_sa/tristan_da_ cunha/tristan_history.html.

PART VI
SOCIOCULTURAL DIALECTS

Bridging the Great Divide (African American English)

John Baugh

34 Young man in the city. © by Doug Logan.

The linguistic legacy of the African slave trade has been sorely misunderstood within the United States and throughout the world. Exacerbated by longstanding racial controversies, the linguistic behavior of African Americans, and slave descendants in particular, has been a source of political and educational contention since the birth of the nation. Many of the linguistic stereotypes that abound regarding African Americans are misleading and grossly exaggerated; indeed, American slave descendants do not constitute a linguistically homogeneous group. Thus, blacks who grew up in isolated rural farming communities speak quite differently from African Americans who grew up in heavily populated inner-city neighborhoods and older African Americans typically use language differently from younger African Americans.

Slave descendants share a unique linguistic history that sets them apart from those whose American ancestors were not enslaved Africans. Whereas typical immigrants to the United States may have come to America in poverty, speaking a language other than English, they usually did so with others who shared a common language and culture. The vast majority of Americans can trace their family ancestry to homelands where the languages of their ancestors are well known. Such is not the case for the typical slave descendant of African origin.

The explanation for this unique historical linguistic circumstance is fairly straightforward, as are the racial consequences of this legacy. Only blacks from Africa were imported as slaves throughout North and South America. Whenever possible, slave traders separated captives who spoke the same language. This practice, a crude form of language planning, attempted to disrupt communication among slaves to prevent uprisings during the Atlantic crossing and thereafter. Once placed on the auction block, slaves were then denied access to schools and literacy by law. Again, this linguistic heritage is unlike the vast majority of other immigrants who were exposed to Standard American English within their local public schools.

Because the linguistic consequences of slavery are not well known, many United States citizens, regardless of racial background, do not fully understand why vernacular African American dialects persist, particularly when public figures like Bryant Gumbel or Condoleezza Rice demonstrate full, fluent, and facile command of Standard English. Their linguistic example implies that speaking proficiency is a matter of personal choice, rather than historical circumstances. However, despite the existence of thousands of African Americans who have mastered Standard English, or, in more popular parlance, the fact that "many blacks sound white," it is all too easy to lose sight of the historical linguistic dislocation born of slavery that has made it far more difficult for slave descendants to blend into the melting pot. While the vast majority of American immigrants had the luxury of sharing a minority (non-English) language upon their arrival to America, such was not the case for slaves. Indeed, no indigenous African language survived the Atlantic passage intact, giving rise to a host of African- and European-based pidgin and creole languages that resulted directly from the slave trade.

Due substantially to the lingering inequality that is the legacy of slavery, educators, politicians, and linguists have had highly contentious debates about how best to address the education of black students, and, more precisely, how best to improve literacy among American slave descendants. Does the problem lie with individual students, or are there other, systemic explanations for racial disparities in educational achievement, that lie beyond the control of individual students or those who care for them? While a full understanding of the linguistic behavior of African Americans will not resolve these pressing educational problems, it can shed light on many of the challenges that still face those who sincerely seek ways to overcome racial inequality.

Honest differences of opinion derived from the Ebonics controversy that began in Oakland, California in 1996 may help to clarify the linguistic and educational dilemma that exacerbates racial gaps in academic achievement throughout the nation. Without question, the sociopolitical controversy that erupted in the wake of the Ebonics debate proved to be one of the most contentious linguistic episodes ever to jolt America. Readers may recall that the Oakland, California school board passed a resolution declaring Ebonics to be the language of the 28,000 African American students who attended public schools within that district. The public outcry denouncing Ebonics and its advocates was swift and defied easy racial classification. Maya Angelou was among the first and most vocal of Ebonics' detractors, followed by Kweisi Mfume and other notable African Americans who decried any suggestion that African Americans speak a language other than English.

Although Oakland school officials eventually denied accusations that their resolution was intended to justify claims to obtain federal bilingual education funding, their official policy statement was explicit in this regard, claiming that "African-American pupils are equally entitled to be tested and where appropriate, shall be provided general funds and State and Federal (Title VII) bilingual education and ESL (English as a Second Language) programs to specifically address the needs of their limited English proficiency/no English proficiency" (Oakland African American Task Force Policy Statement).

In addition, some of the most contentious political commentary was derived from an assertion contained within the original Oakland resolution stating that "African Language Systems are genetically based and not a dialect of English." This poorly chosen remark stirred the smoldering embers of Arthur Jensen's incendiary claims, published in the *Harvard Educational Review* of February, 1969, that African American students were cognitively inferior to white students because of genetic differences and that this inferiority was affirmed by standardized test results.

The Linguistic Society of America (LSA) waded into both the Jensen and Ebonics controversies, each time passing resolutions that sought to quell racially charged controversies surrounding the language of African Americans. In the first instance, following remarks authored by William Labov and Anthony Kroch, the LSA observed that:

> The writings of Arthur Jensen which argue that many lower-class people are born with an inferior type of intelligence contain unfounded claims which are harmful to many members of our society. Jensen and others have introduced into the arena of public debate the theory that the population of the United States is divided by genetic inheritance into two levels of intelligence ability: one defined by the ability to form concepts freely, the other limited in this area and confined primarily to the association of ideas.

While these statements served to undercut unsubstantiated genetic claims in Jensen's comments, Oakland's resolution inadvertently reintroduced Jensen's genetic folly, although Oakland educators eventually claimed that their reference to genetics was restricted to linguistic classification and had nothing whatsoever to do with the racial genealogy of African Americans. In this instance the LSA, under the guidance of John Rickford, passed a resolution intended to affirm the linguistic integrity of African American Vernacular English, stating:

> The variety known as "Ebonics," "African American Vernacular English" (AAVE), and "Vernacular Black English" and by other names is systematic and rule-governed like all natural speech varieties.

In so doing the LSA was able to accomplish two important tasks: first, and foremost, it affirmed the linguistic integrity of black American speech, and second, it asserted that Ebonics should be viewed as a dialect of English, and not as a separate language without essential English derivation. Shortly after the LSA passed their resolution, the Oakland school board released a revised Ebonics resolution that deleted all references to genetic classification and conceded, albeit somewhat grudgingly, that Ebonics is "not merely a dialect of English."

The discussion of recent and longstanding historical linguistic controversies surrounding African Americans is necessary to fully appreciate that neither linguists nor educators have yet completely resolved these matters. The Ebonics episode in Oakland generated so much ill-will and hostility that educators and politicians have been loath to reconsider the topic; that is, despite the fact that many of the educational problems that are suffered by numerous African American students owe their existence to the very linguistic misunderstanding that lies at the heart of the Ebonics debate.

Some brief linguistic illustrations demonstrate the subtle but substantive barriers that many African American students face as they strive to succeed within an educational system that makes no accommodation for the dialect that so many of them bring to school. One of the most common dialect features of African American Vernacular English is that of habitual *be*, as found in *They be happy* or *She be staying at home*. An uncritical reflection might wrongly assume that these sentences are identical to Standard English *They are happy* or *She is staying at home*. In the first instance many speakers of vernacular African American English make a productive distinction between temporary and habitual states of affairs. Thus, *They('re) happy* and *They be happy* are not synonymous; the former conveys a temporary state of affairs while the latter conveys a habitual state of happiness. Similarly, *She is staying at home* can convey a temporary state of affairs in contrast to *She stays at home*, which suggests a habitual event. Speakers of AAVE can productively distinguish between *She('s) staying at home* (as a temporary state) and *She be staying at home* (as a habitual state).

Some insightful students of African American English have likewise observed that some African languages make similar "stative" versus "habitual" contrasts that they believe were integrated into the speech of slaves and their descendants. These forms were then linguistically codified under racial segregation and willful attempts to restrict literacy among slaves, thereby denying extensive exposure to written norms for Standard English.

Another linguistic illustration that is not exclusive to African Americans refers to standard versus nonstandard uses of *ain't* and other forms of negative agreement. Whereas many speakers of American English may say and comprehend the meaning of *I ain't got no money*, few Americans (other than speakers of AAVE) use *ain't* as equivalent to *didn't* as in *I ain't drop the book*. As such, the English teacher working with a classroom of students from diverse American English backgrounds could easily launch into a carefully planned lesson intended to illustrate distinctions between *ain't* and other negatives such as *isn't* or *don't* without ever realizing that African American students also use *ain't* as equivalent to *didn't*.

An additional example, with strong African historical roots, illustrates some of the linguistic challenges that educators and their African American students face in school. If, for example, an African American student wrote a non-standard sentence that stated, *He been sad*, a teacher might readily "correct" this sentence to state *He was sad*. However, it is quite possible – even likely – that the student had intended to convey not only that was he sad but that he has continued to be sad for an extended period of time.

Many African languages convey changes in meaning through tonal contrasts; that is to say, they are "tone languages," and this allows their speakers to convey different meanings for the same word depending upon tone, stress, or emphasis. Speakers of AAVE and other American English dialects have come to adopt a tonal contrast regarding the use of the word *been*. In the preceding example, if the student had intended to say that *He been sad* was a temporary past event, they would have intended for an unstressed form of *been* to be implied. However, had it been the writer's intention to convey that "He is not only sad at this moment, but he has been sad for quite some time," then a stressed form of *been* as in *He BEEN sad* would have been the intention.

Other examples from AAVE are numerous, and generally occupy a complete monograph, but table 34.1 illustrates some of the examples worthy of educational attention. As with non-standard uses of *ain't* many such examples are not exclusive to AAVE. However, all of the examples that are identified in table 34.1 are common to speakers of vernacular African American English.

The contrastive examples illustrated in table 34.1 offer a small hint of the vast array of subtle-to-substantial linguistic variation that exists between AAVE and Standard American English. Slight though these examples may be, they serve to highlight the linguistic vestiges of the African slave trade that serve to remind us of the bygone era of overt racial discrimination that was sanctioned by Jim Crow laws and longstanding patterns of residential and educational segregation.

Table 34.1 Some common linguistic examples of African American Vernacular English (AAVE)

Standard English	AAVE
Reduction of final consonant clusters	
cold	col'
left	lef'
mind	min'
desk	des'
Suffix -s absence	
cents	cent
He has ten cents	He has ten cent
brother's	brother
My brother's book	My brother book
likes	like
He likes music	He like music
Post-vocalic r absence	
door	do'
car	ca'
Absence of present-tense auxiliary and linking verbs	
He is here	He here
We are leaving	We leaving
Phonological inversion	
Did you ask a question?	Did you aks a question?
Syntactic alternation	
What time is it?	What time it is?
How can you do that?	How you can do that?
What is the problem?	What the problem is?
Non-standard Negation	
I don't have any cards	I ain't got no cards.
He didn't leave any keys	He ain't leave no keys.

I offer these linguistic, historical, and sociopolitical observations in the hope of shedding additional light on the unique linguistic circumstances born of the African slave trade, and an ensuing recognition that legislators have yet to demonstrate the political will to adequately address the educational abyss that persists between black and white educational performance throughout the nation. Academic excellence does not demand that we attempt to eradicate AAVE; rather, by recognizing that many black students come to school using linguistic patterns that differ substantially from academic varieties of English, we can better prepare them and their teachers to bridge the linguistic and cultural gaps that will ultimately ensure that no child is ever left behind.

When Linguistic Worlds Collide (African American English)

Walt Wolfram and Benjamin Torbert

35 Boy in a field. © by Lise Gagne.

Debate about language origins and evolution is common, but the history of race relations in American society makes the case of African American English, popularly known as *Ebonics*, somewhat special. The broad path of historical development seems obvious. Africans speaking a rich assortment of West African languages such as Mandinka, Mende, and Gola – among many others – learned English subsequent to their shackled emigration from Africa to North America. But the process of this shift and the possibility of lingering linguistic effects centuries later from the ancestral languages of West Africa remains a matter of controversy and intrigue.

Describing the early development of African American speech presents a historical, linguistic, and political challenge. Slave traders were hardly thinking of documenting their exploitation of human cargo for the historical record, and most references to speech in the early slave trade were connected to its role in moving and marketing human merchandise. For linguists, the reliance on limited historical records written for purposes other than linguistic documentation is always problematic, but the difficulties are compounded for vernacular speech that society has deemed unworthy of preservation. Writing was an illegal skill for early African Americans in North America, making first-hand accounts rare and questionable in terms of accuracy with respect to vernacular speech. But there are also questions of authenticity about other recorders of black speech, and its representation runs the gamut – from racist caricatures that exaggerate stereotypical differences to inclusive portrayals that over-look any possible ethnic differences in speech. Observations about African American speech have never been far removed from the politics of race in American society, so that it is hardly surprising that the status of African American English (AAE) has been – and continues to be – highly contentious and politically sensitive.

Competing Explanations

Two major explanations have dominated the modern debate over the origin and early development of AAE. The "Anglicist Hypothesis," originally set forth by prominent American dialectologists during the mid-twentieth century, argues that the origin of AAE can be traced to the same sources as earlier European American dialects of English – the varieties of English spoken in the British Isles. This position assumes that slaves speaking different African languages simply learned the regional and social varieties of the adjacent groups of white speakers as they acquired English. It further assumes that over the course of a couple of generations only a few minor traces of these ancestral languages remained, as in the typical American immigrant model of language shift.

In the mid-1960s and the 1970s, the Anglicist position was challenged by the "Creolist Hypothesis." Researchers of creole languages noted that the early language situation for African descendants circumscribed by the conditions of slavery was hardly like that of Europeans who came by choice and blended with other European groups. Instead, the extreme circumstances of subordination and segregation led to the development of a "creole language," a specially adapted language formed when groups not sharing a common language need to communicate. Typically, the lexical stock of the creole comes from the language of the socially dominant group. The Creolist Hypothesis asserts that an English-based creole language spread throughout the African diaspora, and today creoles are still spoken in regions that extend from West African countries such as Sierra Leone and Liberia through the Caribbean to the Sea Islands of South Carolina and Georgia, where the creole language Gullah is spoken (see chapter 28, "Gullah Gullah Islands"). This creole spread to the sprawling plantations of the American South, becoming the prototype for the development of AAE. The Creolist viewpoint argues that the speech of African Americans in North America has changed greatly over the centuries, but that the imprint of its creole past is still found in a number of language traits: the absence of the linking verb *be* (e.g., *You ugly*), the loss of inflection suffixes such as the *-s* on verbs (e.g. *She like school*), possessives (e.g., *the dog mouth*), and plurals (*many time*), as well as the distinctive verb particles such as the use of *done* to indicate completed action (e.g., *He done went*) and the use of *been* to indicate distant time (e.g., *She been known him forever*). All of these traits are typical of well-known, English-based creoles – from Gullah to Jamaican Creole, and to Krio, the dominant language of Sierra Leone.

Revising the Hypothesis

New historical and linguistic information has brought the traditional positions on the origin of AAE under intensified scrutiny. One source of information comes from the ever-expanding written records of ex-slaves, including an extensive set of ex-slave narratives collected under the Works Project Administration (WPA), newly uncovered letters written by semi-literate ex-slaves in the mid-1800s; and other specialized texts, for example, an extensive set of interviews conducted with black practitioners of voodoo in the 1930s known as the Hyatt texts. In addition to these written texts, limited sets of archival audio recordings have been uncovered, including a set of tapes made by WPA workers with ex-slaves in the 1930s.

A quite different source of new information comes from the examination of the speech of groups of black expatriates who have lived in relative isolation since their exodus from the United States. For example, in the 1820s, a group of blacks migrated from Philadelphia, Pennsylvania, to the peninsula of Samaná in the Dominican Republic, where the descendants of this community continue to live today in relative seclusion. A significant population of African Americans also migrated from the United States to Canada in the early 1800s, and some of their descendants continue to live in remote, out-of-the-way regions of Nova Scotia. It is commonly assumed that secluded groups will be relatively conservative in their use of language and thus may provide a window into the earlier state of a language. The examination of speech in these transplanted, black-enclave communities has shown a striking resemblance to the speech of earlier European American varieties spoken in North America, reviving support for the Anglicist Hypothesis. However, there is an important difference between the British-origins position of a half-century ago and the current position referred to as the "Neo-Anglicist Hypothesis." The original Anglicist position concluded that the early accommodation of European American speech by African American speakers has been maintained to the present, so that there remain no essential differences between the speech of comparable groups of African Americans and European Americans in the rural American South, the regional source of the earliest African American speech in the United States. The Neo-Anglicist position, however, argues that AAE has diverged from European American varieties over the years, so that present-day AAE is now quite different from contemporary benchmark European American dialects. The differences are not due to earlier language history, but to the evolving nature of African American speech during the twentieth century.

Resolving the Controversy

For almost a decade now, a team of researchers from North Carolina State University has been re-examining the development of AAE based on yet another set of historical circumstances – longstanding, enclave African American communities in geographically remote areas of the United States. As in studies of expatriate situations, the lack of everyday contact with outside groups may provide insight into the history of African American speech. In one respect, these communities in the US may be preferable to expatriate situations because they offer the advantage of long-term continuity in a regional context. For example, in Hyde County, North Carolina, a sparsely populated coastal region characterized by the unique Outer Banks dialect (see, for example, chapter 30, "Dialect in Danger"), African Americans and European Americans have co-existed since the first decade of the 1700s. Until the mid-twentieth century, the marshland terrain made it difficult to travel overland and there was little movement into and out of the region. The long-term seclusion and stable bi-ethnic settlement that included a 25 to 50 percent African American population for three centuries present an ideal laboratory for examining the development of language over time. Through our interviews with more than a hundred speakers ranging in age from 5 to 102, we can project what the earlier language was probably like for both African Americans and European Americans, as well as how it might have changed during the course of the twentieth century. Similar communities have also been examined in other regional settings of the South, including a couple of geographically remote communities of African American speakers in Appalachia, where their speech is surrounded by a dialect influenced historically by Scots-Irish (see, for example, chapter 3, "Defining Appalachian English", and chapter 4, "If These Hills Could Talk").

The research shows that the speech of older African Americans was more influenced by the regional dialect of the area than that of younger speakers. For example, in Hyde County, where the unique Outer Banks dialect features the pronunciation of *high tide* as *hoi toid* and the formation of negative sentences with *be* as *I weren't there* or *She weren't there*, older black and white speakers sound much alike. In Appalachia, older African Americans and European Americans share characteristic regional features such as the pronunciation of *fire* as *far*, the use of the prefix *uh-* in *He was a-huntin' and a-fishin'* and the use of *-s* on verbs in *People goes there all the time*. In fact, when we play excerpts of speech from these older speakers to outside listeners, they are often unable to identify the ethnicity of the speaker. This kind of evidence would seem to support the Anglicist position as the correct historical interpretation.

Closer inspection indicates that matters are not as simple as they might appear at first glance. The detailed investigation of different kinds of language structures shows that there are some features that have continuously distinguished speakers ethnically, though these are sometimes more subtle than the more salient items found in the current urban version of AAE. For example, we find a few pronunciation and grammatical features that apparently have been ethnically distinctive for centuries, co-existing comfortably with a shared set of regional features. Though older African Americans and European Americans may have the same regional traits, they have differentiated themselves in the pronunciation of consonant blends before a vowel such as the loss of the final consonant in *wes' en'* for *west end*. The groups have also been different in the pronunciation of consonant sequences such as *skr* for *str*, in *skreet* for *street*. In grammar, the patterned absence of *be* in sentences such as *He ugly* and the absence of various inflectional suffixes in *she go, the boy hat,* or *many time* have probably differentiated black and white speech in some outlying Southern regions for as far back as we can project in the history of American English. Many of the traits that have distinguished black and white speech for centuries are directly or indirectly traceable to the early contact situation between English and West African languages. As African languages and English collided, there was an obvious accommodation to the regional manifestations of English, but the imprint of the original impact also remained indelible. This is hardly remarkable in language contact situations. The English vowels of some Minnesotans, for example, still bear the language marks of the earlier Scandinavian settlers, and southeastern Pennsylvanians continue to reflect German language influence in constructions such as *Are you going with* for *Are you going with me?* and *It's all* for *It's all gone* long after German was used regularly in the area – or, after German is all.

AAE has been influenced both by its earlier regional context in the US and its heritage language situation, making a clear-cut winner in Anglicist-Creolist debate difficult to pick. As is often the case in such debates, both sides have a point – and the truth lies somewhere in between. The position presented here, which admits both earlier regional influence and the persistent influence of the original language contact situation, is referred to as the "Substrate Hypothesis" simply to distinguish it from other positions.

The Evolution of Contemporary AAE

The story of AAE is an ongoing one. In fact, its modern path of change is every bit as intriguing as its earlier history. Current studies show that the distinctive traits of AAE are probably stronger at the beginning of the twenty-first century than they were a century earlier. Older speakers in remote regional contexts may still sound quite local, but their younger counterparts are likely to sound more like their transregional urban AAE counterparts. Younger speakers in the outlying region of Hyde County, for example, usually reject the regional pronunciation of *high tide* as *hoi toid* and the use of *weren't* for *wasn't* as they pick up the use of habitual action *be* in sentences like *Sometimes they be trippin'* and intensify the absence of the -*s* suffix on verbs in sentences like *She go* for *She goes*. In the process, AAE has become a transregional variety that is more ethnically distinct today than it was a century ago. The fact that ethnicity now usually trumps region in African American speech is one of the great stories of modern dialectology.

There are a couple of reasons for the emergence of AAE as a super-regional, ethnically based variety of English. The expanded mobility of African Americans in the last century linked speakers from different regions, making it easier for interregional language spread to take place. At the same time, the pattern of persistent segregation in American society served as a fertile social environment for developing and maintaining a distinct ethnic variety. Many Northern urban areas are, in fact, more densely populated by African Americans today than they were several decades ago, and the informal social networks of many urban African Americans remain highly segregated. Population demographics, however, do not tell the only story. Over the past half-century, there has been a growing sense of ethnic identity associated with AAE, supported through a variety of social mechanisms that range from community-based social networks to stereotypical media projections of African American speech. In the process, regional dialects – and Standard English – have become associated with "white speech." The development of "oppositional identity," in which behavior with strong associations with white norms is avoided, became an important part of the ethnic divide. Though it might seem ironic that the association of Standard English with white speech would develop in a social and educational context that steadfastly rejects vernacular speech of any type – and African American English most vigorously of all – it is a true testament to the symbolic role of language in the African American experience. It is also an indication of the enduring cultural clash between white-dominant mainstream institutions and people of color in American society. In an important sense, there is no greater testament to the durability of African American culture than the vitality of the past and present voice of African American English.

Acknowledgment

North Carolina. National Science Foundation grants BCS 9910224 and 0236838 supported the research reported here.

Further Reading

Even the most restricted list of the articles and books on African American English would be excessive to cite here. The Substrate Hypothesis is presented in great technical detail in Walt Wolfram and Erik Thomas, *The Development of African American English* (Blackwell, 2002). Shana Poplack and Sali Tagliamonte, in *African American English in the Diaspora* (Blackwell, 2001), set forth the Neo-Anglicist position in equal technical detail. A more accessible description of the history and development of AAE is John Russell Rickford and Russell John Rickford's book, *Spoken Soul: The Story of Black English* (Wiley, 2000).

Talkin' with mi Gente (Chicano English)

Carmen Fought

36 Time out on the railroad tracks. © by Jamison Boyer.

A coworker of mine asked me recently, "Why do so many Mexican American students seem to have such a hard time speaking English, even if they were born here in the US?" I realized that her comment was based on a mistaken impression. She heard some students speaking English with what sounded like a Spanish accent, and assumed that Spanish was their first language. Instead, what she was hearing was probably Chicano English. Chicano English is a dialect spoken mainly by people of Mexican ethnic origin in California and the Southwest. There are other varieties associated with Latino communities as well. In New York City, for example, one finds Puerto Rican English, which shares some properties with Chicano English, but is different in other ways.

Why Study Chicano English?

One of the factors that makes Chicano English worth a long linguistic look is the fact that it "grew up" in a bilingual setting. As immigrants from Mexico came to California and other parts of the Southwest, communities developed which included many people who spoke only Spanish. Many of these speakers began to learn English and, like other learners of a language, they spoke a non-native variety which included sounds and grammatical constructions from their first language, Spanish. But the children of these immigrants grew up using both English and Spanish, and as the communities began to stabilize, so did a new dialect of English.

Because of its origins, Chicano English does have many features, especially in the phonology, that show the influence of Spanish. For example, the *a* sound in words like *pasta* or *saw* sounds much more like the Spanish *a* than in other dialects of English. In the ending on words like *going* or *talking*, Chicano English speakers tend to have a higher vowel, more like the *i* of Spanish (as in *sí*), so that the words end up sounding more like *goween* and *talkeen*. There is also a special use of the word *barely* in Chicano English to mean 'had just recently' as in *These were expensive when they barely came out.* (In my dialect, this would be translated as *These were expensive at the beginning, when they had just come out.*) This may come from the Spanish adverb *apenas*, which can mean that something almost did not happen but then it did (which is what *barely* means in many English dialects), or it can mean that something happened just recently. This latter meaning can sometimes be attached to *barely* in other dialects of English (*Don't leave; you barely got here!*) but not always (e.g., *I barely broke my leg*, which speakers of most other dialects don't say, but which is acceptable in Chicano English).

Is Chicano English Just the Non-native English of Spanish Speakers?

It would be a mistake to characterize Chicano English as "learner English," somehow imperfect and non-native. Chicano English is a stable and fully formed dialect, linguistically and structurally equivalent to other dialects of English, such as the varieties spoken by Anglos in the same regions. Like the coworker I mentioned earlier, many people hear Chicano English and assume that what they are hearing is the "accent" of someone whose first language is Spanish. The problem with this theory is that many speakers of Chicano English are not bilingual; they may not know any Spanish at all. Despite the mistaken impression that many people have, these Mexican American speakers have in fact learned English natively and fluently, like most children growing up in the US. They just happened to have learned a non-standard variety that retains indicators of contact with Spanish.

My students often insist that they can tell whether someone is bilingual or not from their English. To test this, I have made up a tape of short segments (in English) spoken by four Chicano English speakers from my fieldwork in Los Angeles in the mid-1990s. Two of the speakers are bilingual, and two speak only English. I play this tape for the students and ask them to identify each speaker as bilingual or monolingual. In every class where I have done this test, the students are unable to classify the speakers correctly. The most non-standard sounding speaker, for example, is usually labeled by a majority of the class as bilingual, yet I discovered in the interview that the most he can do in Spanish is count to ten. The truth is that you don't need to know any Spanish to speak Chicano English.

Chicano English also includes features that are not clearly attributable to Spanish. An example is multiple negation (*She didn't tell me nothing about it*) which could be related to Spanish, but could just as easily have come from other non-standard dialects spoken by working-class African Americans or Anglos, for example.

More recently, it has been discovered that some Chicano English speakers also incorporate features from the local Anglo dialect, a California variety known colloquially as the "Valley Girl" dialect. Additionally, some speakers use features from African American English.

Of course, not everyone in a particular Mexican American community speaks Chicano English, and there is also a wide range of styles encompassed by this label, as is the case with other dialects, including standard ones. Some middle-class speakers in a Mexican American community may speak a variety that is grammatically fairly similar to more standard dialects, but retains a special phonology, while other middle-class speakers might not speak Chicano English at all. Women, in general, speak Chicano English a bit differently than men. The language used by young speakers who are gang members includes terms that other members of the community do not use.

What is "Spanglish"?

Also characteristic of Chicano English is the use of Spanish lexical items. Even speakers who do not know much Spanish will occasionally throw in a word or phrase like *ándale* or *hasta la vista* as a kind of identity marker. This occasional use of a Spanish word is different from code-switching – the more complex mixing of lexical items and structures from English and Spanish in a single sentence. An example of code-switching would be *Es un little boy* (*It's a little boy*). This pattern is most common among speakers who are highly fluent in both languages. It can also occur among Chicano speakers who don't speak Chicano English, but mix Spanish with some other dialect of English.

Linguists have discovered that there is code-switching in most communities where two languages are spoken on a regular basis. It seems to be a basic human reaction to the everyday use of two languages in a society, and is subject to rules and norms just like any other part of language. Nonetheless, people often have a negative reaction to it, and assign it a negative label. In the communities where Chicano English is spoken, the term used for code-switching is usually "Spanglish." I think of this term as a somewhat negative one. However, I was surprised to find that the attitude toward Spanglish among the young adult speakers I talked to in Los Angeles was very positive.

David, 17, for example, told me, "Two languages sounds better for us Mexicans." Jorge, 18, told me he liked code-switching, and explained to me that it is what distinguishes Chicanos or Mexican Americans from people actually living in Mexico. He referred to code-switching as "Chicano language." Several other young Chicano speakers described this way of talking as "cool." So in some sense, one might say that fluency in Chicano English includes the acceptance of using Spanish and English in the same sentence, whether or not one does it.

Is Chicano English Influencing Other Dialects?

We know that Chicano English has been influenced by other dialects, such as Valley Girl English or African American English. An interesting question is to what extent that influence has gone in the other direction. The pronunciation of *going* as *goween*, for example, is something that I hear increasingly among California Anglo students. Did this come from Chicano English? I don't know the answer to this question, but in the meantime, I will keep a sharp eye on *barely* to see what happens in the future.

Stirring the Linguistic Gumbo (Cajun English)

Megan E. Melançon

37 Boaters at the mouth of Bayou Cane, Louisiana. © by Darryl Lodato.

"Get down out dat car and come have a coffee"

Cajun English speaker

The ingredients in the gumbo that is southern Louisiana's linguistic heritage include several varieties of French (seventeenth-century, Cajun, and Creole), Canary Island Spanish, German, and, the most recent addition to the dish, English. All of these ingredients have flavored the speech of

French Louisiana, yielding a unique dialect called Cajun English. The dialect is spoken mainly in southern Louisiana, although migrations to southern Texas and southern Mississippi have resulted in pockets of Cajuns living in those areas. The Cajuns have been called a "linguistic curiosity," and, in fact, their versions of English and French differ from American English and the French spoken in France. So, who are the Cajuns, and where did they come from?

History of the Cajuns

Cajuns are descendants of French settlers who moved into the area of Canada known as Acadia (modern day Nova Scotia) in the early 1600s. For many years, the territory was ceded back and forth between France and England as the spoils of war, and the settlers were left virtually undisturbed. In 1713, however, the Treaty of Utrecht permanently sealed the fate of the small colony – it became a permanent possession of the British. The Acadians were allowed to live in peace for a period of time, but because of their friendship with the Native Americans living in the area, and also because of an influx of British settlers, the British crown decreed that all persons of French ancestry must pledge allegiance to the British government. Beginning in 1755, those who refused to do so were deported and scattered across various coastlines in the American colonies in what their descendants still refer to as *le grand dérangement*.

There are pockets of French culture and language surviving in diverse areas of the United States as a result of this forced migration, including Maine, South Carolina, Georgia, Mississippi and Louisiana. Some deportees also ended up in the then French-ruled Caribbean islands of Martinique, Guadeloupe, and Haiti, while others went back to Europe.

The Acadians (shortened by English speakers to 'Cadians and then to Cajuns) were reviled and feared by their English-speaking Protestant neighbors in the American colonies, so they sought out isolated communities where they could practice their religion and teach their native language to their children. This isolation led to the preservation of some elements of French as it was spoken in the mid-1700s. In fact, some of the lexical items in Cajun French today are essentially unchanged from the French of that era, e.g. *le maringouin* 'mosquito' (modern French *le moustique*).

The English that the Cajuns acquired for trading and economic purposes has been strongly influenced by their native French. The dialect has also been affected by the assimilation of the Cajun culture by various other ethnic groups living in the region: Native American tribes, German and Irish immigrants, African and Caribbean slaves, and the Spanish-speaking *Isleños* from the Canary Islands. More recently, forced schooling in English pursuant to the 1921 Louisiana constitution (which established English as the official language of the state), and the intrusion of mass media into even the most isolated bayou communities, have led to fewer and fewer people speaking French, with a consequent rise in the use of English. Today's reality is that English is just as much a part of the culture as French, and English is rapidly overtaking many of the sociocultural parts of the Cajun heritage.

Characteristics of Cajun English

Although there are many dialectal oddities in Cajun English, five features strike the listener right away: vowel pronunciation, stress changes, the lack of the *th* phonemes, non-aspiration of *p*, *t*, and *k*, and lexical differences. The use of these features has resulted in no southern drawl at all in Cajun English. Cajuns talk extremely fast, their vowels are clipped, and French terms abound in their speech. These variations have been studied by a few linguists, more folklorists, and, in a casual way, many more tourists.

The vocal differences of Cajun English are both qualitative and quantitative. The qualitative differences (the differences between the standard forms of English vowels and Cajun English vowels) are easily identifiable. Quantitative differences are changes that are across-the-board and non-random in the speech of most Cajuns. Some examples? Diphthongs (or dual-vowel sounds) change to monophthongs (single vowels) in words such as *high*. Standard American English uses a diphthong *i* as in *tie* while Cajun English speakers use an unglided vowel as in *tah*. The word *tape*, pronounced in English as *ta-eep* is pronounced without the *ee* glide, as *tehp*. In addition, many Cajun English speakers use the tense version of English vowels, making words like *hill* and *heel* "homophones," or words which have the same pronunciation – *heel*.

Intonation and stress are so striking in Cajun English that entire joke repertoires have been based on them. The French spoken by the older

Cajuns was passed on to their descendants, who found it necessary to speak English for socioeconomic reasons, and the syllable-final/phrase-final stress of French persists to this day in the speech of Cajuns. Bilingual stress patterns often exhibit a form of mutual borrowing, and even though many Cajuns do not speak French at the present time, or speak it very poorly, the patterns of French are still imprinted on the dialect. As has been found in French Canada, English-like stress patterns are invading the French of the Cajuns, while the syllable-final stress pattern of the French has seeped into the English of the former Canadians. This leads to words such as *Marksville*, normally pronounced with the stress on the first syllable, being pronounced with stress on the second syllable (with a shortened and raised final vowel sound).

Voiceless and voiced *th* replacements occur frequently in the speech of non-standard speakers, and the Cajuns are no exception. In fact, the replacement of the *th* sounds with a *t* or a *d* sound is another source of the numerous jokes and imitations of Cajun speech made by others (and sometimes by Cajuns themselves, as in the "Cajun Night Before Christmas" recording made by Jules D'Hemecourt). Although many southern English and African American English speakers use *f* or *v* in place of the *th* phonemes, both Creole and Cajun English speakers use the voiceless and voiced alveolar stops *t* and *d*. Many bilingual French-Canadians exhibit this same linguistic behavior with regard to the *th* phonemes, while standard French speakers tend to use *s* or *z* in place of a *th* sound.

Standard English speakers normally aspirate (exhale a breath of air) when pronouncing the stop consonants *p*, *t*, and *k* in stressed, syllable-initial position. Cajun English speakers do not, yielding words like *pat* sounding much like the word *bat*, with a shortened vowel sound. The source of this is probably the French language. French speakers do not aspirate the voiceless stops. The mystery is why the Cajun English speakers in Louisiana, many of whom do not speak French, and who are more than 300 years removed from contact with French speakers, still retain this feature in their speech.

Lexical differences are perhaps the most apparent to the casual observer: *boudin, lagniappe, making groceries,* and *get down out of* (a vehicle) are all unacceptable to modern-day spell- or grammar-checkers, yet are quite normal in southern Louisiana (meaning 'a rice and sausage mixture wrapped in an intestinal sack', 'a little something extra', 'going grocery shopping', and 'get out of', respectively). Some (like *boudin* and *lagniappe*) are borrowings from French; others are calques, or direct translations, from French (e.g. *making groceries*, from the French *faire les courses* and *get down out of* the car/truck/bus from French *descendre*). In addition, various areas of southern Louisiana have vocabulary items and pronunciations which are specific to the community, such as *zink* for *sink* in the New Orleans area. The French influence is also apparent in the use of definite and indefinite articles. One has *a* coffee during a visit (and, given the strength of the coffee, one is grateful not to have "some"!). French endearments (*cher*, a short form of *chéri(e)*, pronounced *sha*), curse words, and conjunctions are often sprinkled into conversations ("*mais* I don't know, me").

Current state of the language

Despite being subjected to abuse and stigmatization for many years, Cajun English speakers abound. Why would this be? Why would a dialect which was considered a mark of ignorance until very recently be heard on the lips of Cajuns young and old? The explanation most applicable to Cajun English is that the language is seen as a marker of being an insider to the community. This is seen most clearly when the French language ability of Cajuns is assessed: that language is dying, and is now only used among the older folks in the community. However, Cajun English use has been documented among even the youngest Cajun descendants, a fact that is easy to verify simply by going to any café in any small town in south Louisiana. To be a Cajun these days, the necessary and sufficient condition seems to be that you must speak Cajun English.

In many communities, a culture survives long after the language associated with it dies. In the case of the Cajuns, the differences from the surrounding Anglophone community are quite marked, making it easier to resist the encroachment of English culture. The retention of the unique music, food, and religion of the Cajuns has been aided by a history of endogamous marriages, geographical isolation, and stigmatization by the Anglophone community. Despite the fact that these things have changed tremendously in the past 40 years, Cajun people young and old still retain a distinctive flavor in their speech. So, the culture may survive. As long as Cajun English is used as a dividing line between the Anglophones and the long-exiled French Canadians, Cajun English will continue to flourish.

Some Cajun Phrases

alors pas of course not
cahbin bathroom
co faire? why?
dit mon la verite! tell me the truth!
en colaire angry
fais do-do go to sleep
he's got the gumbo his pants are too big in the seat
hot, hot very hot
magazin store
make a bill buy groceries
Mo chagren I'm sorry
my eye! (or my foot!) no way!
slow the TV turn down the volume
speed up the TV turn up the volume
sussette pacifier
une piastre a dollar

Resources

A useful resource on Cajun English is Dubois and Horvath, "From accent to marker in Cajun English: A study of dialect formation in progress," *English World-Wide* 19(2), 161–88 (1998). Dubois and Melançon discuss Cajun French in "Cajun is dead – long live Cajun: Shifting from a linguistic to a cultural community," *Journal of Sociolinguistics* 1(1) (1997). Father Jules O. Daigle published *A Dictionary of the Cajun Language* in 1984.

Action Cadienne was formed in April, 1996. It is a non-profit volunteer association dedicated to the preservation and promotion of the French language and the Cadien (Cajun) culture of Louisiana. Its website is at www.actioncadienne. org/. Other websites of interest are: Council for the Development of French in Louisiana (CODOFIL), www.codofil.org/ and Kreyol Lwiziyen: The Language of French Louisiana, www.angelfire.com/ky/LeCorde/cajun.html.

From the Brickhouse to the Swamp (Lumbee Vernacular English)

Walt Wolfram

38 Lumbee girls. © by Neal Hutcheson.

Native American languages are in a cultural crisis. Many once-vibrant languages are now used by only a handful of elderly speakers, and as those last speakers die, their languages die with them. Despite efforts by some community members and linguists to maintain and revitalize these indigenous languages, they often simply disappear with the passing years. As a result, only a few of the Native American languages that were spoken in the 1800s are still spoken today, and the remaining ones are disappearing at an alarming rate.

What happens to the speech of Native American groups when their heritage language base erodes? Do they simply adopt the speech of the surrounding non-native community and blend into the English mainstream, or do they develop a distinct vernacular? In many cases, Native Americans have adopted the English dialect of the surrounding community. But there are also some instances where Native Americans have carved out a unique dialect niche – a kind of "American Indian English." No group is more representative of this latter category than the Lumbee Indians of North Carolina.

Who are the Lumbee?

The Lumbee are the largest Native American group east of the Mississippi and the seventh largest Native American group in the United States, with over 50,000 members listed on the tribal rolls. Although Lumbees can be found throughout the nation, they are concentrated in Robeson County, North Carolina, and are relatively unknown outside of southeastern North Carolina. In Robeson County they make up 40% of the population, and some communities in Robeson County are over 95% Lumbee. In contrast, European Americans comprise about 35% and African Americans approximately 25% of the Robeson County population, making the county a stable tri-ethnic area.

One of the curious aspects of the Lumbee is how little is known about their exact historical origins. There is ample archaeological evidence that Native Americans have inhabited the Robeson County region for thousands of years. In colonial times, the Carolinas were inhabited by speakers of several different major families of Native American languages, including Siouan, Iroquoian, and Algonquian languages. The Lumbee were among the first Native American Indians to learn English during the early English settlement of the Carolina coastal plain and were reported to be speaking English as early as the first half of the 1700s. With the growth of European settlements in the region, some tribes may have relocated or blended together, making it even more difficult to identify a specific ancestral dialect lineage for the Lumbee. Although some Lumbees believe their history can be traced to the famous Lost Colony on Roanoke Island, most scholars think that they are an amalgam of several different Native American groups.

The Lumbee were officially recognized as a tribe by a congressional act in 1956. Unfortunately, while the act recognized the Lumbee as an Indian tribe, it explicitly denied them entitlements usually afforded to recognized tribes, such as federal funding or reservation land. In fact, the Lumbees' ambiguous status as a tribe may be the ironic and unfortunate result of their early adoption of English, and their uncertain historical origin. They are one of the few Native American groups to be assigned such an ambiguous status. The Lumbees' century-long quest for full recognition is certainly one of the unheralded stories of the Native American struggle to maintain cultural identity and integrity.

Lumbee English

Since the loss of their heritage language generations ago, the Lumbee have perpetuated their identity through the development of a distinctive dialect of English. Even the congressional act of 1956 acknowledged their distinct dialect by noting that Lumbees could be identified by a "distinctive appearance and manner of speech." Residents of the area also recognize the existence of Lumbee English, which differs from the speech of the neighboring African American and European American communities in Robeson County. Given tape-recorded samples of African American, European American, and Lumbee residents, listeners from Robeson County correctly identified Lumbees over 80 percent of the time – a higher rate than their correct identification of European Americans in the county. Although patterns of social and cultural segregation, population density, and historical continuity have contributed to the development of Lumbee English, there is an important sense in which the dialect is a constructed identity, by which they have defined themselves as neither white nor black – a cultural "other" in the ideology of the bi-racial Southeastern US. Like other dialects, Lumbee English has distinct lexicon, pronunciation, and grammar. Although it possesses a few unique words and phrases, Lumbee English is defined more by the combination of words and structures that set it apart from Southern white and black varieties of English than by the existence of exclusive Lumbee lexicon. A few distinctive terms, such as *ellick* 'coffee with sugar', *juvember* 'slingshot', and *yerker* 'mischievous child', are mostly restricted to the Lumbee, but words like *fatback* 'fat meat of a hog', *mommuck* 'mess up', and *headiness* 'very bad' are shared with other dialects in the Southern coastal plains. As is often the case in enclave communities, a number of social designations are also embodied in some of the vocabulary items. Thus, the term *daddy* is used for close friends as well as a parent, and teenagers may greet one another with *What's up, Daddy?* The term *Lum*, a clipped form of Lumbee, is reserved for those who have identified with their Lumbee cultural heritage. Social distinctions within the community are captured by terms like *brickhouse Indian* and *swamp Indian*, which refer to higher and lower status in the community.

Pronunciation features of Lumbee English combine patterns from Mid-Atlantic coastal speech and from Appalachian English. For example, older Lumbee Indians in isolated communities pronounce *side* and *time* something like *soid* and *toim*, more like the traditional pronunciation of these vowels on the Outer Banks of North Carolina than the widespread current Southern pronunciation of *sahd* and *tahm*. *Tobacco* and *potato* may be pronounced as *'baccer* and *'tater*, combining the loss of an unstressed syllable and intrusive *r* in the final syllable in a way that parallels both the coastal dialect and Appalachian English. When combined with pronunciations such as *tar* for *tire* and *far* for *fire*, the dialect seems to resemble Appalachian speech to listeners from other regions.

Several prominent grammatical features characterize Lumbee English. One of the dialect icons of Lumbee English is the use of *bes* in sentences such as *That's how it bes* or *The dogs bes doing that*. Although the finite use of *be* is often associated with African American Vernacular English, its use in Lumbee English differs from its African American counterpart in two important ways. First, it is inflected with *-s*, whereas *be* in African American English does not take the inflectional *-s*. Second, finite *be* is more expansive in its meaning; it is not restricted to habitual activities as it usually is in African American Vernacular English. In Lumbee English, speakers can say both *She usually bes playing*, as well as *She bes playing right now*. Another prominent feature of Lumbee English is the use of *weren't* as the past tense form of *be* in sentences such as *It weren't me* or *I weren't down there*, a feature shared with coastal dialects in the Mid-Atlantic South. Also, the use of forms of *be* where the perfect use of *have* is found in other dialects, as in *I'm been there already* for *I've been there already* or *He be took the food* for *He has taken the food* characterizes the dialect. Although all of these structures are found in other vernacular dialects of English, the particular combination of traits sets Lumbee English apart, both from surrounding vernacular dialects and other dialects of English.

Walt Wolfram   247

The Development of Lumbee English

No single source can account for the development of Lumbee English. There may be some residual effects from the ancestral language, but if so, they are very subtle and not readily apparent. This is hardly surprising given the tribes' early acquisition of English, and the fact that all traces of a heritage language can be lost within a couple of generations. Instead, Lumbee English has been molded primarily from the available models of English used by the Europeans settled in the area. For example, structures like *I weren't there* and the pronunciation of *fire* as *far* were apparently adopted originally from the regional dialects in the vicinity. In the 1700s and 1800s, Lumbee English was connected with the coastal dialects of North Carolina, and this historical connection is still reflected in some dialect features. At the same time, there is obvious influence from the Scots-Irish who spread eastward from the Appalachian region, as well as from the Highland Scots who settled in the region during the eighteenth century. Some of the features incorporated into the dialect are retentions of earlier forms that were once widespread in the English language, such as the use of forms of *be* for *have* in sentences like *I'm been there* or the use of the prefix *a-* in *She's a-fishin'*. The final ingredient added to the dialect mix includes innovations that took place within the Lumbee community itself, such as the development of some of the specialized meanings of lexical items. The resulting dialect is a distinctive mix blended from the various dialects in the region and some internal, community-based dialect development.

The Future of Lumbee English

Although many historically isolated dialect communities are now diminishing because of outside influences, this is not as evident in Lumbee English as it is in some other dialects. The set of identifying structures has shifted over time, but the dialect is still vibrant. In fact, the use of some dialect structures is actually increasing rather than receding. The use of *be* for *have* and the use of *weren't* as in *I weren't there* are still quite robust in the speech of some young people, even in the face of school-imposed standard English norms. As one Lumbee educator put it, "Since the 1880s, when they started the Indian schools, they have been trying to teach us standard English and they haven't succeeded yet."

The non-mainstream status of Lumbee Vernacular English has subjected the Lumbee to a type of double jeopardy. The community lost its ancestral language heritage originally to accommodate the sociopolitical and economic exigencies of European encroachment. Regrettably, their early adoption of English was subsequently used against them, as they were denied full recognition as an Indian tribe. There is little doubt that the Lumbee would be fully recognized by the US government today if they had maintained their heritage language. But they have not lost their linguistic identity. Instead, they creatively molded the English language to mark their ethnic distinctiveness. Their dialect supports their unflagging confidence that they are simply and utterly Indian. Unfortunately, many ill-informed individuals considered the dialect to have no linguistic integrity and dismissed it as an unworthy approximation of standard varieties of English. While Lumbee Vernacular English is undeniably different from standard English, it is much more than just another non-standard dialect of English. It remains one of the most transparent and authentic markers of cultural and ethnic identity for the Lumbee, even as they embrace other dimensions of the Native American cultural renaissance.

Despite persistent institutional efforts to repress and obliterate any linguistic traces of cultural distinctiveness in their language and dialect, the Lumbee have creatively maintained a distinct manner of speech as a symbolic indicator of their identity. As local artist Hayes Allan Locklear put it: "That [the dialect]'s how we recognize who we are, not only by looking at someone. We know just who we are by our language. You recognize someone is from Spain because they speak Spanish, or from France because they speak French, and that's how we recognize Lumbees. If we're anywhere in the country and hear ourselves speak, we know exactly who we are."

Lumbee Vocabulary Quiz

		Word List		
bate	brickhouse	buddyrow	chicken bog	ellick
headiness	jubious	juvember	Lum	on the swamp
mommuck	sorry in the world	swanny	toten	yerker

1. He acts like a real _____.
2. She ate a _____ of greens.

3. You're my _____ for doing me the favor.
4. Come on down and we'll have some _____.
5. How are things _____?
6. I felt right _____ after I saw the haint.
7. Don't _____ the room.
8. She was _____ when her horse died.
9. They tell stories about how she heard a _____.
10. Fetch me some _____; I need to wake up.
11. They made a _____ from some branches they found.
12. I know you made this mess, you little _____.
13. She made the _____ mess in her room.
14. I _____ that I'll punish you if you don't behave!
15. He thinks that he is a _____ Indian.

Answers

1. Lum (Lumbee) 2. bate (lot) 3. buddyrow (friend) 4. chicken bog (chicken and rice) 5. on the swamp (neighborhood) 6. jubious (strange) 7. mommuck (mess up) 8. sorry in the world (sad) 9. toten (ghost) 10. ellick (coffee) 11. juvember (slingshot) 12. yerker (mischievous child) 13. headiness (very bad) 14. swanny (swear) 15. brickhouse (upper status).

Resources

A more technical description of Lumbee English can be found in Walt Wolfram and Clare Dannenberg, "Dialect identity in a tri-ethnic context: The case of Lumbee American Indian English, *English World-Wide* 20: 79–116 (1999), and in the various publications by the staff of the North Carolina Language and Life Project. These are listed at www.ncsu.edu/linguistics, along with audio samples of representative speakers. For additional information on Lumbee history and culture, visit web sites at www.lumbee.com and www.uncp.edu/nativemuseum. More information on Native American varieties of English in general can be found in William A. Leap's book *American Indian English* (University of Utah Press, 1993). The video documentary on Lumbee English, *Indian by Birth: The Lumbee Dialect* (2000), can be ordered at www.uncp.edu/nativemuseum.

More than Just Yada Yada Yada (Jewish English)

Cynthia Bernstein

39 Young Orthodox Jews. © by Eddie Gerald/Alamy.

Yinglish, Yidgin English, Yidlish, Yiddiglish, Ameridish, Anglish, Heblish, Engdish, Engliddish, Engbrew, Englibrew, Jewish English, Jewish Dialect, Frumspeak, Yeshivish, Hebonics: all of these terms have been used to name a variety of English spoken by Jews in the United States. Of course, not all Jews speak alike, and many use the same variety of English as their non-Jewish counterparts; but those who identify closely with religious and cultural aspects of Jewish life often represent their affiliation in speech.

Among the most observant Jews, almost all aspects of life are associated with group membership. Since driving on the Sabbath is forbidden, they live within walking distance of their place of worship, creating a strong sense of community among group members. A physical boundary, called an *eruv*, delineates an area outside of which objects are not carried on the Sabbath and high holidays. Orthodox Jews meet at shared schools, synagogues, kosher restaurants, and kosher grocery stores. They talk, study, read, pray, and sing together; and all these linguistic performances serve to reinforce shared dialect features. Specialized vocabulary names religious objects, holidays, rituals, household items, clothing, food, and other objects and activities associated with the culture. Shared ancestral languages, particularly Hebrew and Yiddish, also contribute to the dialect we typically refer to in America today as Jewish English.

History

Two main varieties of Jewish English emerged in America, originating from two regionally distinct European groups: Sephardim and Ashkenazim. Sephardic Jews immigrated to America from Spain and Portugal, beginning in the 1600s, and from the Ottoman Empire during the late 1800s and early 1900s. In addition to the languages of their native countries, Sephardic immigrants brought with them a language known as Dzhudezmo (or Judezmo) and its literary counterpart, Ladino. Although the linguistic heritage of these groups is represented in the pronunciation of modern Hebrew, Sephardic speech has had less influence on English in the United States, where many assimilated among non-Jews as well as among the more populous Ashkenazim.

Ashkenazic Jews began arriving in large numbers during the early 1800s from Western Europe: Germany, Holland, Alsace, Bohemia, Switzerland, and western Hungary. Later in the 1800s, there were increasing numbers from Eastern Europe: Russia, Austria-Hungary, Romania, and Poland. Both groups of Ashkenazim spoke Yiddish, in addition to the separate national languages of their countries. Although Yiddish relates linguistically most closely to German, among Western Ashkenazim the language was disappearing in favor of the speakers' national languages prior to their arrival in America. It was primarily the Eastern Ashkenazic group that maintained Yiddish in America.

Yiddish appeared in newspapers, plays, songs, and prose fiction. It was used for scholarly writings in education, history, and folklore. Although Hebrew was considered a more learned language, Yiddish translations of scripture and prayer were available. Among second and third generations in the United States, however, use of Yiddish began to decline. English, intermingled with Yiddish and Hebrew features, became more common, especially among Jews attending public schools. For many descendants of Eastern Ashkenazim, Jewish English thus emerged as the primary language. Like other dialects defined geographically, socially, or ethnically, features of vocabulary, pronunciation, grammar, and discourse set Jewish English apart from other varieties of English.

Vocabulary

The Jewish English lexicon ranges from items in the mainstream of American English to ones that are highly specialized. Large numbers of words have spread from Jewish English into more general American usage: *kosher* 'ritually clean, legitimate', *glitch* 'slip-up', *bagel* 'doughnut-shaped roll', *maven* 'expert', *schlock* 'junk', *mensch* 'decent person', *klutz* 'clumsy person', *schmooze* 'chat, gossip', *chutzpah* 'impudence, guts', *tchotchke* 'knick-knack', *schmuck* 'jerk, prick', *kvetch* 'whine', *nebbish* 'nonentity, nerd', *kibitz* 'to observe, as in a card game, and give unwanted advice'. Hebrew names for popular holidays and celebrations, such as *Chanukah* and *bar mitzvah* are used among Jews and non-Jews alike. Blends with English words are readily formed, as in *Chanukah card* or *matzo ball soup*.

Some terms have both Hebrew and Yiddish variants that are used interchangeably. The skullcap worn by Orthodox and Conservative Jews, for example, may be referred to as either a *kippah* (Hebrew) or a *yarmulka* (Yiddish). Some variants, however, convey subtle differences in Jewish identity: in referring to their place of worship, for example, Reform Jews typically refer to *temple*, Conservative Jews to *synagogue*, and Orthodox and Chasidic Jews to *shul*. Holidays may be named either in English (*Passover*) or in Hebrew (*Pesach*), depending on speaker and speaking situation. This distinction is exploited by Alfred Uhry, in *The Last Night of Ballyhoo*, in a conversation between Joe, an observant New York Jew, who uses the word *Pesach*, and Lala, a Southern Jew whose family is trying desperately to assimilate, who understands only when he translates for her, *Passover*.

Names for many holidays as well as everyday activities are unfamiliar outside the religious Jewish community: religious holidays, e.g., *Tisha B'Av* 'Ninth of Av', a fast day; marriage, e.g., *shadchen* 'matchmaker'; death, e.g., *ovel* 'mourner'; study, e.g., *limud* 'learning'; prayer, e.g., *tallis* 'prayer shawl'; and kinship, e.g., *zeide* 'grandfather'. Expressions include wishful terms, e.g., *halevai* 'would that it were so', greetings, e.g., *boruch habo* 'welcome', curses, e.g., *yemach shemo* 'may his name be blotted out', and interjections, e.g., *nu* 'well, so'.

Pronunciation

Pronunciation of Jewish English is most closely associated with New York City. Early studies found the following features of pronunciation to be most closely associated with Jewish English: raising of pitch and emphatic exploding of *t* and *d*; slight lisping of *s* and *z*; strong hissing of *s*; substitution of *th* or *sh* for *s*; pronunciation of a hard *g* sound in *ing* words, so that the *ing* of *singer* sounds like that of *finger* or *Long Island* sounds like *Long Guy Land*; and occasional substitution of *k* for *g* as in *sink* for *sing*. Some features were common to both Jews and non-Jews of New York: loss of distinction between *wh* and *w*, so that *which* and *witch* sound the same; intrusive *r*, as in *idear* for *idea*; and several substitutions in vowel sounds.

Current research supports the maintenance of Jewish English pronunciation. According to Tom McArthur, editor of *The Oxford Companion to the English Language*, some New York City descendants of the Eastern Ashkenazic immigrant population still pronounce *circle*, *nervous*, and *first* as *soikel*, *noivis*, and *foist*. McArthur notes hard *g* in *-ing* words, over-aspiration of *t*, variations in *s* and *z* sounds, and certain Yiddish-derived vowel substitutions. Other pronunciation features derived from Yiddish include loudness, exaggerated intonation, and a fast rate of speech.

Grammar

When Yiddish or Hebrew words become part of Jewish English, they may be integrated through the use of English suffixes. Yiddish verbs, for example, typically lose the *-(e)n* Yiddish infinitive and take on English inflections: Yiddish *bentshn* has become *bentsh* 'to recite the Grace after

Meals'; *dav(e)nen, dav(e)n* 'to pray'; *kvetshn, kvetsh* 'to complain'; *shlepn, shlep* 'to drag, carry'. These are conjugated, then, as English verbs: *bentshes, bentshed, bentshing; shleps, shlepped, shlepping.* English suffixes are also used to change the part of speech of Yiddish and Hebrew words integrated into Jewish English. The verb *shlep* may be converted into the adjectives *shleppy* or *shleppish,* the adverbs *shleppily* or *shleppishly,* or the noun *shleppiness.* Yiddish nouns, like English, take an *-s* plural; others use *-im* or *-lekh.* In Jewish English, Yiddish *kneidel* 'dumpling' may be pluralized either as *kneidels* or as *kneidlekh; shtetl* 'small town' may be *shtetls* or *shtetlekh.* In Hebrew, masculine nouns typically pluralize *-im* and feminine, *-os(t).* The plural of the word *tallis* (Hebrew and Yiddish for 'prayer shawl') may be rendered in Jewish English as *tallises* or as *talleisim.* The plural of *kippah* (Hebrew for 'skullcap') may be either *kippahs* or *kippot.*

Sometimes Yiddish suffixes are added to English or Hebrew words. For example, the noun-forming Yiddish (from Slavic) *-nik* (ardent practitioner, believer, lover, cultist or devotee) has given American English *beatnik, peacenik,* and *no-goodnik.* The diminutive suffixes *-chik* and *-el(e)* are common and may even be combined: *boychik, boyele,* and *boychikel* (plural *boychiklekh*) are all fond names for a little boy.

Word-formation processes of Jewish English can be effective in creating a variety of phrases. One example is the use of Yiddish-sounding *s(c)hm-* rhymed with an English word to suggest playful dismissiveness, captured by the title of Fran Drescher's book, *Cancer Schmancer,* which describes her triumphant attitude toward her battle with cancer. Bridge champion Marty Bergen offers the book *Points Schmoints,* which conveys his dismissive attitude toward the point-count system of bidding popularized by Charles Goren. The process has become popular in general American English, as noted in the *USA Today* headline, "Deficit schmeficit: Not a Bush priority."

Jewish English verb phrases often combine Hebrew or Yiddish nouns with English verbs. English *say* and *make* are particularly productive. One *says kaddish* 'recites mourners' prayer' or *yizkor* 'memorial prayer' and makes *kiddush* 'recites prayer over wine' or *(ha)motzi* '[the] prayer over bread'.

Some Jewish English expressions, including ones that have found their way into mainstream English, are direct translations of Yiddish sayings: *[I need it like] a hole in the head* (*loch in kop*); *Get lost!* (*ver favalgert, ver farblondhet*); *[You should live] until a hundred and twenty* (*biz hundert un tsvantsik*).

A syntactic feature called "Yiddish Movement," used to convey sarcasm, calls for moving an adjective, adverb, or noun that would ordinarily appear at the end of a sentence to the beginning and stressing it, as in

Smart, he isn't. In Philip Roth's *Goodbye Columbus*, Aunt Gladys criticizes her adult nephew for not having adequately clean underwear. "By hand you can't get it clean," she argues. When he tells her not to be concerned, she exclaims derisively, "Shmutz [dirt] he lives in and I shouldn't worry!"

Discourse

Discourse features associated with Jewish English fall into three general categories. First, Jewish speech is characterized as being loud and fast. Popular linguistic writer Deborah Tannen describes New York Jewish conversational style as overlapping, loud, high-pitched, fast-paced, and accompanied by exaggerated gesture. Another conversational analyst describes Jewish speech style as involving sociable disagreement, non-alignment, and competition for turns. Third, and above all, Jewish discourse is associated with sometimes self-effacing humor. Lawrence J. Epstein, author of *The Haunted Smile: The Story of Jewish Comedians in America* (Cambridge, MA: Perseus Books Group, 2001), attributes this to the experience of Jews as immigrants; comedy is a way to counter poverty and discrimination. Ironically, Jewish comedians often adopt personas consistent with anti-Semitic stereotypes: Jack Benny, the cheapskate; Ed Wynn and Rodney Dangerfield, the fool; Woody Allen, the neurotic. Jewish humor, according to Epstein, is characterized by wit and wordplay, a style attributable to the importance of language in Jewish culture. A center for the display of Jewish comedy from the late 1930s through the early 1960s evolved as the "Borscht Belt," a string of Catskill Mountain resorts given their moniker from the beet soup enjoyed by many Russian Jewish immigrants. Among the names Epstein associates with that entertainment circuit are Milton Berle, Fanny Brice, Mel Brooks, George Burns, Carl Reiner, Neil Simon, Red Buttons, Danny Kaye, Judy Holliday, Jackie Mason, Alan King, Henny Youngman, Buddy Hackett, Joan Rivers, Jerry Lewis, Woody Allen, Sid Caesar, and Joey Bishop.

Jewish English in American Culture

Evidence of Jewish ethnic identity is still present in American culture today. Jewish comedians frequent the airwaves, their styles ranging from the loud and confrontational Howard Stern to the quiet and mild Jerry Seinfeld. Stereotypes of Jewish women, such as the Yiddishe Mama and the Jewish American Princess, are reflected in the comic antics of television characters Roseanne in *Roseanne* and Fran Drescher in *The Nanny*. Some of these stereotypes are the subject of David Zurawik's *The Jews of Prime Time* (Brandeis University Press, 2003), which takes issue with the misrepresentation of Jews in the media. Public awareness of Jewish tradition has been enhanced by adaptations of stories originally written in Yiddish: Sholom Aleichem's character Tevye the Dairyman gained fame as the title character in the musical *Fiddler on the Roof*; Isaac Bashevis Singer's story "Yentl the Yeshiva Boy" was popularized by Barbra Streisand's film version, *Yentl*. A revival of klezmer bands, begun in the 1970s, has given Jewish secular music a place among popular varieties of styles. All of these have increased public awareness of Jewish language and how it is used to represent Jewish identity. Through print media, theater, film, music, and the Internet, people of all ethnic backgrounds share in Jewish English words, sounds, sentences, and styles that have become part of American language.

Resources

Leo Rosten's books are popular for extensive explanation and examples: *The Joys of Yiddish* (McGraw-Hill, 1967), revised by Lawrence Bush and published as *The New Joys of Yiddish* (Random House, 2001); *Hooray for Yiddish: A Book about English* (Simon and Schuster, 1982); *The Joys of Yinglish* (Penguin Books, 1990). A wonderful collection of Yiddish words, proverbs, insults, and blessings is Payson R. Stevens, Charles M. Levine, and Sol Steinmetz, *Meshuggenary: Celebrating the World of Yiddish* (Simon and Schuster, 2002). A collection rich with examples from songs, comic strips, novels, and book reviews is Gene Bluestein, *Anglish/Yinglish: Yiddish in American Life and Literature* (2nd edition, University of Nebraska Press, 1998). Chaim M. Weiser, *Frumspeak: The First Dictionary of Yeshivish* (Jason Aronson, 1995) specializes in religious vocabulary. In addition, valuable online glossaries may be found at www.koshernosh. com/dictiona.htm (includes voiced pronunciations); www.jewfaq.org/glossary.htm; www.ou.org/about/judaism.

Fading Future for Ferhoodled English (Pennsylvania German)

Marion Lois Huffines

40 An Amish buggy in Lancaster County, Pennsylvania. © by Diane Diederich.

If you ask the waitress for cherry pie and she says, "It's all," if the local butcher shop is advertising Ponhous, and if the supermarket puts out a sign declaring "Fastnacht donuts at $1.69 a dozen," then you can be sure you are in Pennsylvania Dutch country.

The Pennsylvania Dutch are, of course, not Dutch. They are descendants of German and Swiss immigrants who called themselves Deitsch, a dialect word for "German." Americans who heard Deitsch thought they heard the word "Dutch," and the label stuck. The language they speak is a German dialect and is closely related to dialects of southern Germany along the Rhine. So while they are popularly known as Pennsylvania Dutch, they are really Pennsylvania Germans.

The Pennsylvania Germans fall into two major groups: the Plain and the Fancy or, in more technical but equally inexact terms, the "Sectarians" and the "Nonsectarians." The Plain groups include the numerous sects of Amish and Mennonites who settled in southeastern Pennsylvania in the early 1700s seeking religious freedom. The Fancy Pennsylvania Germans include mainstream Lutherans and members of the Reformed Church who also settled in Pennsylvania before the Revolutionary War. Although estimates vary, the Germans outnumbered every other national or ethnic group in colonial Pennsylvania during their peak years of immigration (1749–54), with the possible exception of the English.

Pennsylvania German is still spoken natively by Old Order Amish and a majority of Old Order Mennonites. Members of these Plain separatist groups speak Pennsylvania German in their homes and communities. They learn English, which they use when conversing with outsiders, in school, usually in one-room schoolhouses maintained by their own community. Although members of the Old Orders continue to use Pennsylvania German, there are indications that they may not do so in the future. The increasing number of preschoolers who speak some English indicates that it is being used to some extent in the home. English also serves the Plain communities for reading and writing so that friends and family members who normally speak Pennsylvania German must write each other in English. Less conservative Amish and Mennonites use more English in their daily lives than do the Old Orders, and this parallels their greater acceptance of modern society in their lifestyle.

The nonplain Pennsylvania Germans are often called the "church people" because they worship in church buildings instead of private homes, or the "gay" or "fancy" Dutch because they wear colorful clothing. Among these nonplain people, the shift to English is pervasive. The number of native speakers is decreasing. Though some can understand it, the vast majority of young Pennsylvania Germans do not speak the language at all. In nonplain communities Pennsylvania German is used to speak with certain elderly members of the family and neighborhood and in an attempt to keep secrets from children and grandchildren. There are young speakers, but they typically learn Pennsylvania German as a second language and do not speak it very well.

Why did parents stop speaking Pennsylvania German to their children? Most indicate that they chose to raise their children to speak English specifically because English is the language of the school system. Many people did not speak Pennsylvania German to their children because they believed it would "ruin their English." As a consequence, the younger generation exhibits little mastery of Pennsylvania German. Older people tell stories of being mercilessly teased about their so-called "Dutchy accent" by their peers and even by school officials. One man related that a teacher literally washed out his mouth with lye soap because he spoke Pennsylvania German at school, a story also heard about others. Because of this abuse, many people not only stopped speaking their language, but also suppressed their accents in order to hide their origins.

The "Dutch accent" expresses itself in a number of ways: in the words that are chosen, in the sounds that make up the words, in how those words are put together to make sentences, and in the melody of those sentences.

Pronunciation

Elderly people who learned Pennsylvania German as their first language have a number of sounds in their English that generally do not occur in the speech of younger generations. For example, a *j* may sound like *ch*, and the words *jars, juice* are pronounced *chars, chuice*; the *th* of *with* and *thing* may be pronounced *wiss* and *sing*; the *v* sound in *visit* and *available* may sound like *w* as in *wisit* and *awailable*; the vowels of *butter, nothing*, and *until* sound like *bawter, nawthing*, and *ontil*; and the vowel sound of *house, mountain*, and *down* are pronounced *haase, maantain*, and *daan*. In some respects these elder Pennsylvania Germans sound like recent German immigrants, but their families have been in the US for over 200 years. These characteristic sounds are slowly dying out but can still be heard in the "Dutchy" areas of Pennsylvania.

Word Usages

Pennsylvania Germans often use Pennsylvania German words in English. For some speakers this usage is a slip of the tongue, as in this example:

"You see him out with the *sens* [scythe] knocking down grass." Other speakers deliberately select a word to invoke humor or to impress the listener with their knowledge of Pennsylvania German, as these examples show:

"I can, but I get *verhuddelt* every now and then."
"I used to try to talk to Daddy in that, but he always felt it was so *verdreht*."
"Now I wish I wouldn't have been so *schtarrkeppich*."

Many Pennsylvania German words have made their way into the English language of the area. These words include: *smearcase* 'cottage cheese', *spritz* 'sprinkle', *toot* 'paper bag', *speck* 'fat, bacon', *snitz* 'slice or cut' (usually apples), *ponhous* 'scrapple', *rutsch* 'squirm, move', *all* 'all gone', *sneaky* 'finicky about food', and *dare* 'to be permitted' as in *I dared go sledding on that hill*. Other Pennsylvania German words in English are less familiar to younger people: *Fastnacht* 'donut eaten on Shrove Tuesday', *dappich* 'clumsy', *strubblich* 'disheveled, unkempt', *fress* 'eat like an animal', and *schusslich* 'in a hurry, scatterbrain'. These words are not "borrowings" in the sense that they are perceived as foreign; they are part of the English language spoken by the Pennsylvania Germans, and many have been integrated into the English language of central Pennsylvania.

Sentence Structures

Probably the most far-reaching Pennsylvania German influence in the English of the region is how sentences are constructed. These features are well established as part of the English of central Pennsylvania and are also recognized as part of the so-called "Dutchy accent" of the area. These structures include:

*   Use of the adverb *already* placed after the verb in the simple past form:
    I helped butcher already.
    I remember she did do that though already.
    I heard different remedies already.
    Other English speakers would have said, *I've already heard different remedies*.

- Use of the adverb *once* with commands, usually at the end of the sentence:

    Explain it to her once.

    Show it to her once.

    Not wait once.

- Use of the present tense for activities begun in the past and continuing in the present:

    She quilted several already now since she's here.

    I live there for quite a few years.

    We're five years here.

    Other English speakers would have said, "*We've been here for five years.*"

- Sentences that include the verbs *to be* and *to have* with a preposition that appears without any expressed object:

    That had a little bit of meat on.

    There's seeds in.

    I didn't know you had anything in.

    The preposition "floats" at the end of the sentence. Other English speakers would have said, *I didn't know you had anything in it.*

- Intonation or sentence melody patterns characteristic of the English of the Pennsylvania Germans that contrast with those of other varieties of English and are very noticeable to people new to the area. These special melodies include yes/no questions with a falling tone of voice at the end instead of a rising questioning tone. In the question *Did you get it?* the voice falls from its high pitch on *get* to a low pitch on *it*. In the question *Are you coming over?* the high pitch is on the first syllable of *over* and falls to a lower pitch on the second syllable. This question melody seems to be spreading beyond the Pennsylvania German community into the English spoken in surrounding areas

Commercial Exploitation

In the Pennsylvania Dutch areas, tourism has sprung up all around the sectarians. This commercialism spills over onto bric-a-brac at gift shops and into so-called "folk festivals" in Nonsectarian areas. These fairs offer Dutch foods and crafts, many of which exist or have been developed only for the tourist. The colorful hex signs, for instance, have been ascribed magical origins, but they appear on barns "just for nice," with no purpose other than that it suits the owners' fancy, and the plain Pennsylvania Germans will not have them at all.

The commercialism also promotes its own variety of so-called "Dutchified English." A booklet entitled *Ferhoodled English: A Collection of Quaintly Amusing Expressions Heard among the Pennsylvania Dutch Folks* has been reprinted numerous times. The unnamed authors cite "quaintly amusing expressions" such as *Amos, come from the woodpile in, mom's on the table and Pop's et himself done already*, or *Aunt Emmy's wonderful sick. She don't feel so pretty good and they've got her laid down yet.* Much of what the booklet insists is typical of this English variety has not been confirmed by fieldwork. Commercial products also display this mythical "Dutchified" English on diner and restaurant placemats, napkins, coasters, kitchen towels, trivets, light-switch plates, and cutting boards. This is commercial stereotyping with a vengeance.

The Future of "Dutchified" English

The Nonsectarian Pennsylvania Germans are currently extending their contact and interaction with the dominant culture beyond the point where it is possible for them to maintain Pennsylvania German as a language. The process of the loss of Pennsylvania German seems deceptively slow because of the dispersion of language enclaves throughout southeastern and central Pennsylvania. However, the shift to English for any individual community is swift, once it begins. Some areas continue to exist in isolation because of their geographical location and agrarian base, but as children attend consolidated high schools and parents work in larger towns and cities, and as the family farms are sold to large agri-businesses, Pennsylvania German will be heard less and less, and its influence on English will wane in the years to come. This may be inevitable, but with its recession will fade one of the rich and longstanding dialect traditions of the United States.

Notes on Contributors

Bridget Anderson is an Assistant Professor of English and Linguistics at the University of Georgia, who does research on Appalachian English in the Smoky Mountains and in transplant communities in Detroit, Michigan. She is from the Smoky Mountains.

Guy Bailey is Provost and Vice-President for Academic Affairs at the University of Texas at San Antonio; he is also a native of Texas who has done extensive surveys of Texas speech over the past couple of decades.

Maciej Baranowski is a Ph.D. student in linguistics at the University of Pennsylvania who conducts research on the changing nature of Charleston speech.

John Baugh is the Margaret Bush Wilson Professor in Arts and Sciences and Chair of African and Afro-American Studies at Washington University in St. Louis. He is the author of several books on African American English, including *Beyond Ebonics: Linguistic Pride and Racial Prejudice* (Oxford, 2000) and *Out of the Mouths of Slaves* (University of Texas, 1999). He has been involved in national debates about linguistic profiling that have been aired on National Public Radio and a number of national television programs.

Cynthia Bernstein is Professor of Linguistics and Coordinator of Applied Linguistics at the University of Memphis. She teaches and researches connections between culture and the features of language used to express it.

Renée Blake, Ph.D., is an Associate Professor in the Department of Linguistics and the Africana Studies Program, New York University who conducts research on Caribbean English and on language and education.

Charles Boberg is an Associate Professor at McGill University, Montreal, who has done extensive research and co-authored (with William Labov) *The Atlas of North American English.*

David Bowie is an Associate Professor of Linguistics and English Language at the University of Central Florida, where he works on the historical development of varieties of English.

Richard Cameron is an Associate Professor in the Department of English and the Department of Spanish, French, Italian, and Portuguese at the University of Illinois at Chicago.

J. K. Chambers, University of Toronto. Jack Chambers is Professor Emeritus of Linguistics at the University of Toronto and a leading researcher on Canadian English and sociolinguistic theory.

Becky Childs, is an Assistant Professor in the Department of Linguistics, Memorial University of Newfoundland, St. John's, Canada. She has researched the speech of small communities in the Smoky Mountains and in coastal North Carolina as well as black and white speech in Abaco in the Bahamas.

Sandra Clarke is a Professor in the Department of Linguistics, Memorial University of Newfoundland, St. John's, Canada, who has been researching the varieties of Newfoundland English for several decades.

Jeff Conn is a visiting Assistant Professor at Portland State University, where he is studying the emergence of the Portland dialect.

Connie Eble is a Professor of English at the University of North Carolina, Chapel Hill. She is originally from the New Orleans area of Louisiana and an authority on slang.

Penelope Eckert is a Professor of Linguistics at Stanford University where she works on language change among teenagers. She is well known for her studies of language and gender, and is the co-author of *Language and Gender* (Cambridge University Press 2003). She is also the author of *Language as Social Practice* (Blackwell 2000).

Jim Fitzpatrick, a graduate student in sociolinguistics at North Carolina State University, grew up in the friendly environs of Boston where he took the native dialect and culture of the area for granted.

Beverly Olson Flanigan is Associate Professor of Linguistics at Ohio University in Athens, where she teaches courses in sociolinguistics and dialectology along with her research on Ohioan speech.

Ellen Fluharty, West Virginia Dialect Project, West Virginia University, lives in Morgantown, West Virginia. She studied at West Virginia University with Kirk Hazen.

Carmen Fought is an Associate Professor of Linguistics at Pitzer College in Claremont, California and author of *Chicano English in Context* (Palgrave/Macmillan 2003). She is well known for her studies of language and ethnicity.

Timothy C. Frazer, Professor, Department of English and Journalism, Western Illinois University, has done research on the speech of residents of small towns in the Midwest who move to larger cities.

Valerie Fridland is an Associate Professor at the University of Nevada at Reno and a native of Memphis who conducts research on Southern vowels in general and the vowels of Memphis in particular.

Matthew J. Gordon is an Associate Professor of Linguistics in the Department of English at the University of Missouri–Columbia. He has written extensively on the vowel patterns of the Midwest.

Lauren Hall-Lew is a Ph.D. student in linguistics at Stanford who has been studying the differences between urban and rural dialects of Arizona.

Kirk Hazen is the founder of the West Virginia Dialect Project at West Virginia University and Associate Professor of Linguistics in the English Department at West Virginia University. He has conducted research on Appalachian English in West Virginia and on rural speech communities in North Carolina.

Marion Lois Huffines is Associate Vice President for Academic Affairs and Professor of German and Linguistics at Bucknell University in Lewisburg, Pennsylvania. She has conducted extensive research on Pennsylvania German.

Neal Hutcheson is a videographer with the North Carolina Language and Life Project at North Carolina State University; he recently produced the documentary *Mountain Talk*, as well as a number of other dialect documentaries that have aired on public television. His products are available at www.talkingnc.com.

Barbara Johnstone is a sociolinguist who teaches at Carnegie Mellon University. In addition to her recent research on Pittsburghese, she has done extensive research on discourse as well as the role of the individual in the speech community.

Scott Kiesling is a sociolinguist who teaches at the University of Pittsburgh. He has conducted research on the use of language by members of fraternity groups.

Christine Mallinson, a Ph.D. student in sociology and anthropology at North Carolina State University, is currently conducting sociolinguistic research in Texana and Murphy, North Carolina.

Megan E. Melançon is a Cajun and a linguist. Her interests and research have centered on Cajun and Creole French and English in southern Louisiana. She is currently Assistant Professor of English in the Department of English, Speech, and Journalism at Georgia College and State University.

Norma Mendoza-Denton is an Associate Professor of Anthropology at the University of Arizona who works on speech style and language and identity.

Miriam Meyerhoff is a Lecturer at the Department of Theoretical and Applied Linguistics, University of Edinburgh, Scotland.

Wendy Morkel completed her master's degree in English with a focus on English language and linguistics at Brigham Young University under the guidance of David Bowie.

Thomas E. Murray was Professor of English at Kansas State University, Manhattan, KS, and has conducted research on the speech of St. Louis, Missouri.

Naomi Nagy is Associate Professor of Sociolinguistics in the Linguistics Program and English Department at the University of New Hampshire. Among her linguistic interests are issues of identity related to New England speech.

Michael Newman is Associate Professor of Linguistics at Queens College, City University of New York, and a member of the CUNY Research Institute for the Study of Language in Urban Society. He currently conducts research on Puerto Rican English in New York City.

Jeffrey Reaser is an Assistant Professor at North Carolina State University who does research on Bahamian English along with his research on language and education.

Julie Roberts is an Associate Professor in the Department of Communication Sciences, University of Vermont. She conducts research on dialects and child language as well as the regional and ethnic dialects of New England.

Claudio Salvucci is an author from Holland, Pennsylvania. His books include *A Grammar of the Philadelphia Dialect*, *The Philadelphia Dialect Dictionary*, and *A Dictionary of Pennsylvanianisms*.

Natalie Schilling-Estes is an Associate Professor of Linguistics at Georgetown University. She is the co-author (with Walt Wolfram) of *American English: Dialects and Variation* (2nd edition, Blackwell, 2005) and *Hoi Toide on the Outer Banks: The Story of the Ocracoke Brogue* (University of North Carolina Press, 1997). She is also co-editor (with J. K. Chambers and Peter Trudgill) of *The Handbook of Language Variation and Change* (Blackwell, 2002).

Daniel Schreier is an Assistant Professor of Linguistics at the University of Regensburg, Germany, who has written several books on the speech of Tristan da Cunha. He is currently conducting research on the speech of St. Helena Island.

Beth Simon is an Associate Professor in the Department of English and Linguistics, Indiana University–Purdue University. She has conducted extensive on the speech of the Upper Peninsula in Michigan.

Jane S. Smith is an Associate Professor of French at the University of Maine. While focusing her research on the French dialects of Maine, she could not ignore the varieties of English that are an integral part of the rich language heritage of Mainers.

Jan Tillery is an Associate Professor of English at the University of Texas at San Antonio who has focused her research on the dialects of Texas.

Benjamin Torbert is an Assistant Professor of English at Mississippi State University who conducted research on AAE in Hyde County and black and white Bahamian English. He also researches perceptual cues in ethnic identification.

Tracey L. Weldon is an Assistant Professor of Linguistics in the English Department at the University of South Carolina and who has conducted research on the Gullah language.

Walt Wolfram is the William C. Friday Distinguished Professor of English Linguistics at North Carolina State University, Director of the North Carolina Language and Life Project, and the general editor of the dialect series for *Language Magazine*. He is co-author (with Natalie Schilling-Estes) of *Hoi Toide on the Outer Banks: The Story of the Ocracoke Brogue* and of *American English: Dialects and Variation*, and executive producer of a number of video documentaries for public television.